BARROW-IN-FURNESS

THROUGH TIME

Gill Jepson

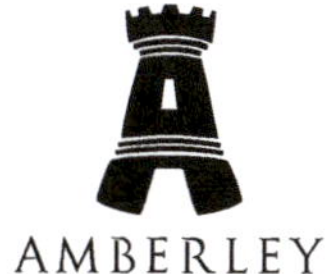

AMBERLEY

Dedicated to my wonderful family and the citizens of Barrow-in-Furness,
who love the town as much as I do.

First published 2016

Amberley Publishing
The Hill, Stroud, Gloucestershire, GL5 4EP
www.amberley-books.com

ISBN 978 1 4456 5910 7 (print)
ISBN 978 1 4456 5911 4 (ebook)

Typesetting by Amberley Publishing.
Printed in Great Britain.

Appointed GPSR EU Representative: Easy Access System
Europe Oü, 16879218
Address: Mustamäe tee 50, 10621, Tallinn, Estonia
Contact Details: gpsr.requests@easproject.com, +358 40
500 3575

Introduction

Before 1845 Barrow (Barrai) was a quiet backwater with only 200 souls. By 1881 the population had jumped to above 47,000. The reason for this was the rapid industrialisation and the influx of workers to the area from places like Ireland, the Midlands and Cornwall. The Furness Railway Company led the way with James Ramsden at its helm and the dukes of Buccleuch and Devonshire as the major investors. They joined with H. W. Schneider, a speculator and mine owner, to develop the town. Ramsden realised that iron ore could be smelted in Barrow and soon Bessemer blast furnaces were processing the ore.

A building programme had to be rapidly undertaken to support the growing population and Ramsden instigated the development of a linear planned town. It boasted a grid of well-built housing, wide roads, modern sanitation and was a model town. The behaviour of its citizens, however, was not. It was rowdy and rough, over-populated by tough labourers with few females. The response to this was the building of a Jute Works that employed women, whom the town fathers hoped would provide a civilising effect and rehabilitate its reputation as the 'Chicago of the North'.

The town aspired to greater things and in 1867 new docks were built and opened by W. E. Gladstone. The town was booming and by 1876 it had the largest steelworks in the world, providing steel rails as far as South Africa and Canada. It was incorporated as the Borough of Barrow in Furness in 1867 and James Ramsden became its first mayor. In 1887 the magnificent sandstone Town Hall was completed, a rival to any in the neighbouring northern cities and expresses something about both the civic pride and confidence of the town.

Industry thrived and diversified and Barrow soon gained a reputation for shipbuilding which continues today. James Ramsden was knighted in 1872 and Barrow was established as an important industrial town. It never quite reached the hopes of Gladstone that it would rival Liverpool and, following First World War, the iron industry declined, causing a slump and unemployment.

Vickers Armstrong Ltd was a significant employer in the Second World War and produced ships, armaments and submarines for the war effort. Barrow was an obvious target for German bombers and in 1941 the town was hit but only peripheral damage was done to the factories and shipyard. Some rebuilding followed after the war as the population grew, encouraging new estates to be built on the outskirts.

Barrow today is a typical post-industrial town. Industry has shrunk but BAE Systems are still one of the largest employers, continuing the tradition of shipbuilding, only now they produce nuclear submarines. Many of the iconic buildings have sadly succumbed to the developers' demolition ball, but Barrow still has a uniquely interesting town with a fascinating history. There are always rumours of regeneration and growth, but these are usually tied closely to the fortunes of the town's main employer. An ambitious if unlikely 'marina' complex and a refurbished town centre is proposed. This would be yet another chapter in Barrow's short yet impressive history, and would certainly live up to the town motto – *Semper Sursum* or 'Always Rising'.

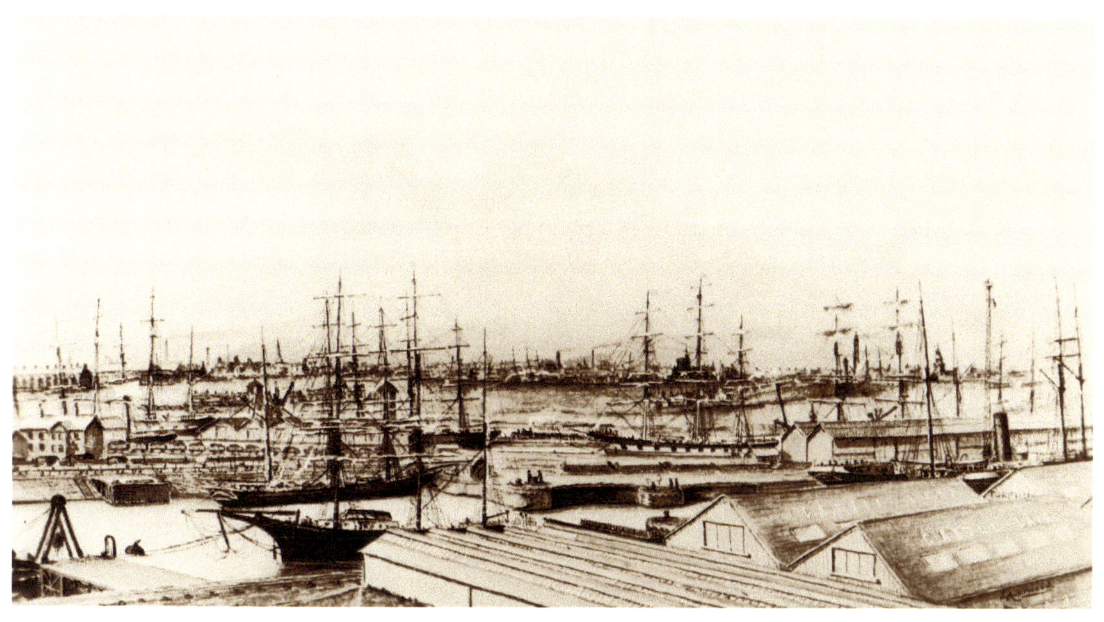

The Port of Barrow

Prior to the appearance of the railway in 1846, Barrow had a number of small jetties and piers to enable the loading of slate and iron ore onto ships. These were positioned along the channel between Barrow Island and the village. The port grew and by 1850 was overcrowded, which led to major harbour improvements. The harbour aspect of the town declined over time and Barrow's significance as a port has diminished.

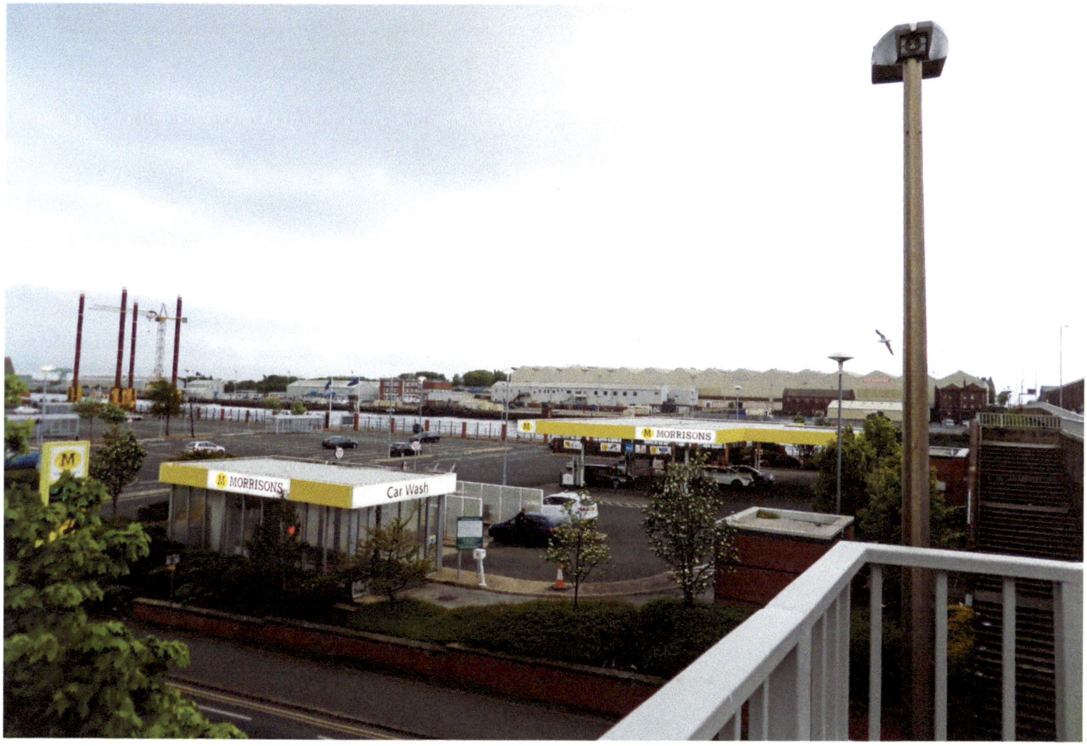

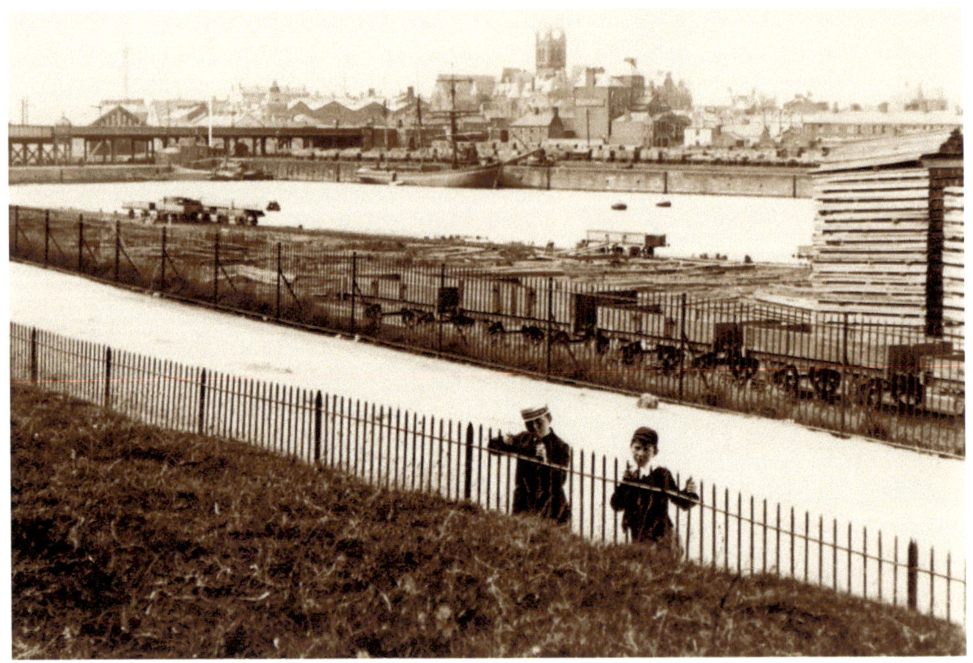

Buccleuch Dock

Around 1886 Buccleuch Dock was built. In the background, the construction of the Town Hall is underway. The Duke of Buccleuch was persuaded to sell more land fronting Barrow Channel to extend the docks and increase capacity. The intention was to increase shipments of iron ore to 300,000 tons. Behind the two boys are Furness Railway sidings and the old Michaelson Road Bridge in the distance. This area now has restricted access and cannot be reached without permission due to security issues.

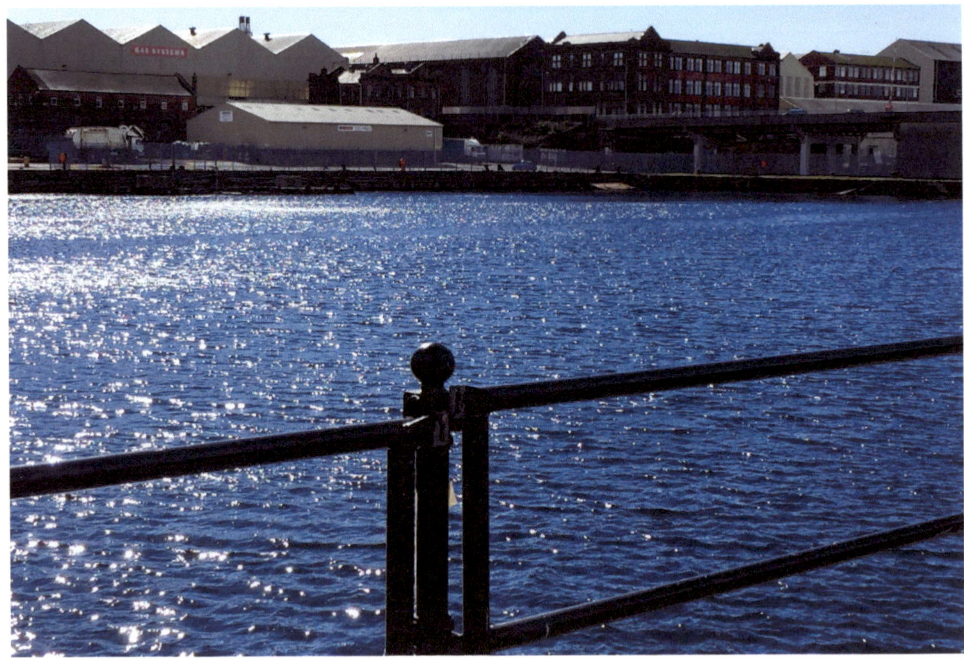

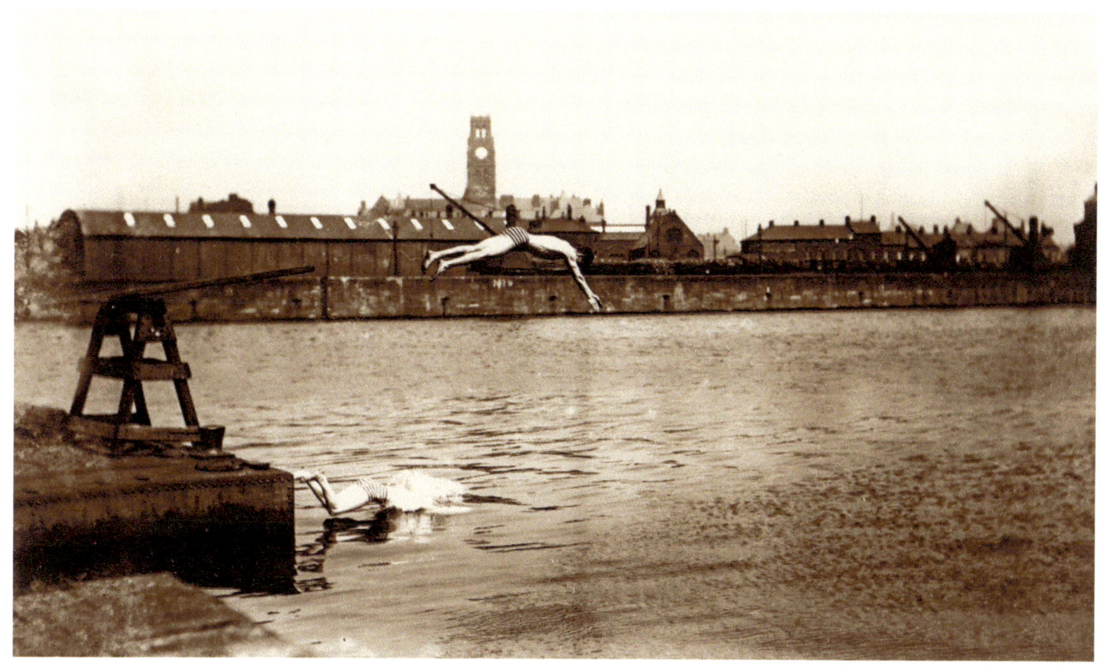

Devonshire Dock

Completed in 1867, Devonshire Dock was brought into use before its official opening in September. Henry Schneider, James Ramsden and their wives were aboard the *Dione* as it towed the first ship through the basin to the dock entrance. The Duke of Devonshire officially opened the dock on 19 September 1867 and William Gladstone was one of many illustrious guests. The boys diving here, however, seem unaware of the significance of this dock. Today the dock has all but disappeared beneath the Devonshire Dock Hall. (Picture courtesy of Martin Millar)

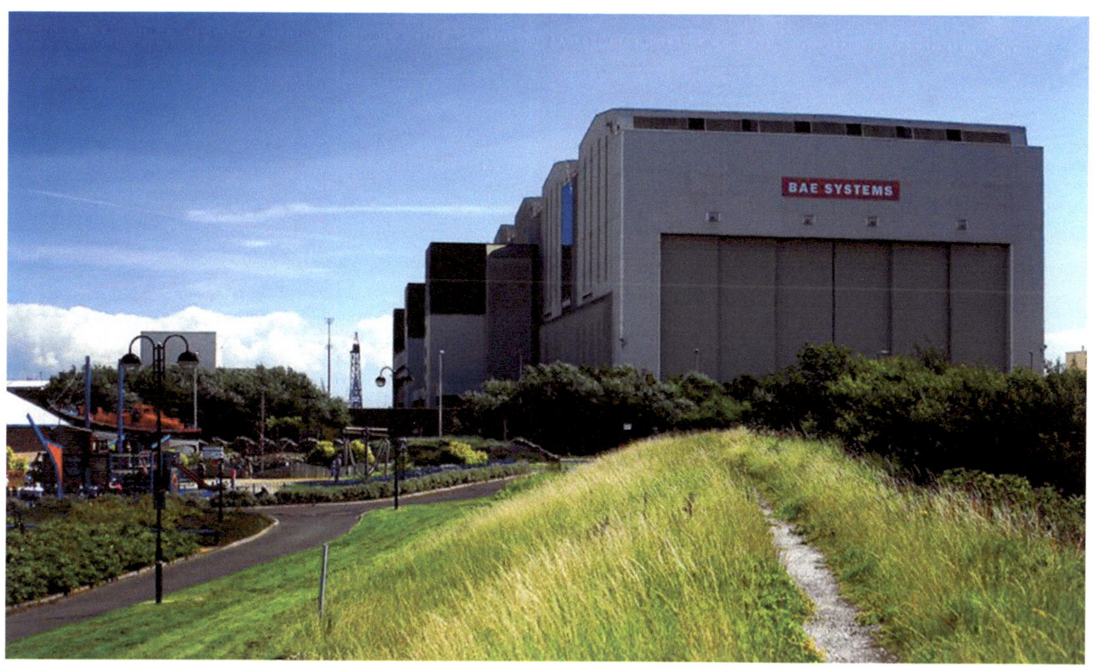

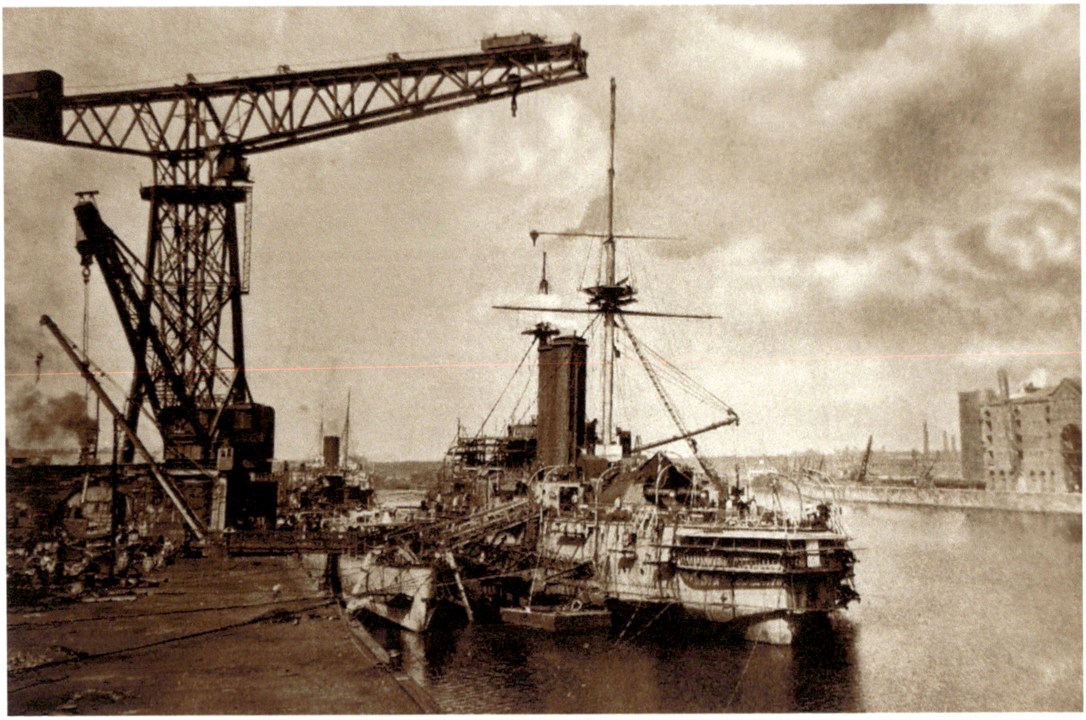

Devonshire Dock

The indoor submarine complex where *Vanguard* and *Astute* submarines were built has subsumed the dock. The huge building was constructed between 1982 and 1986 and dominates the skyline of the town, being visible for miles around. Its continued use is assured with the building of the Trident *Successor* submarines and denotes the largest investment in the shipyard since the Dock Hall was built. (Picture courtesy of Martin Millar)

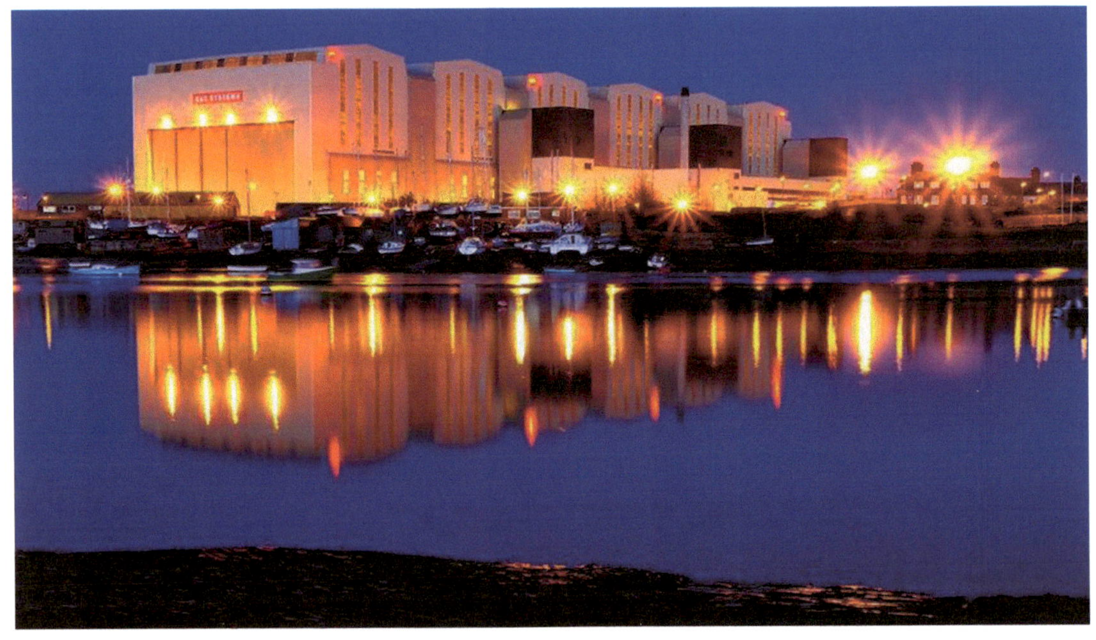

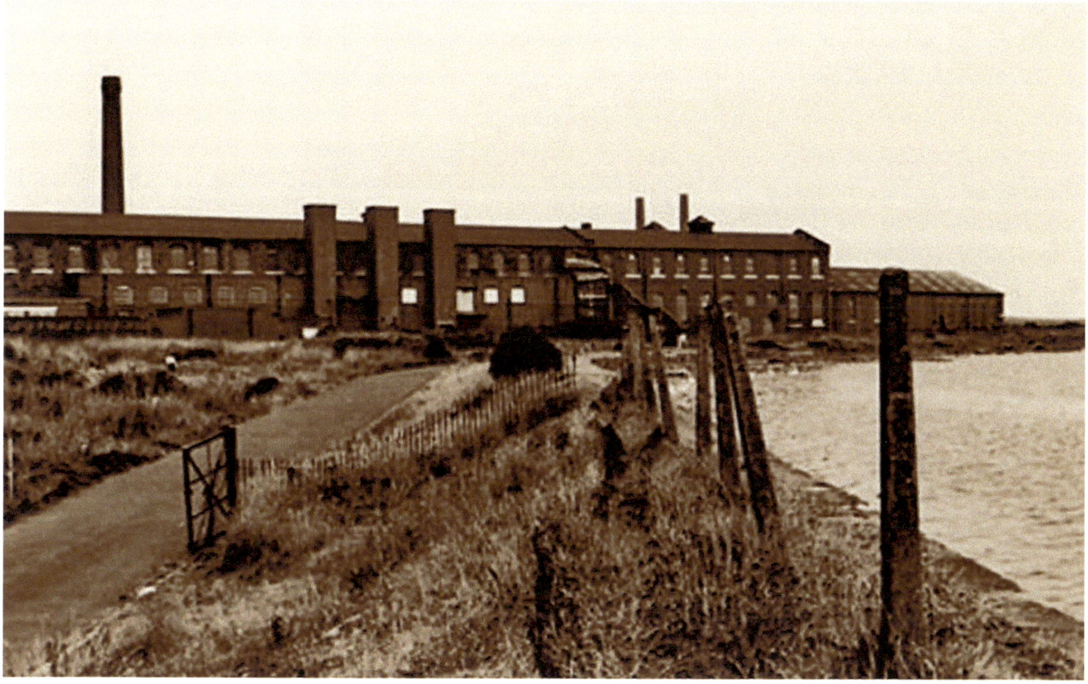

Cavendish Dock

This dock was completed around 1878 but never really came into full use other than as a 'feeder' for other docks. The original plans were designed to rival Liverpool by improving and providing deep water berths to extend the harbour and increase its significance. This never fully came to fruition and the dock now provides a venue for leisure, fishing and walking. (Picture courtesy of Jennifer Foote)

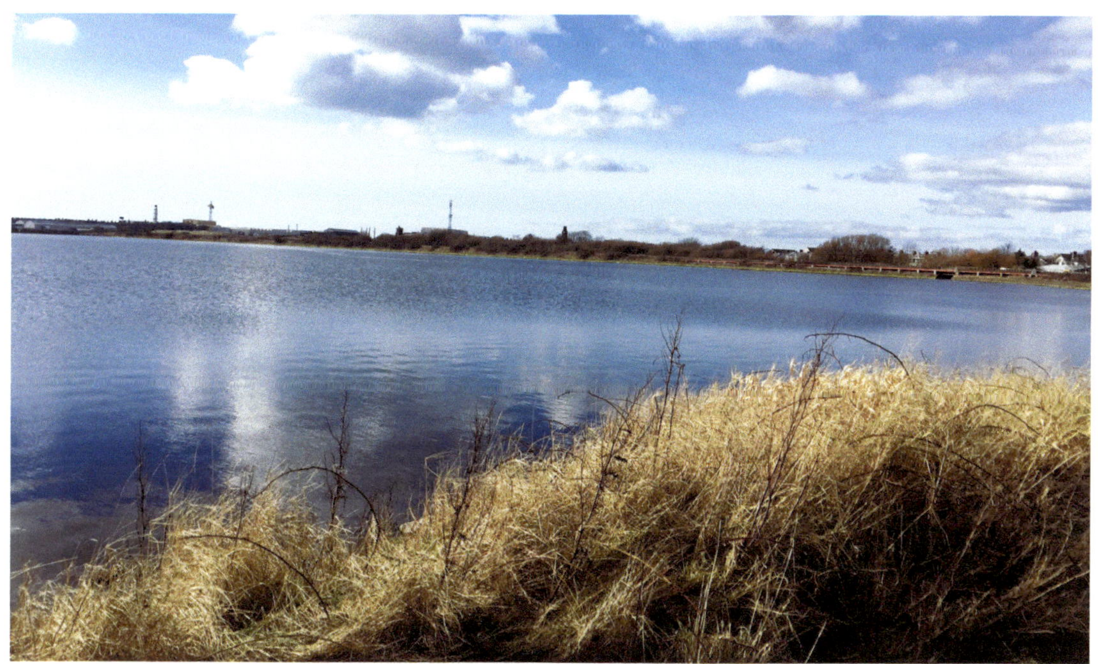

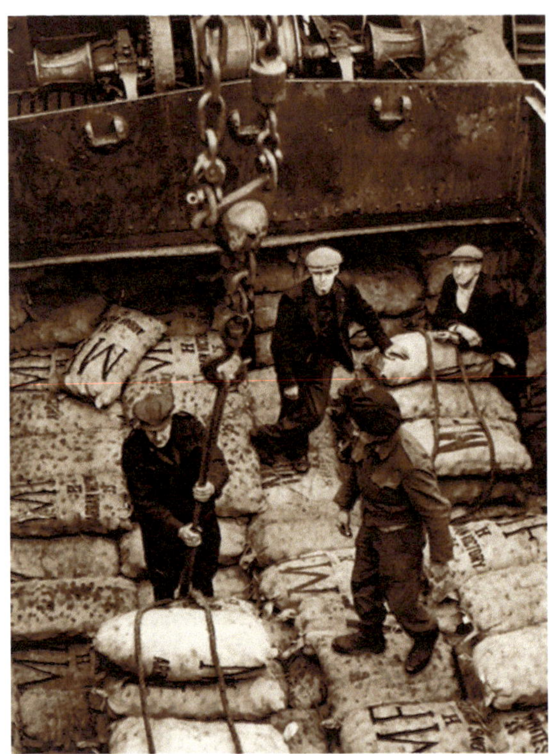

Dockers at Devonshire Dock, 1960s

Dockers had a hard and sometimes dangerous job and there is little evidence of protective clothing in this image. Alfred Hudson, pictured here, died in his sixties from lung cancer contracted from the china clay he unloaded at the docks. He previously served on HMS *Repulse*, which was lost off the coast of Malaya with HMS *Prince of Wales* in 1941. The experience must have been terrifying as the ship was in shark-infested waters when it went down. (Picture courtesy of the *North West Evening Mail*/Janet Pickering) The Spirit of Barrow statue remembers the workers like Alfred who were instrumental in building Barrow and its industry.

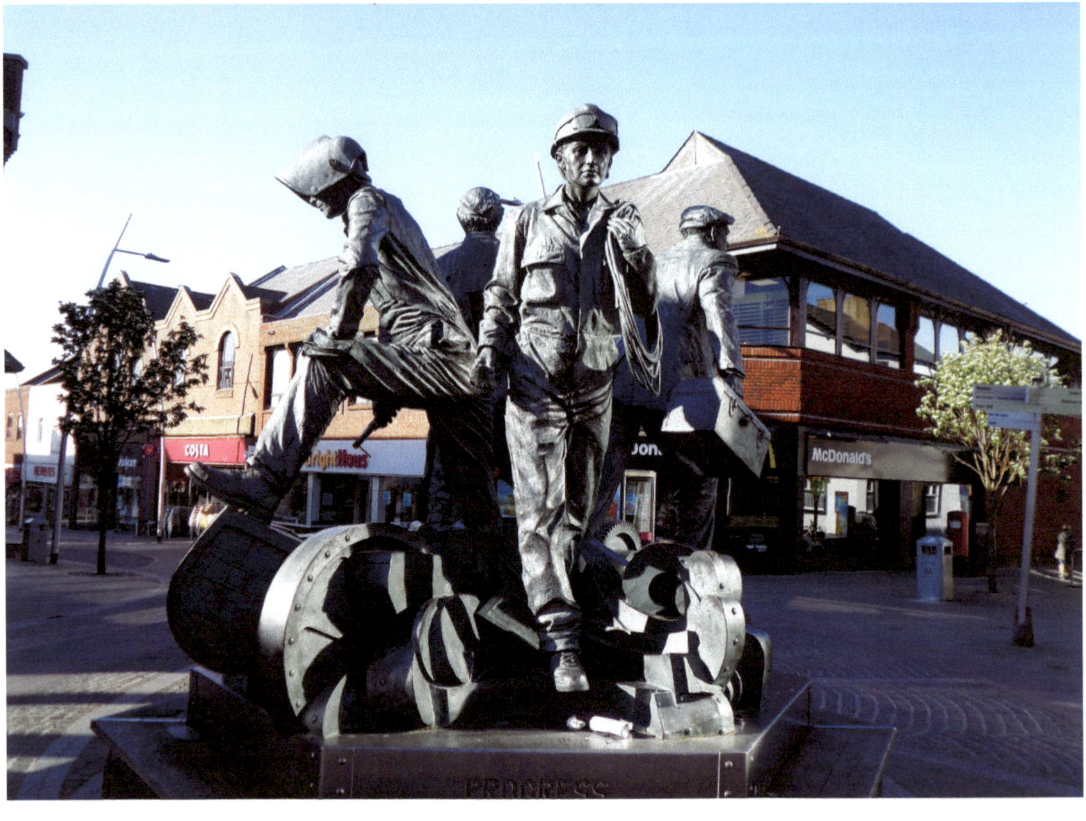

Graving Dock

In 1872 the Graving Dock was built to allow ships to be fitted out and repaired with access to Walney Channel. Built from sandstone and limestone slot, it has tiered steps for workers to access the hull of the ships. It was a dangerous and inhospitable place to work, open to the weather and had narrow walkways that were slippery in wet weather. When the dock fell out of use, the local council transformed it into an unusual museum recording the town's shipbuilding history. (Picture courtesy of the Dock Museum/ Martin Millar)

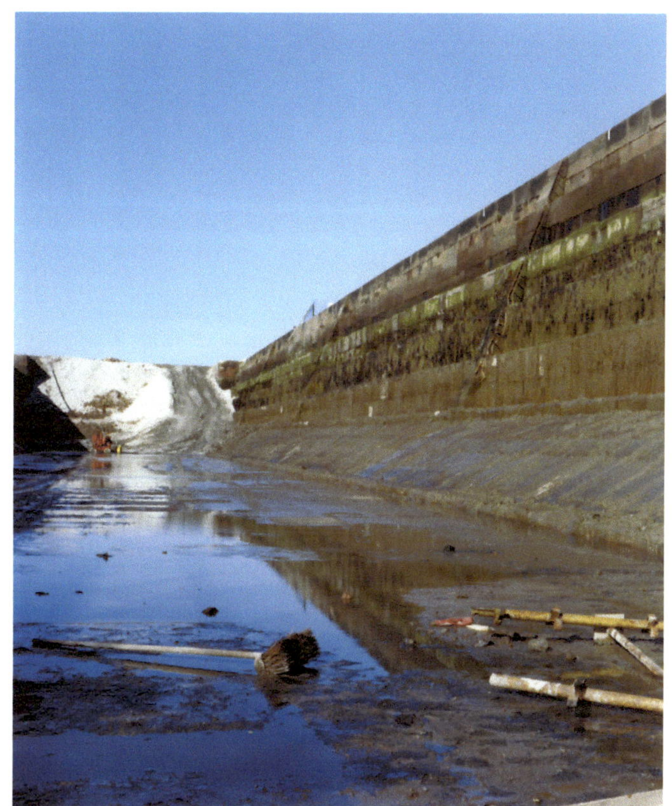

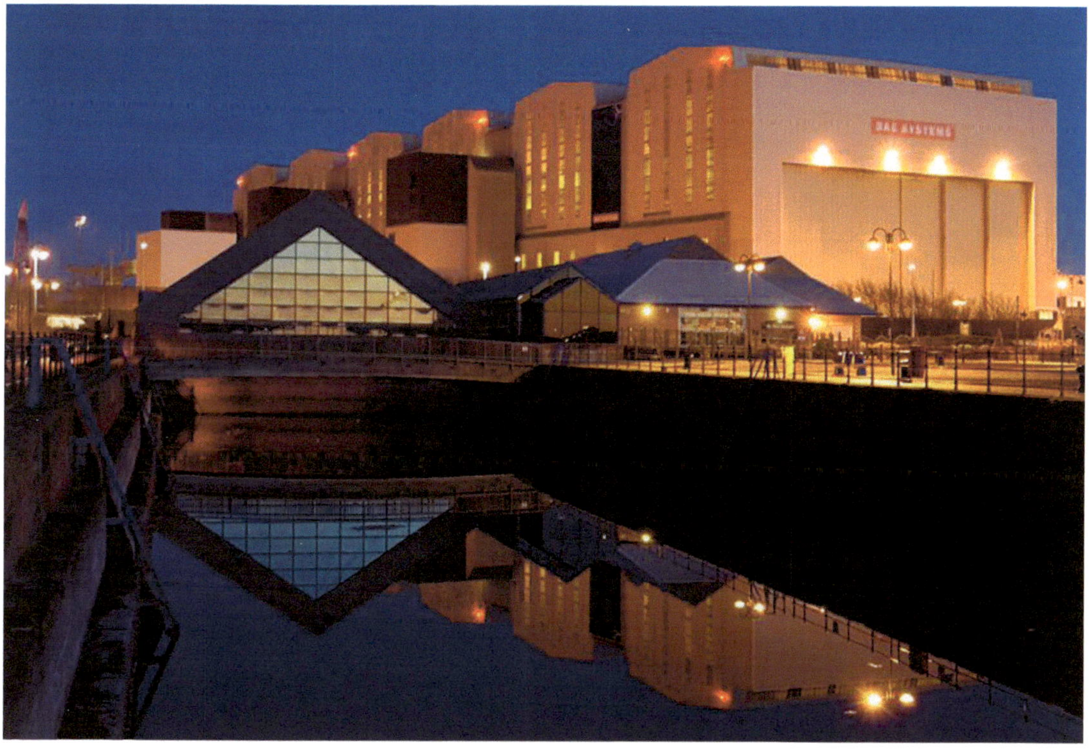

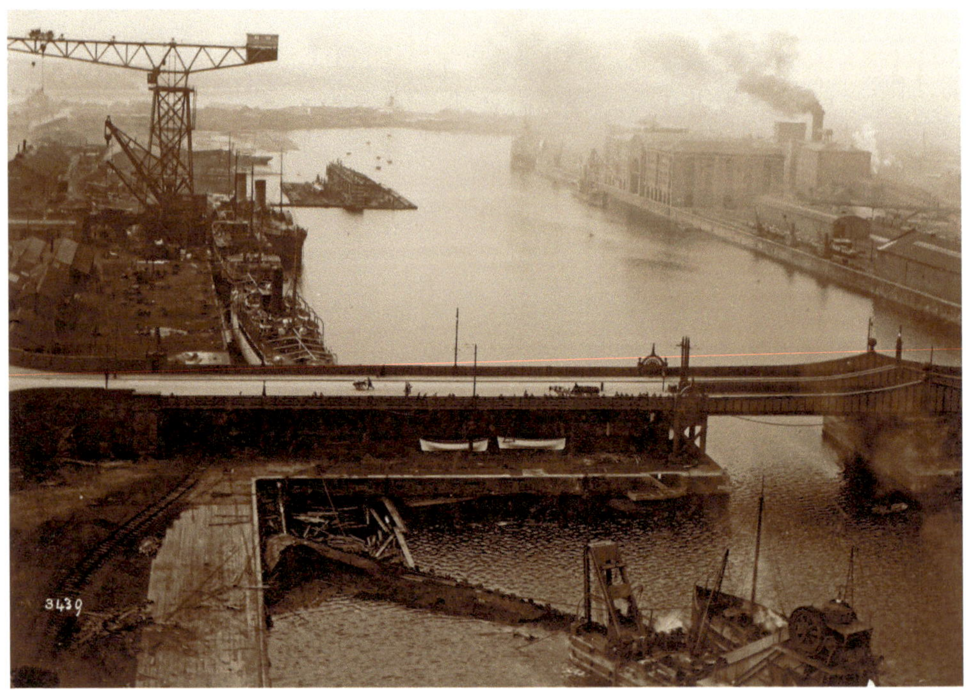

High Level Bridge, Michaelson Road

This impressive bridge was built to connect Barrow Island with the mainland. The island housed the Barrow Shipbuilding Company and the bridge was needed for the workers and transit of goods. The first swing bridge was constructed around 1873 and replaced with a retractable bridge in 1886. The current bridge was built in 1968 and is a steel lift retractable bridge. This was one of the most iconic views in Barrow when thousands of shipyard workers piled across the bridge at finishing time. It is still an important route into Barrow Island and Walney.

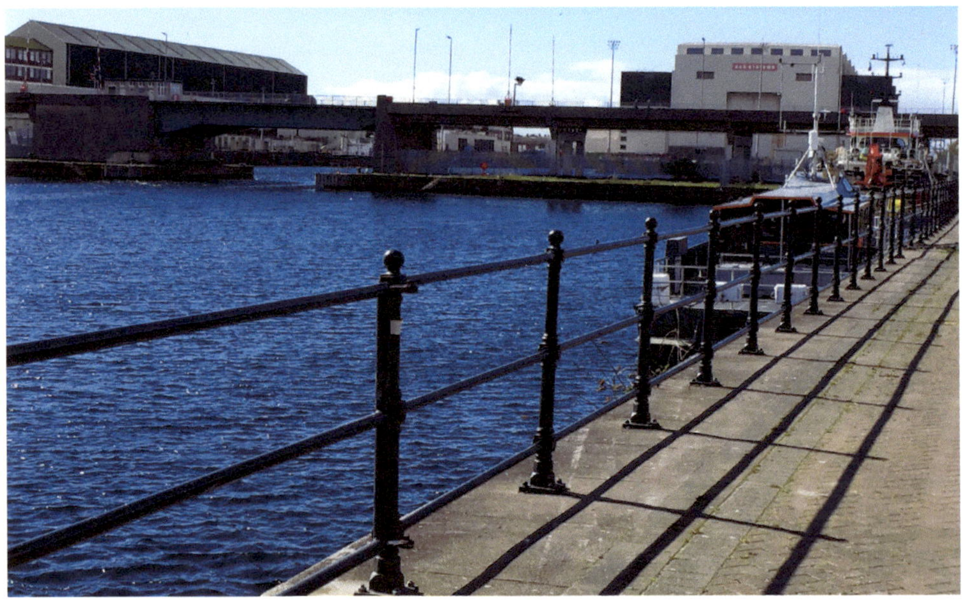

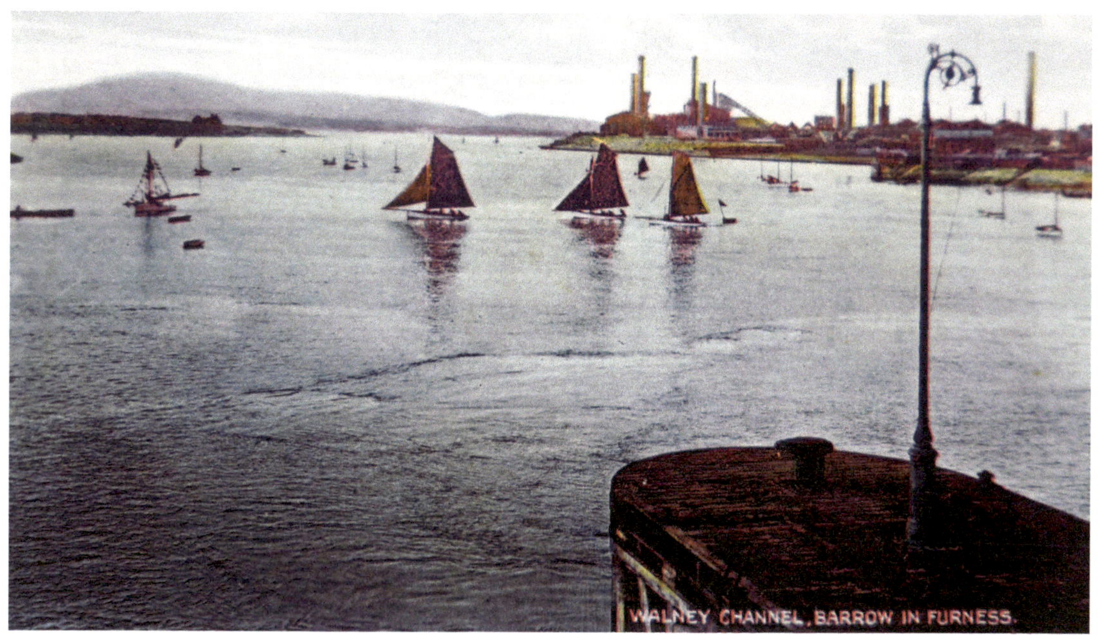

Walney Channel

The channel separates Walney from the rest of Barrow but it is linked by Jubilee Bridge, which provides easy access. However, islanders have been known to be stranded from time to time when the bridge is open. The channel itself is tidal and this view looks towards Black Combe and the western Lake District. Sailing vessels still use the channel but the view has changed dramatically since the demolition of the Iron and Steel works but, once again, this view is dominated by BAE and the DDH. (Picture courtesy of Martin Millar)

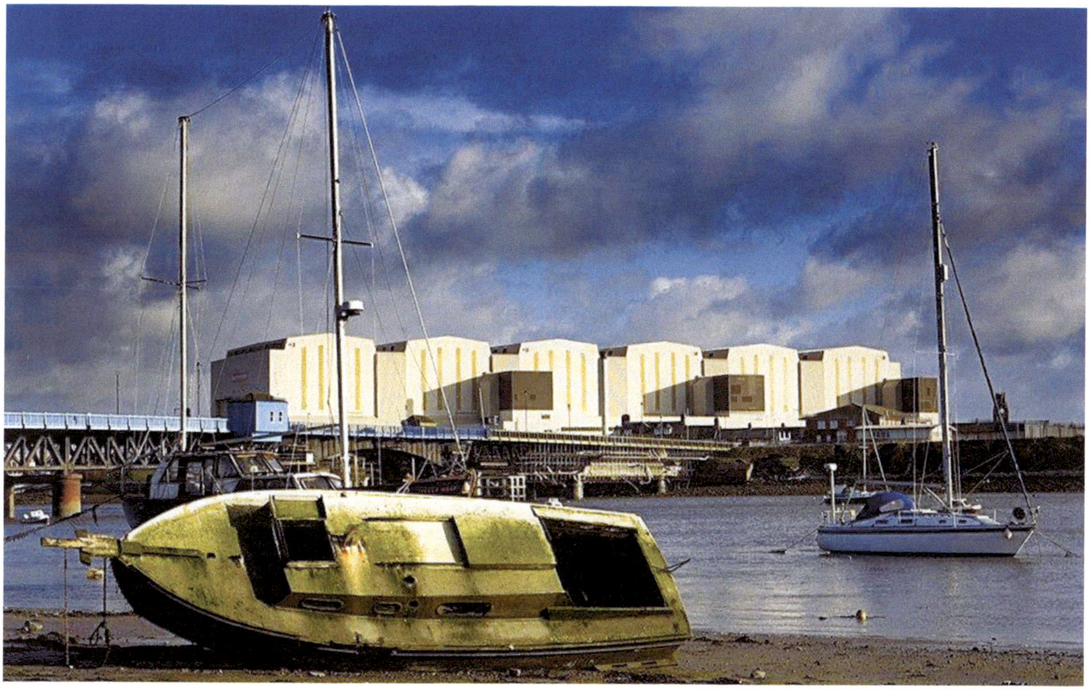

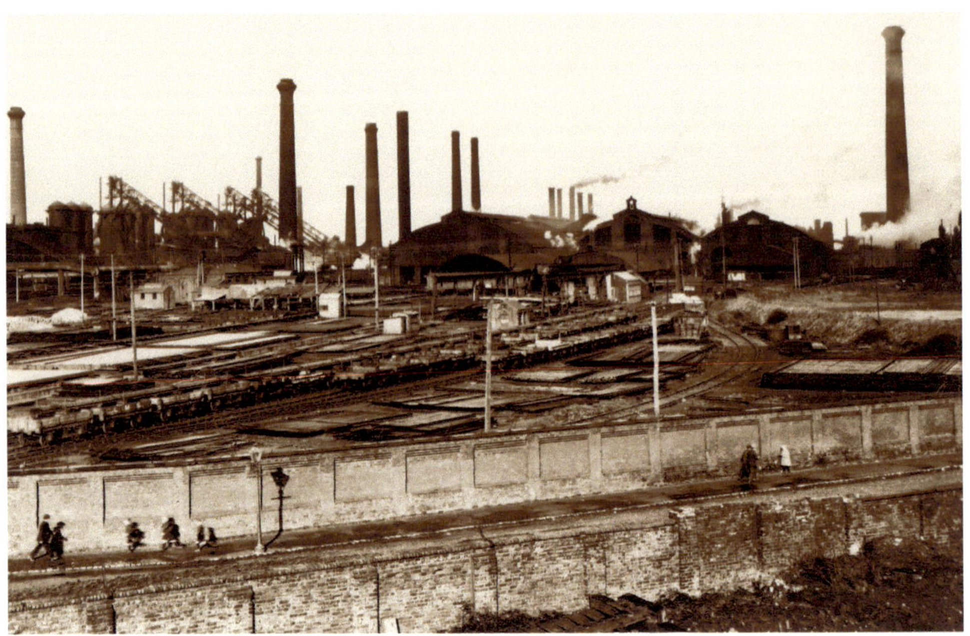

Barrow Ironworks

In 1851, H. W. Schneider discovered a rich seam of iron ore at Askam and output rose rapidly. He saw the possibility and advantages of processing the ore in Barrow and three blast furnaces were built by 1859. The Bessemer-produced high-quality steel was transported all over the world. The industry declined from 1914, the iron works closing in 1963. The steelworks limped on until 1984. Little remains as testament to this industrial period apart from the remnants of the slag bank and the name of Red Man's Walk, which refers to the colour of the iron ore.

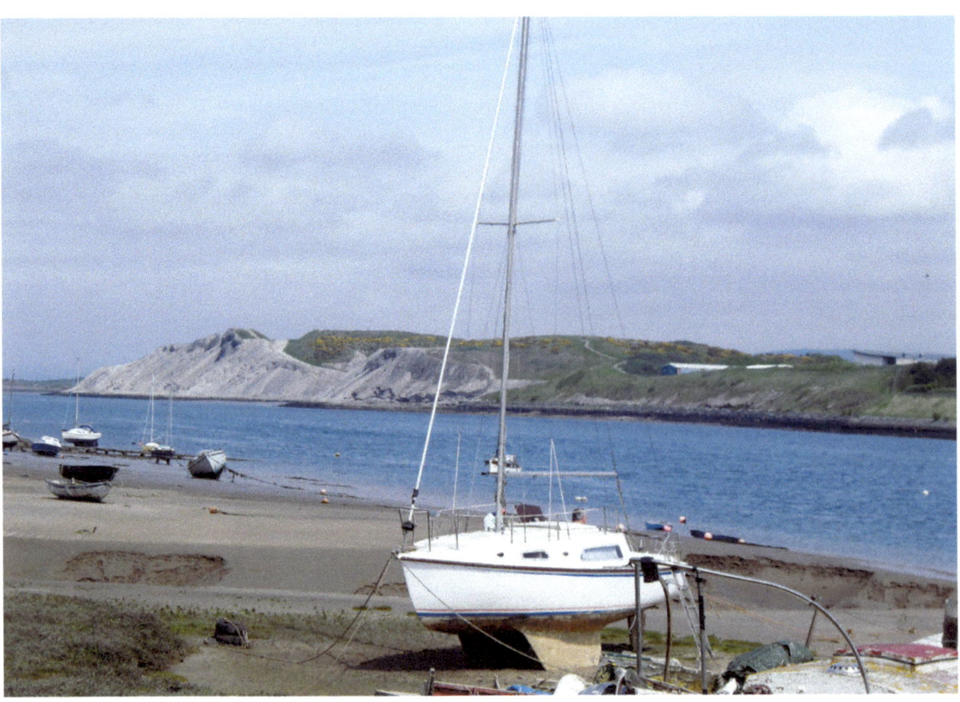

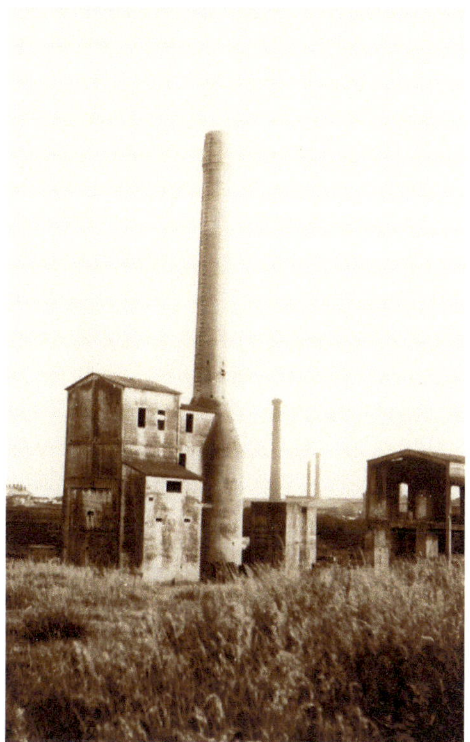

Griffin Chilled Steel Works Chimney

This steel company was one of the companies situated in Hindpool and was important in the early industrial history of Barrow. The Iron and Steel industry faltered by the First World War and, by the mid-1960s, this site was demolished and cleared. Today the land is mainly residential rather than industrial, but the steel works has given its name to a small housing estate as a tangible reminder of its past.

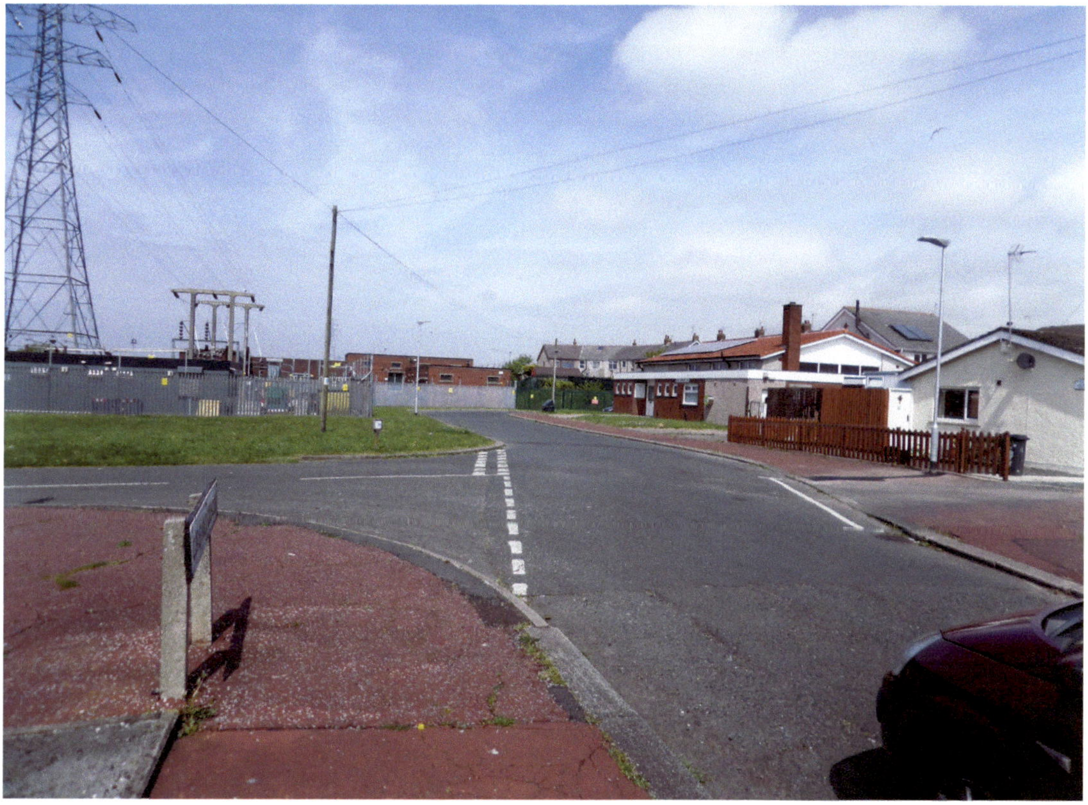

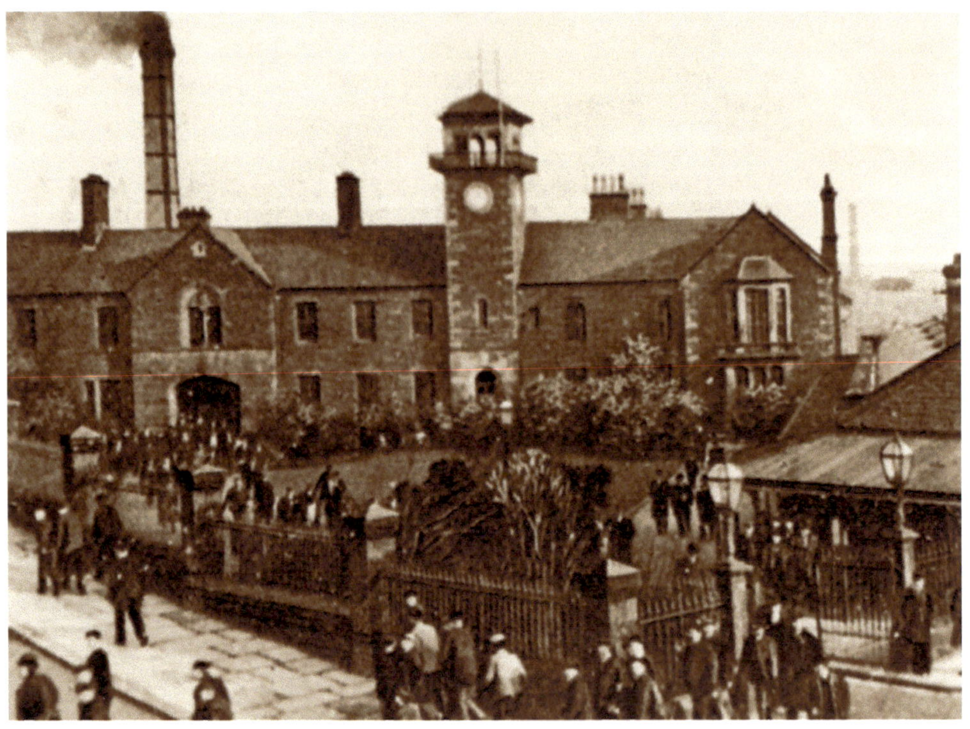

Furness Railway Offices, Rabbit Hill

The Furness Railway Company was the catalyst for the growth and development of Barrow. Its offices were the hub of activity and were at the edge of the original village boundary. James Ramsden arrived as a locomotive superintendent in 1846. His rise was meteoric and his influence over the town was far-reaching. The offices where he worked were demolished and the site is marked for future development as a marina and housing, though it remains derelict at present.

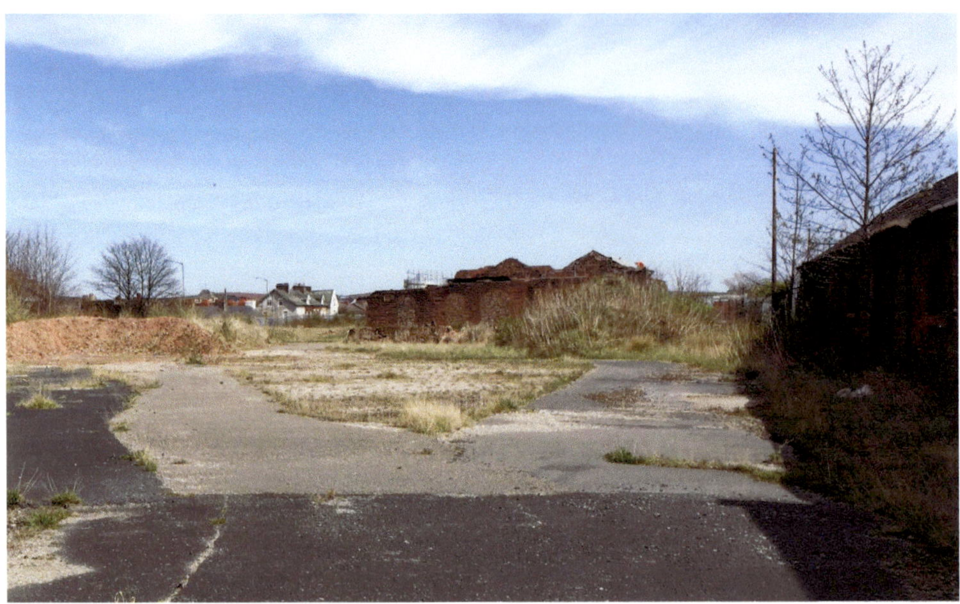

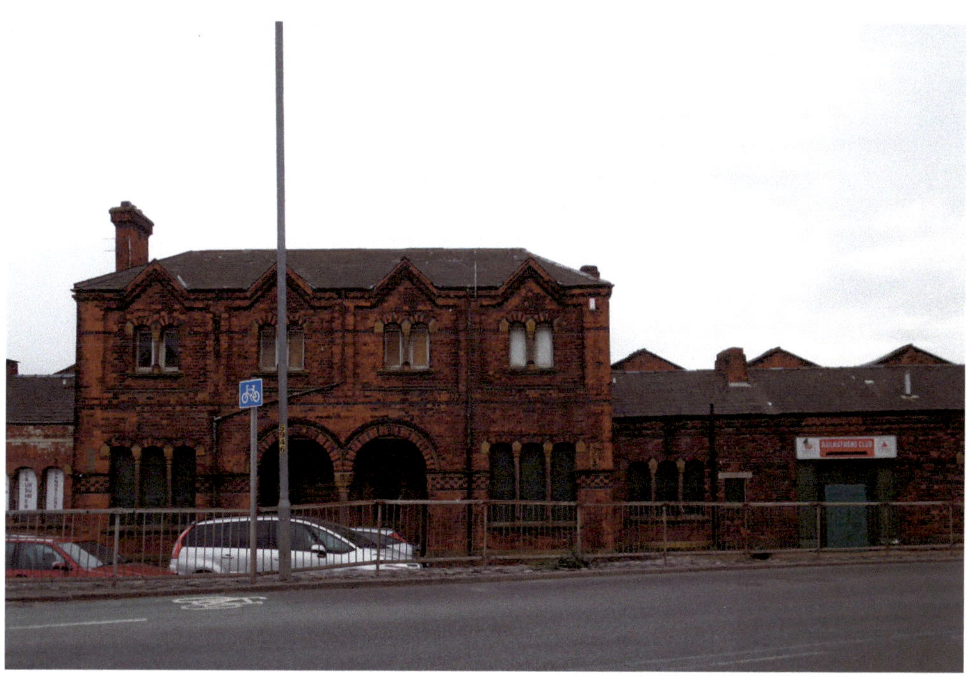

Barrow Railway Station

The first railway station was at the foot of Rabbit Hill and marks the boundary of the original village of Barrow before 1845. The station later moved to its current location behind Holker Street. The first Barrow railway station was centrally placed for rail traffic travelling north along the coast and east towards the interior of the country. The *Coppernob,* an original Furness Railway steam locomotive, was housed outside the station until it was bombed during the Second World War. *Coppernob* was moved to York for safety, sadly never to return. The station was rebuilt after the war in the form we see today, but with some recent modifications.

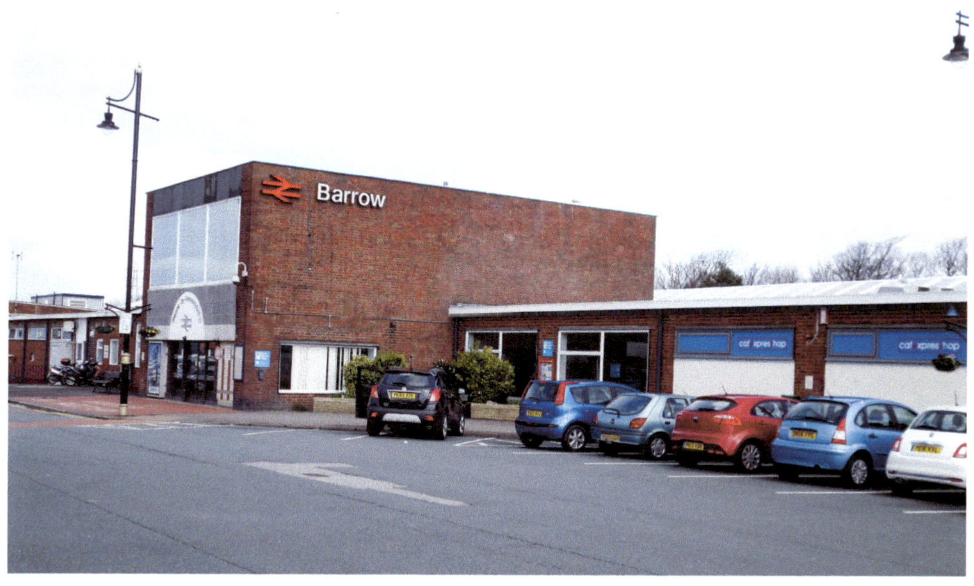

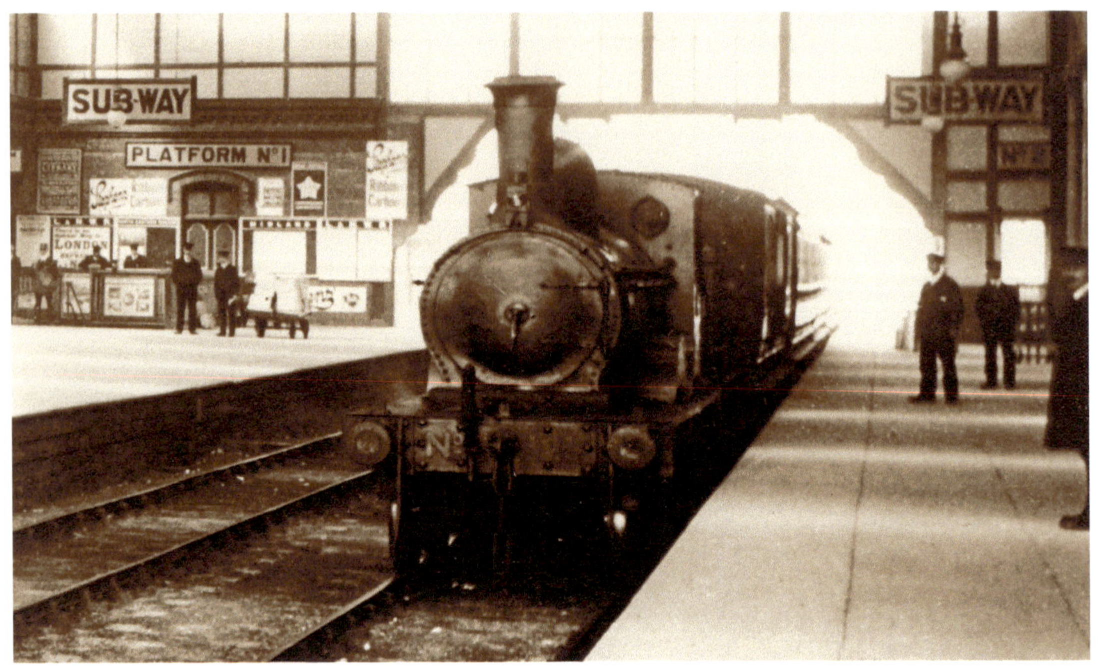

Platform 2, Barrow Station

A steam train halted at Platform 2 ready to collect passengers travelling to Lancaster and stations beyond. It is interesting to note at least nine railway employees waiting on the platforms which must indicate the large volume of trains as well as passengers early in the railway's history. The picture shows the difference in usage of rail travel in current times and indeed how the staffing levels and facilities differ.

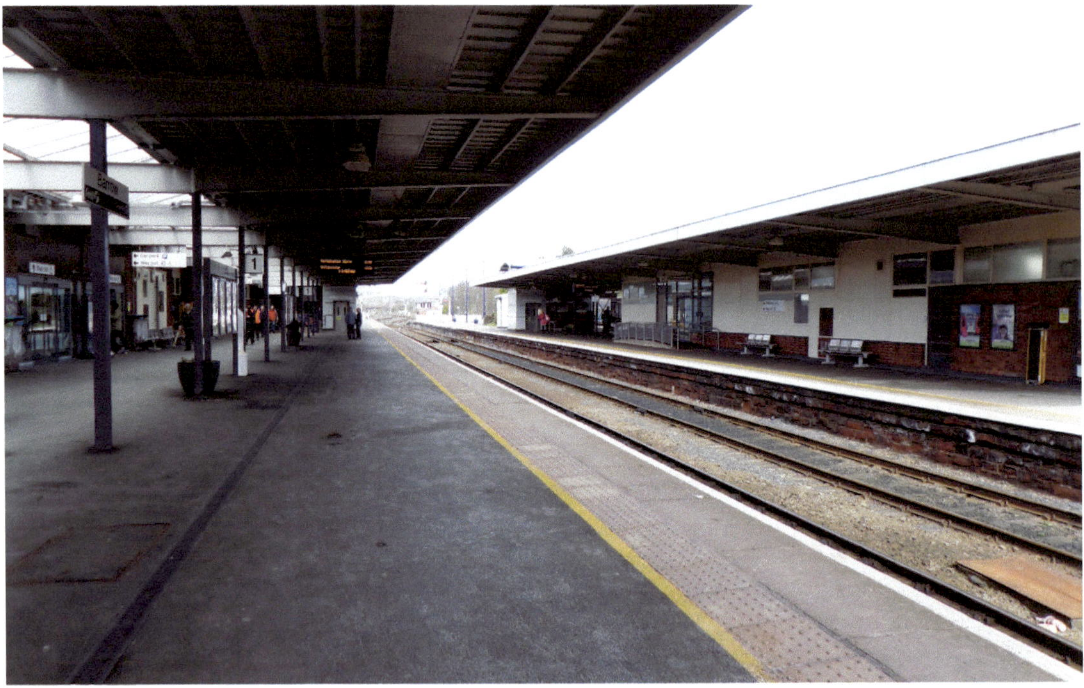

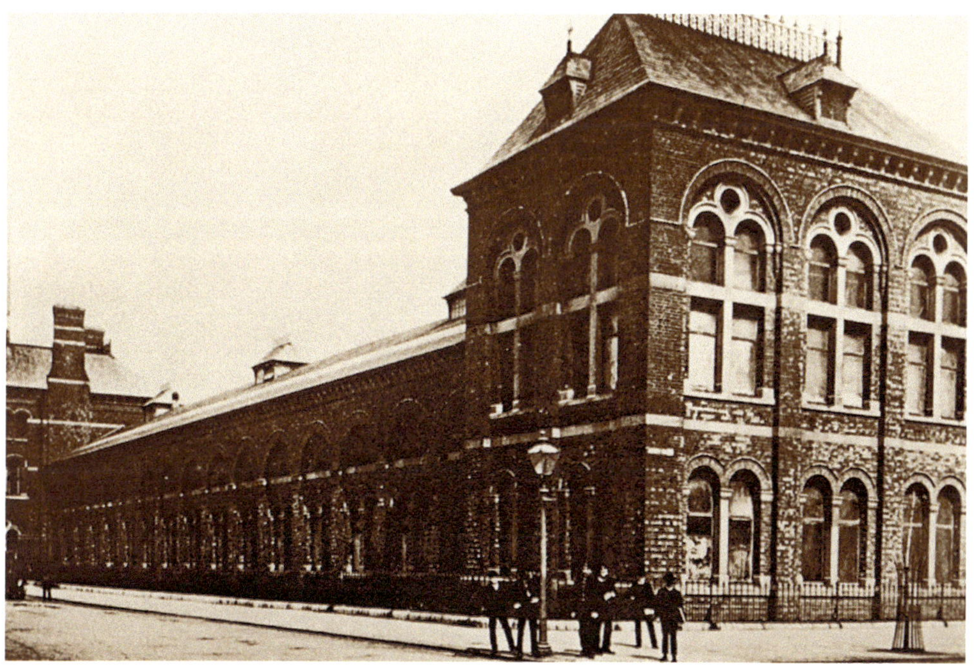

Barrow and Calcutta Jute Works

The Barrow and Calcutta Jute Company was founded by James Ramsden in 1870 to provide diversification and employment for women. It was hoped that the feminine influence would civilise the town. It employed 2,000 women at its peak but could not compete with the Jute Works in Dundee and India. The building was destroyed by fire twice and finally demolished in 1948. The John Whinnerah Institute and Lakeland Laundry occupied the site until they were partially demolished and replaced by a retail outlet and offices.

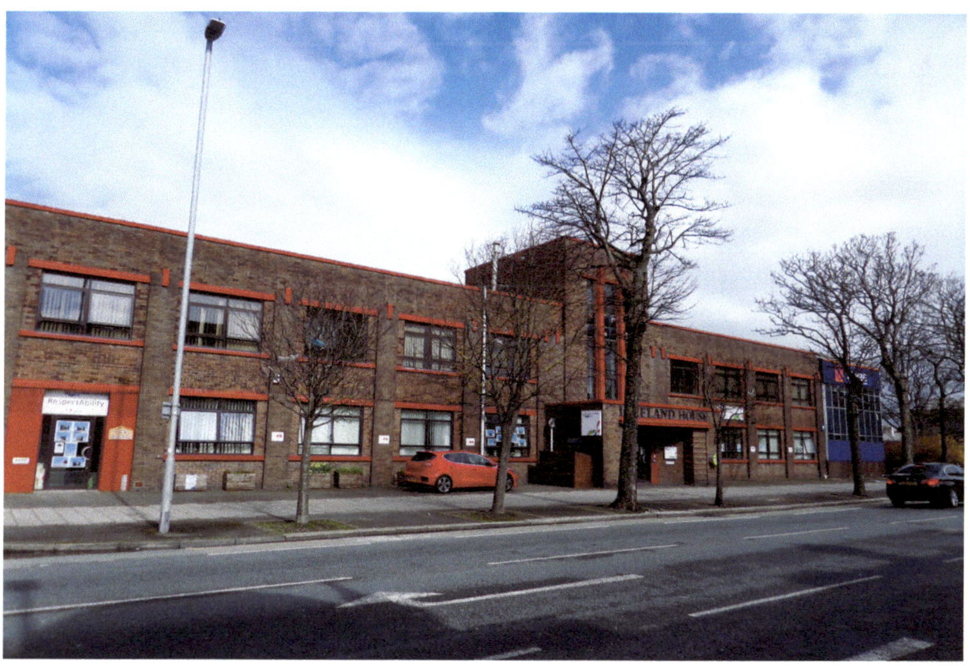

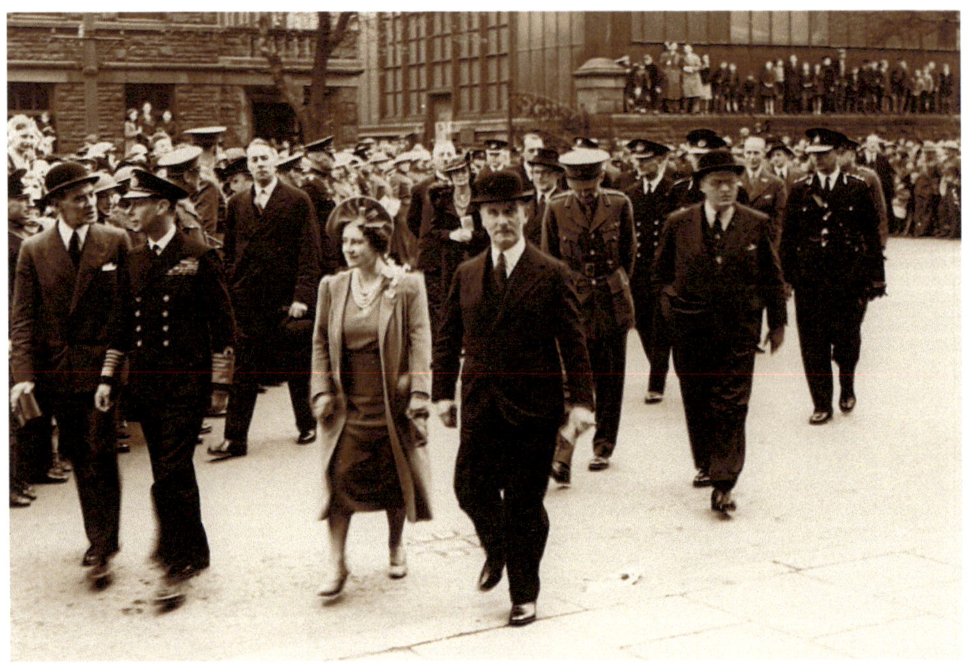

Michaelson Road, Barrow Island

Royal visits to the town were frequent throughout the years, due to the launching of ships. One such visit by George VI and Queen Elizabeth was captured here in 1940. They were visiting Vickers Armstrong Ltd, where ships, armaments and guns were made as part of the war effort during the Second World War. The scene is not dramatically different today, the large Victorian workshops still dominating most of Michaelson Road, which is named after the family who owned the island before industrialisation.

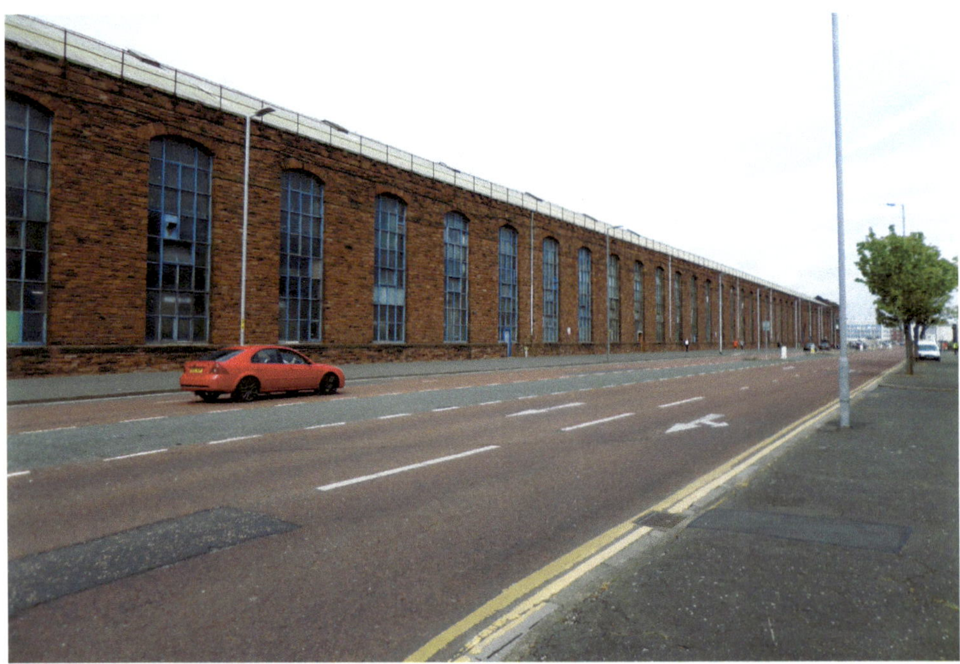

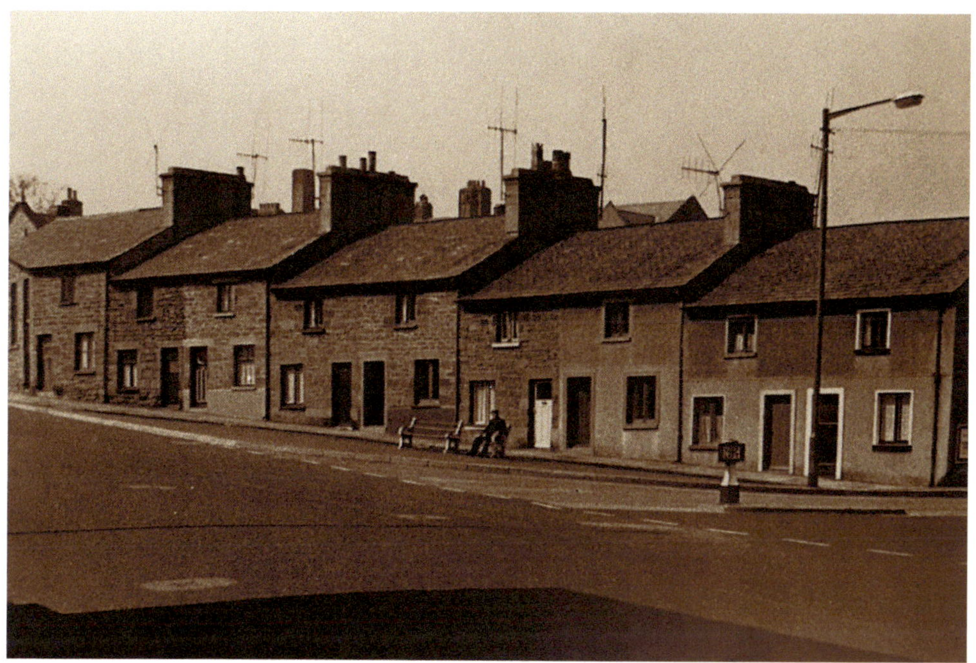

Railway Cottages, Salthouse Road

Originally named Rabbit Hill, Salthouse Road boasts some of the earliest houses built in the new town. They were the Furness Railway cottages and James Ramsden lodged here when he first arrived as Railway Superintendant in 1846. They are all still in use and are a simple reminder of the influence Furness Railway has on the town. They adjoin the school, which is built from the same local red sandstone, and are now listed buildings.

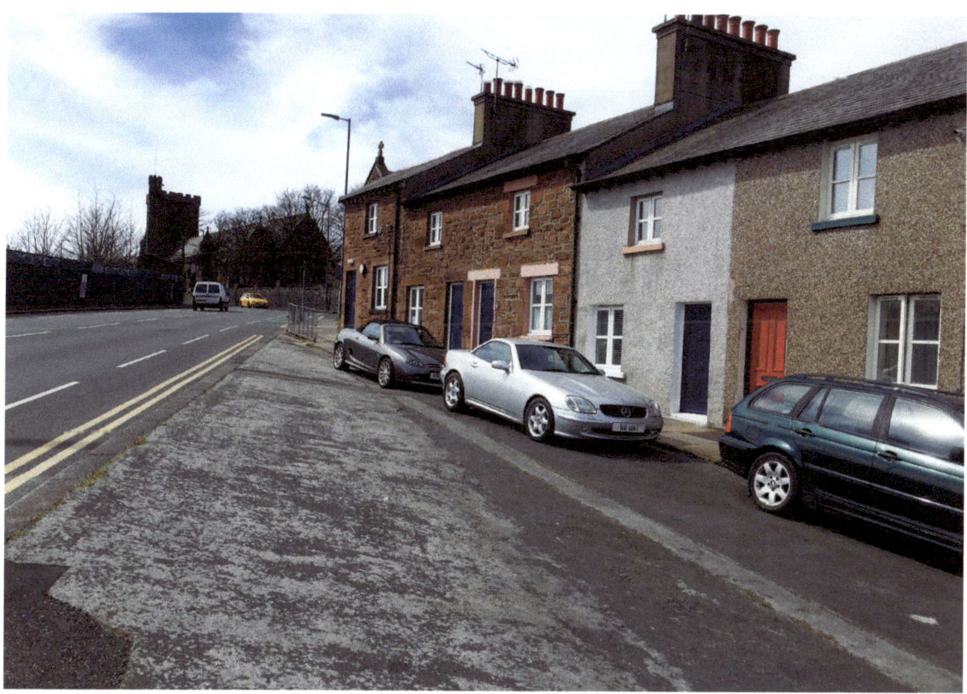

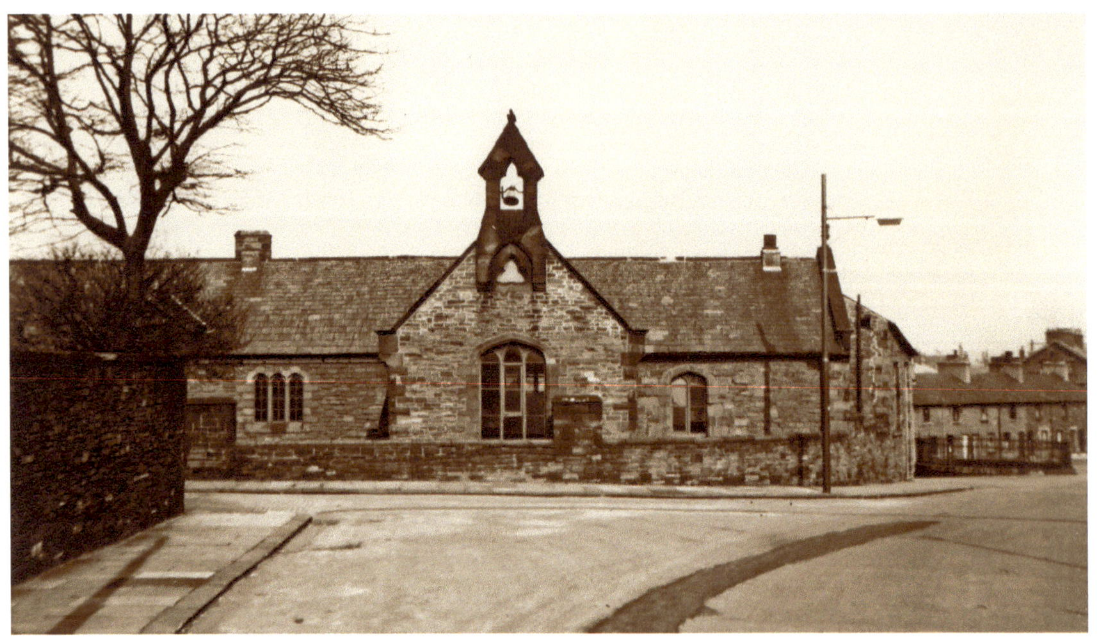

St George's School, Rabbit Hill

Established in 1849, the Church of England primary school is the oldest school in Barrow. Originally, it was a training college for engineers. It has a typical Victorian design with high windows. It is still in use though has been recently remodelled by Cumbria County Council to meet the needs of a modern school and its growing population. The building retains its original appearance but the new entrance in School Street is faced with slate from Burlington slate quarry, which was one of the original resources that first initiated the railway.

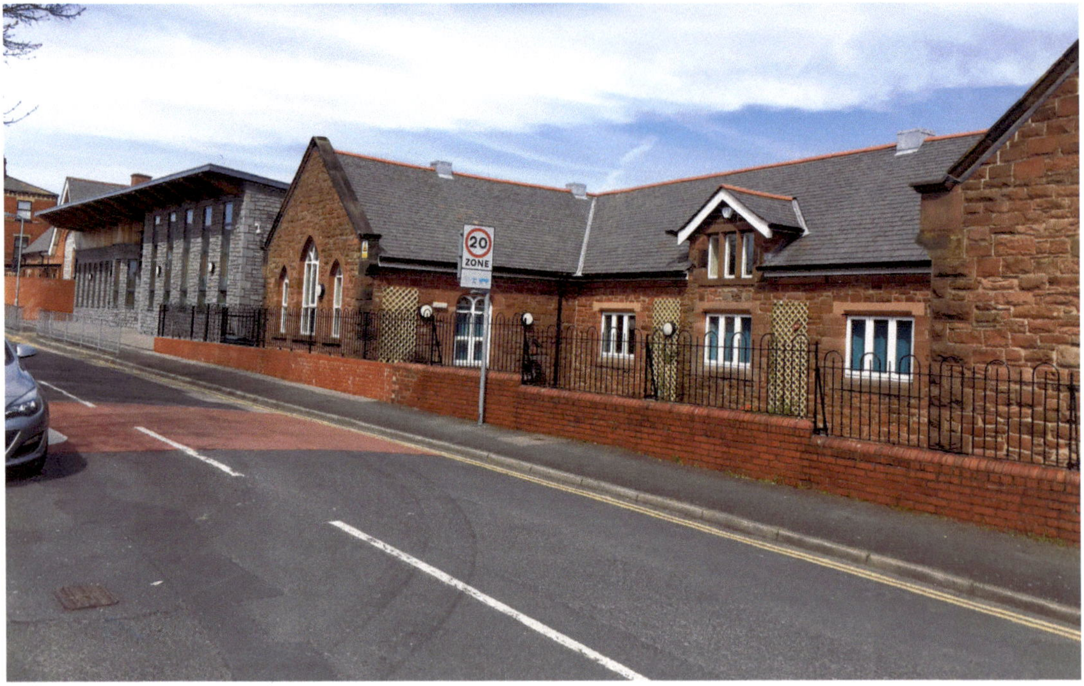

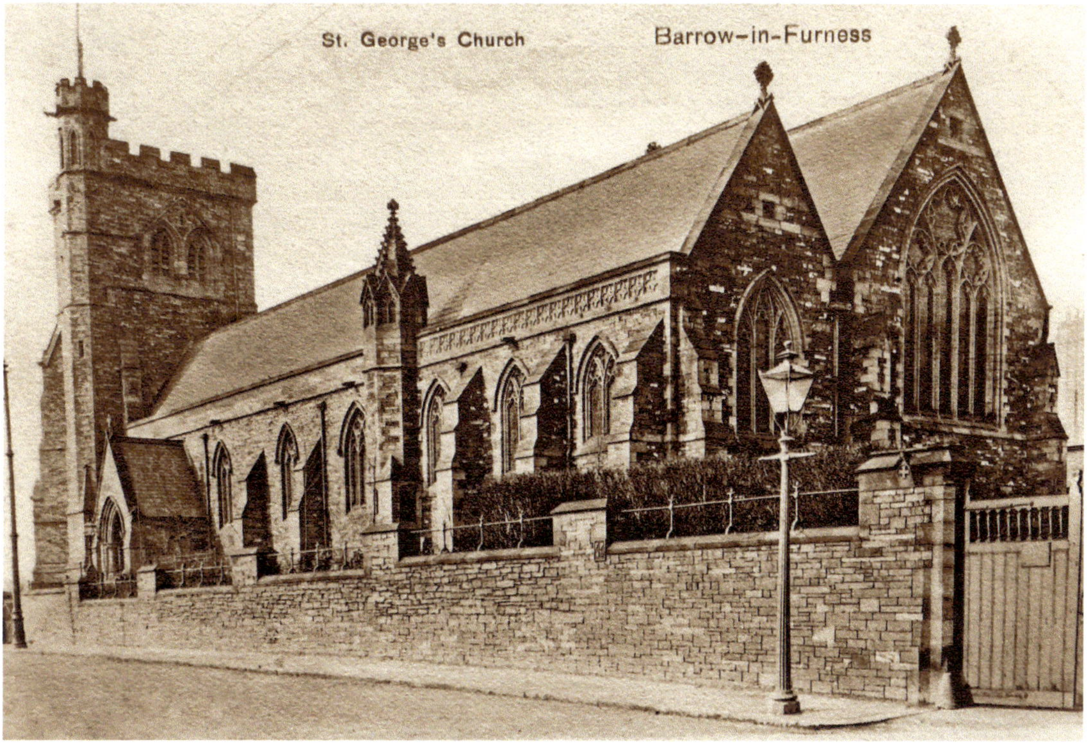

St George's Church, St George's Square

The first Anglican church in Barrow was consecrated in 1861 and sits on top of a mound. Imposingly Gothic and built from Burlington slate, the building was influenced heavily by Ramsden, who had a chapel built on the southern side of the transept. The Ramsden Chapel is used for civic events and has two carvings of James and Lady Ramsden, hinting at his inflated view of his own importance. An elaborate choir stall for local dignitaries was installed as well as a special entrance at the side. Some adaptations have occurred over the years but the church remains impressive.

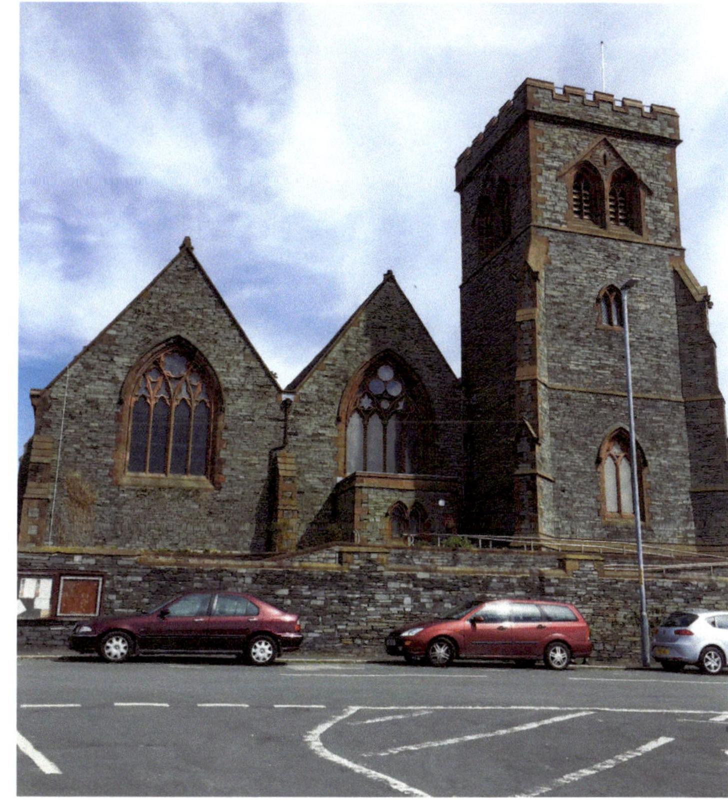

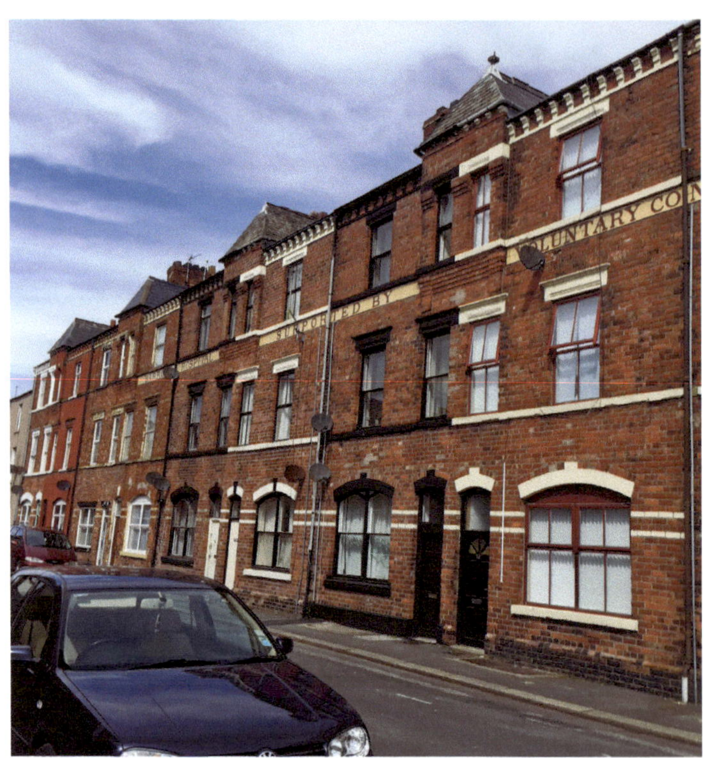

St George's Hospital

The vicar of St George's had established an early hospital in 1866 in a small house on the corner of Cross Street and Albert Street. This was later replaced by a building in School Street. The original sign is still visible along the walls of the terraced row. It boldly declares, 'Barrow Hospital supported by voluntary contributions', a reminder that the National Health Service was still some time away. It is in complete contrast with the modern Furness General Hospital situated on the outskirts of town.

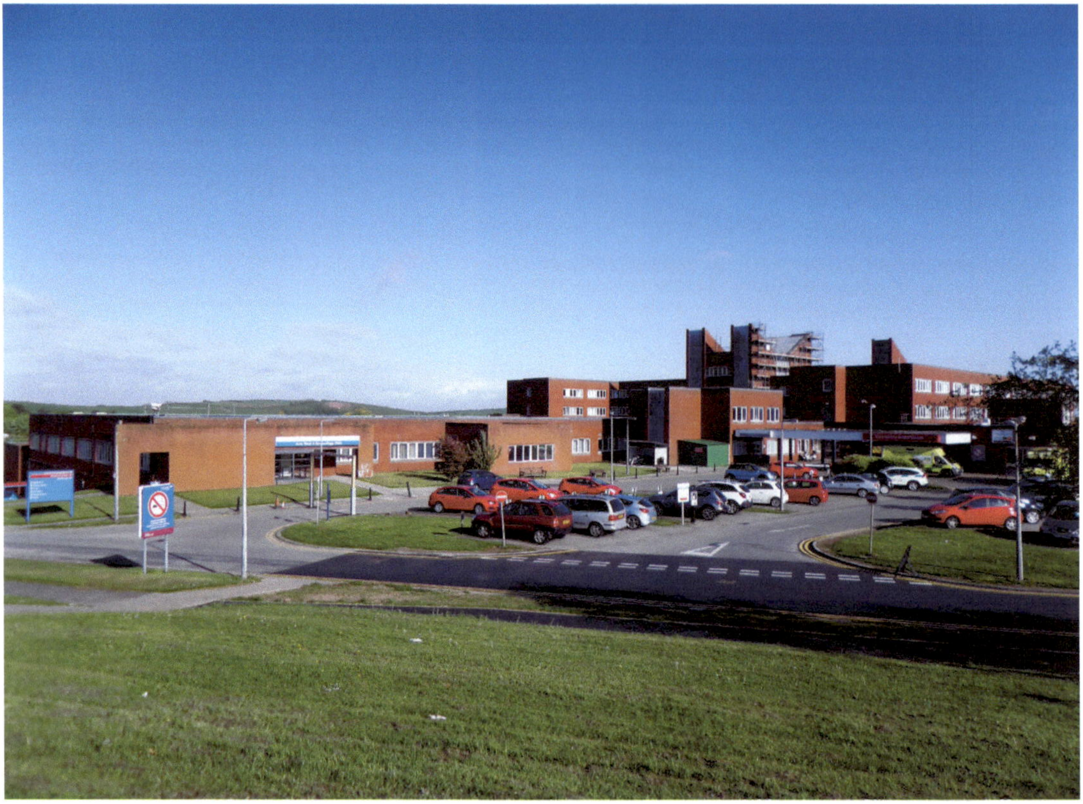

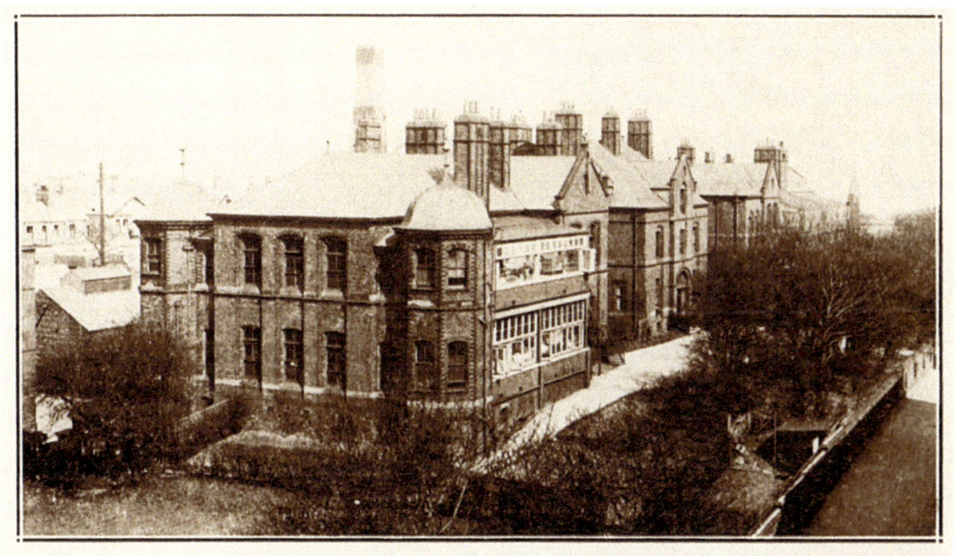

North Lonsdale Hospital, Church Street

North Lonsdale Hospital was opened in 1874. This was a state-of-the-art building with modern facilities and Nightingale wards. It became a training hospital for nurses; the old nurses' quarters in Albert Street are now a care home. The hospital served the community well for 120 years until it became too small and old-fashioned. The site was restricted and the Furness General Hospital was built on the outskirts of town among green fields and close to the main road, providing easier access.

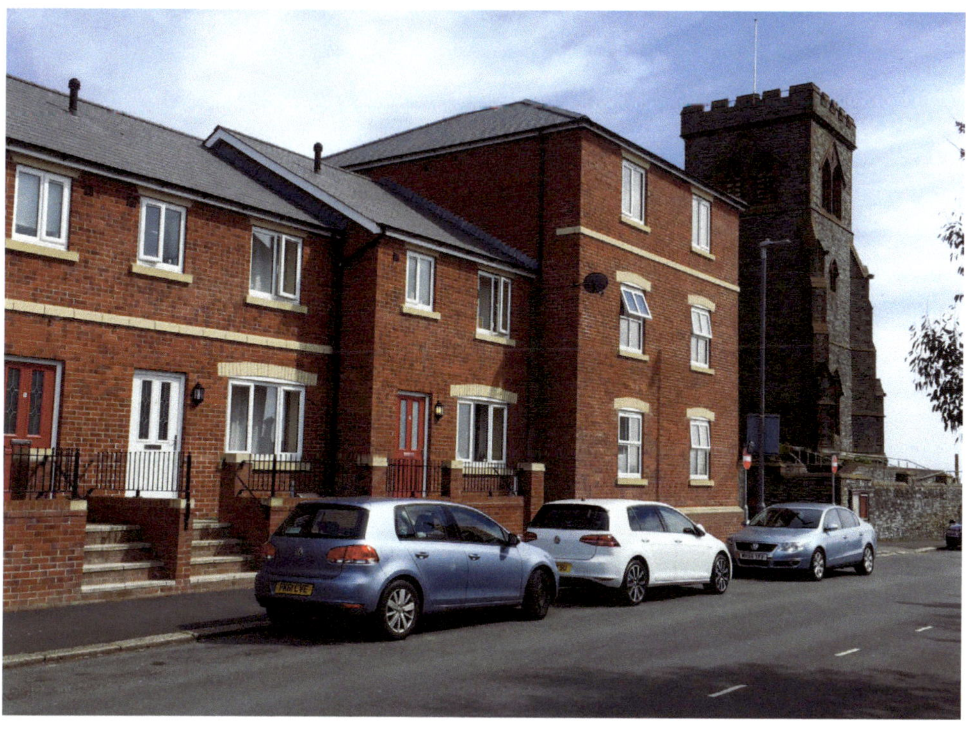

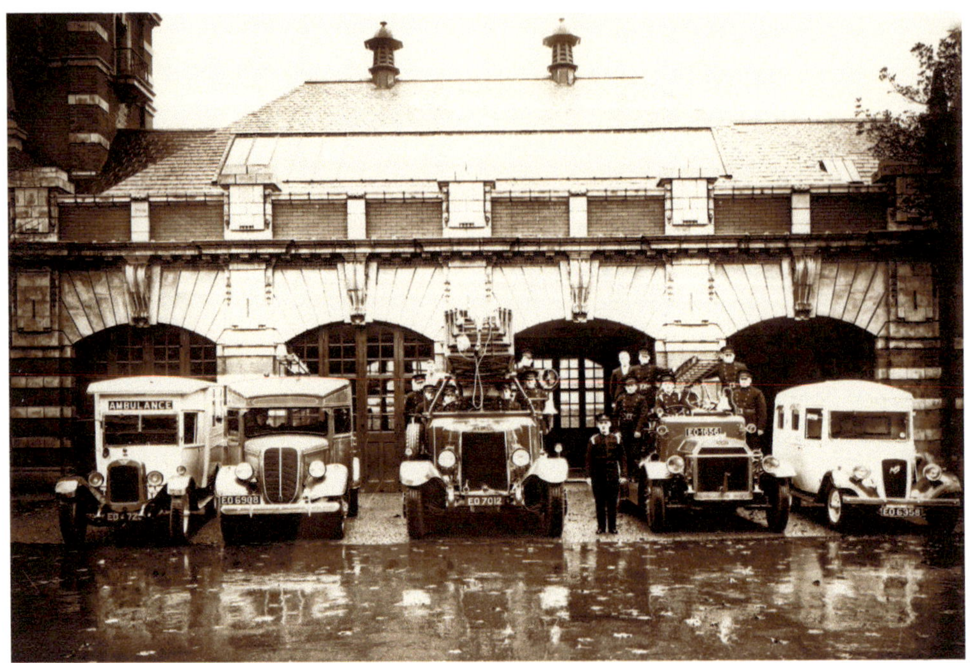

The Fire Station, Abbey Road

A voluntary fire brigade was set up in 1866 and headed by churchwardens of St George's, led by Ramsden. Following incorporation in 1867, the brigade was formalised, firemen appointed and a manual fire engine and other equipment bought. The fire station, built in 1911, was designed for motorised appliances and included a stationmaster's house and accommodation for two drivers. In 1996 it was replaced by a building on Phoenix Road, which has direct access to the main A590 road. Currently, the old Fire Station houses the 'Bed Brigade' store.

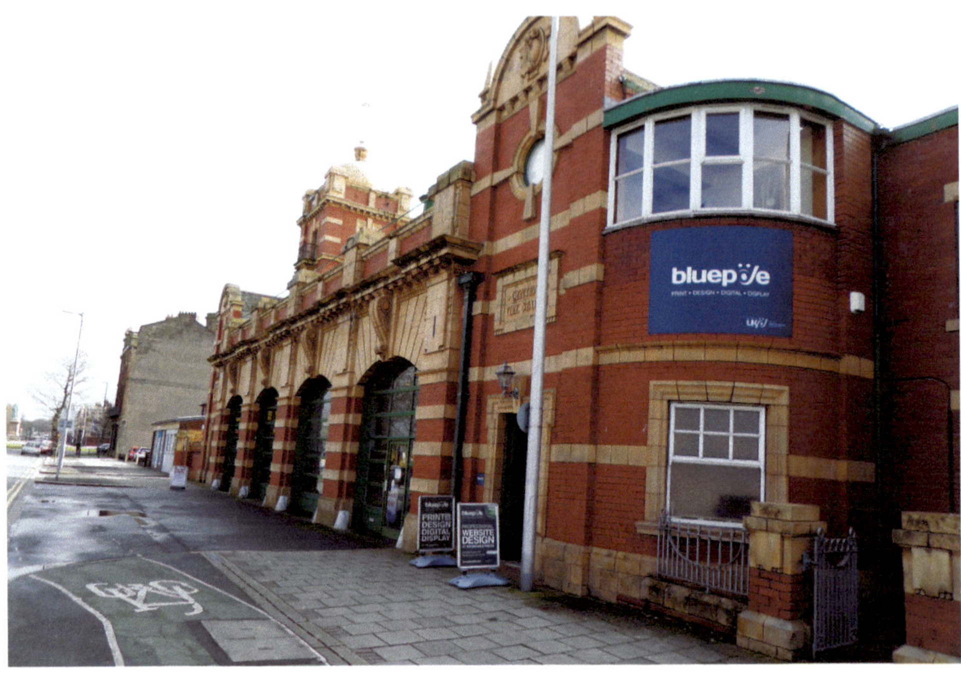

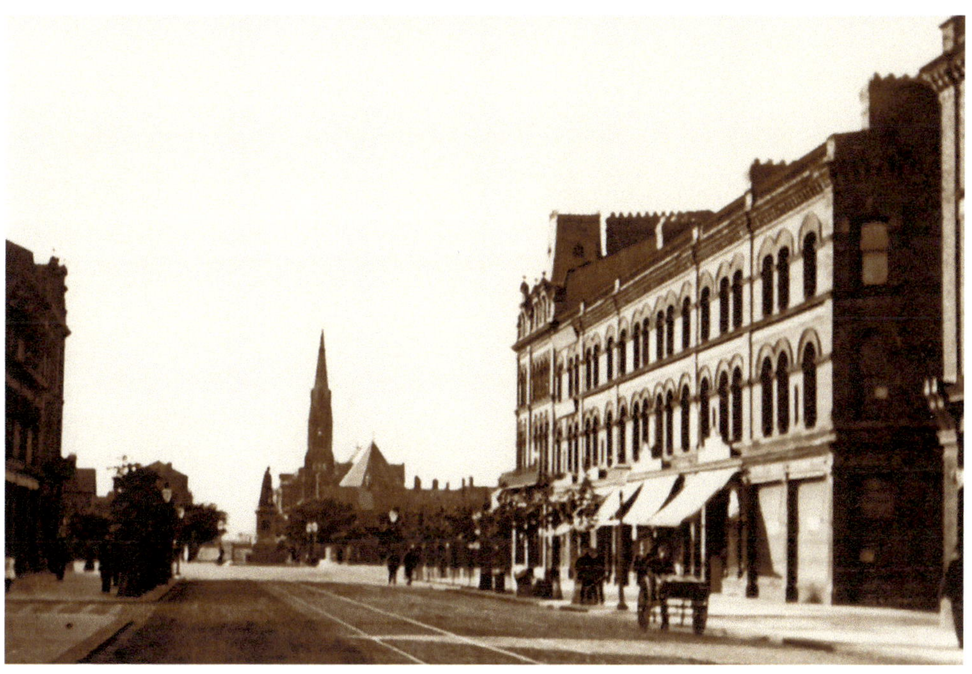

Duke Street, North

Looking towards St Mary's church spire, down Duke Street, one can see a thriving business centre. The busy scene is different today with fewer small shops. This area was once a thriving commercial street with numerous banks and shops, and even a stockbrokers. The chimney of the Jute Works can be seen in the distance.

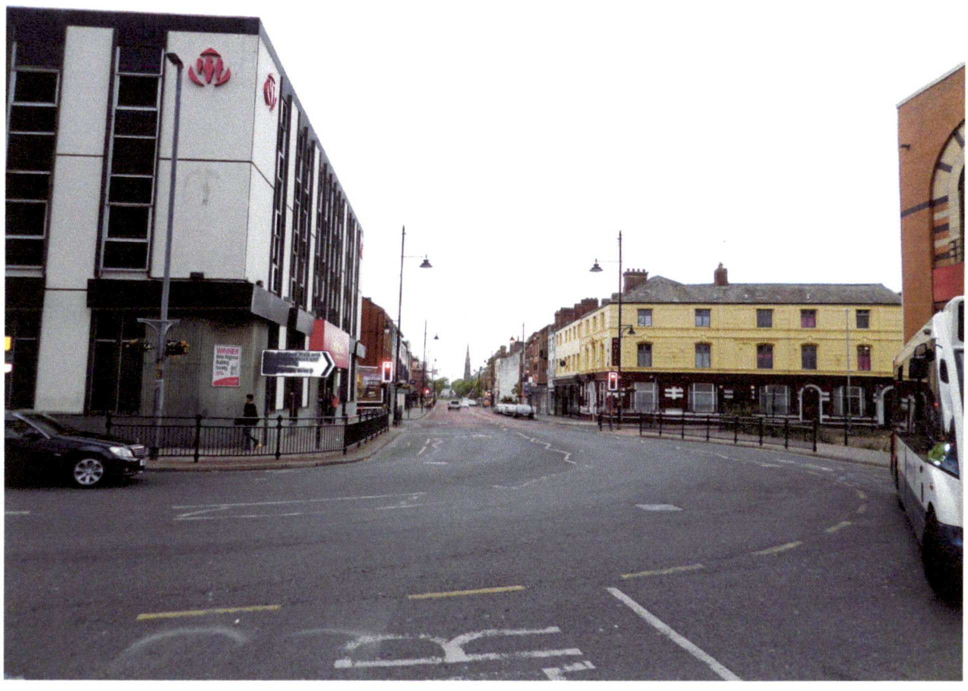

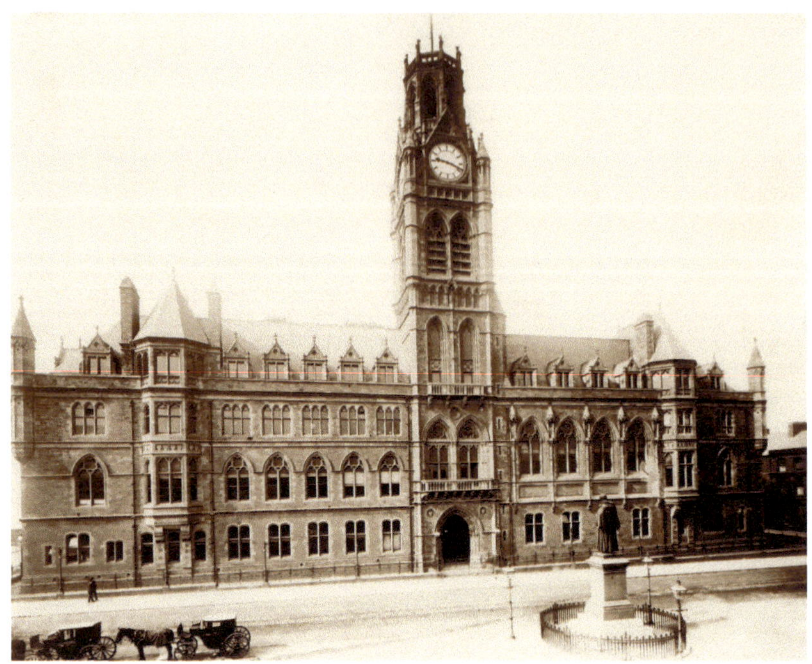

Barrow Town Hall

As Barrow grew, the town sought municipal recognition. The town was made a Borough in 1867 and the town grew in significance and wealth. A magnificent town hall was designed by W.H. Lynn and, after some modifications, was completed in 1887. Built from local sandstone and Westmorland slate in the neo-gothic style, it is a remarkable edifice standing at fifty metres tall. It reflects once again the confidence and self-esteem Barrow had and is a monument to the growth and success of the Victorian industrial town.

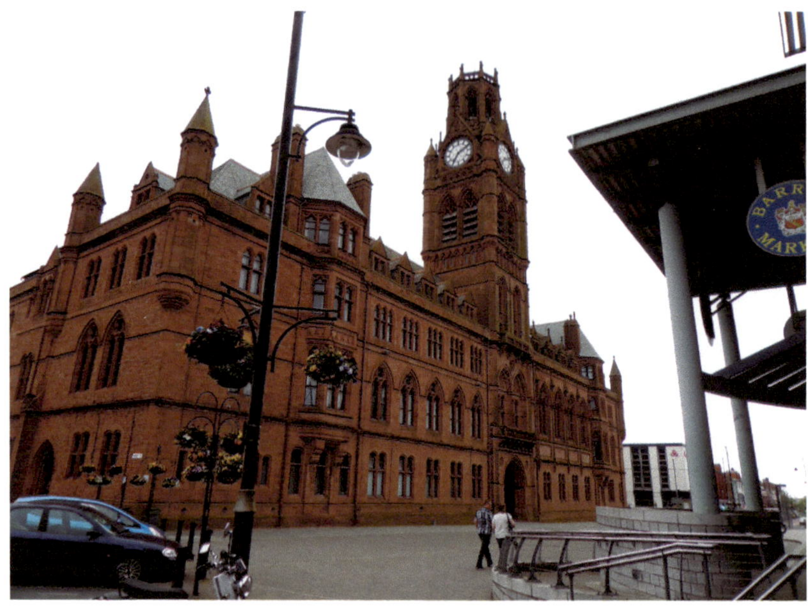

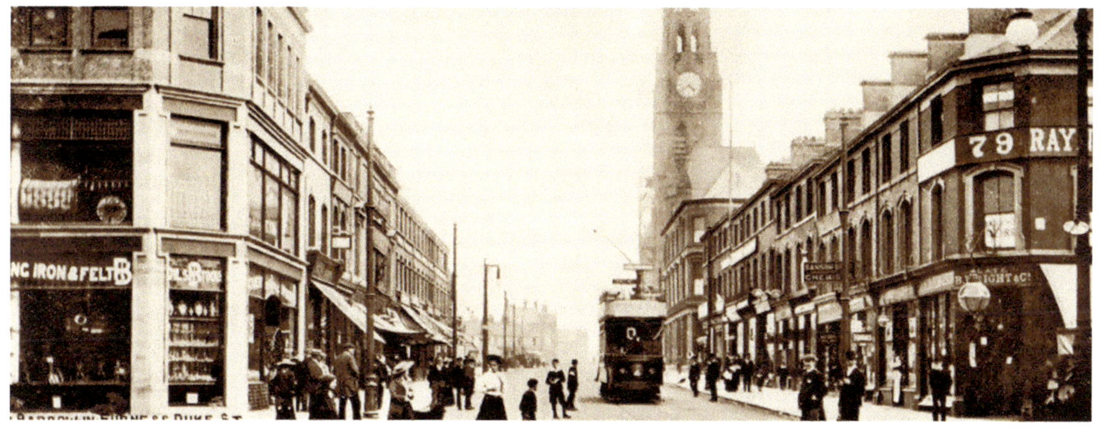

Duke Street, South

Duke Street, looking towards the town hall, reveals shops of many kinds and this appears to have once been a major shopping street. The wide straight road provided the space for trams, which emphasised the modernity of the town. The town hall clock tower dominates the picture and heralds the importance of the Borough of Barrow-in-Furness as a civic entity. It has lost its commercial importance today and most banks are now in Dalton Road.

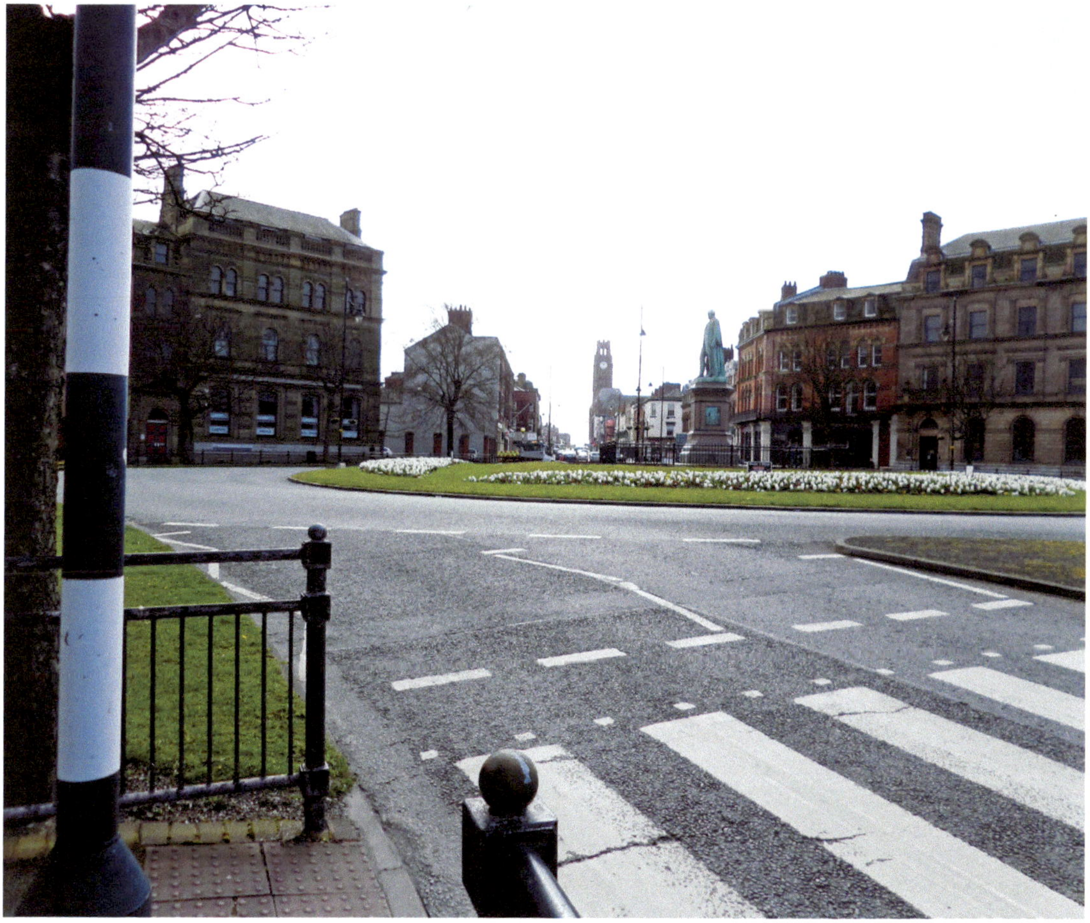

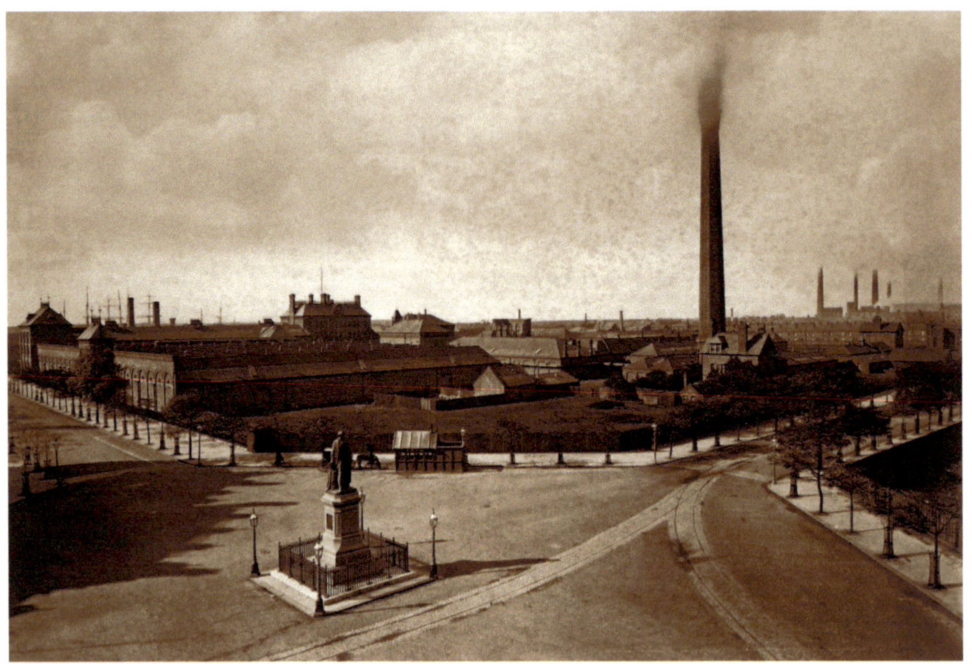

Ramsden Square and the Jute Works

This industrial backdrop is in stark contrast to the current view. Sir James Ramsden's statue faces up Abbey Road, the main route into the town and in the background is the Jute Works, built to provide work for women in an attempt to civilise the mainly male-dominated 'frontier' town. It was so rough and unruly that it was known as the 'Chicago of the North'. The land in the right-hand corner would eventually become the site of Barrow Library.

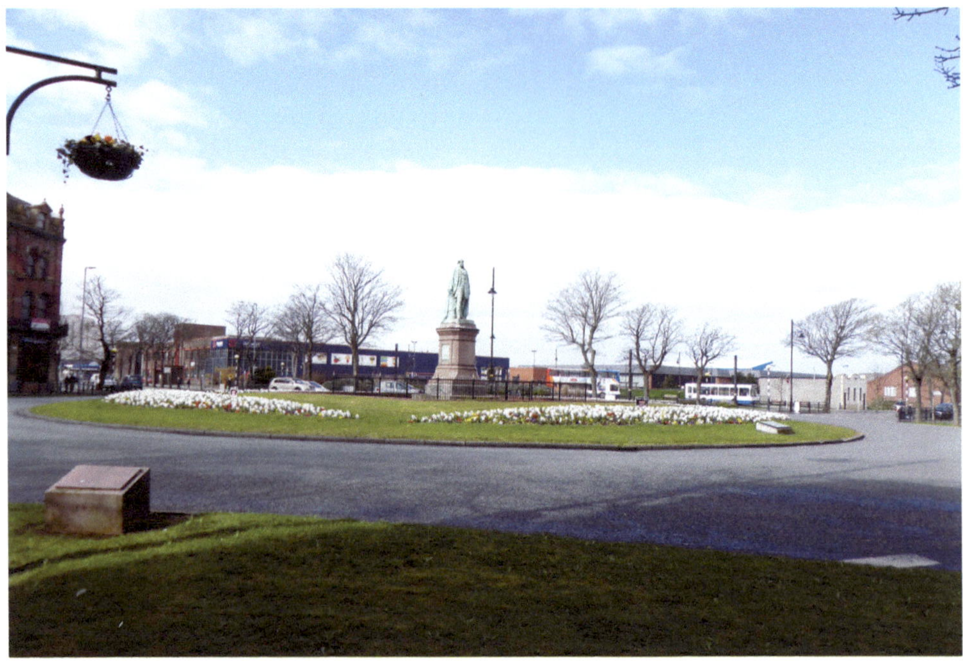

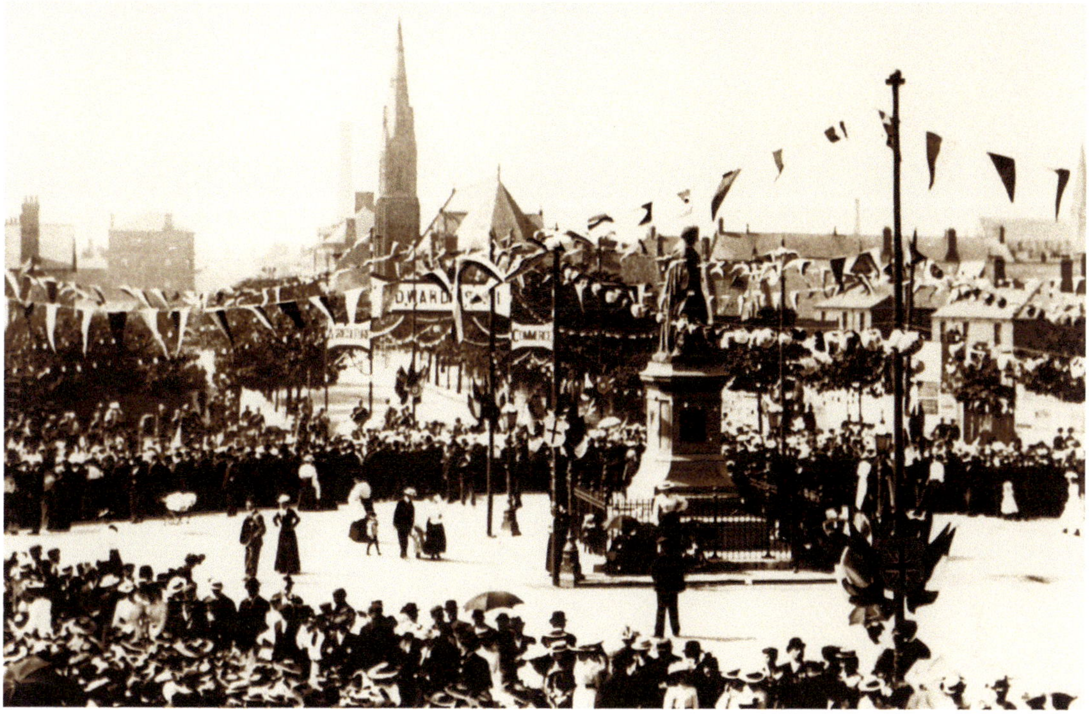

Ramsden Square

The accession of Edward VII heralded a new era. His coronation was on 9 August 1902 and celebrations took place across the country. Naturally, Barrow was no exception. In this picture of Ramsden Square, the local population are out in force for the civic celebrations. Ramsden's statue looks on among the flags and bunting almost as an observer to the passing of the Victorian age which had 'made' Barrow.

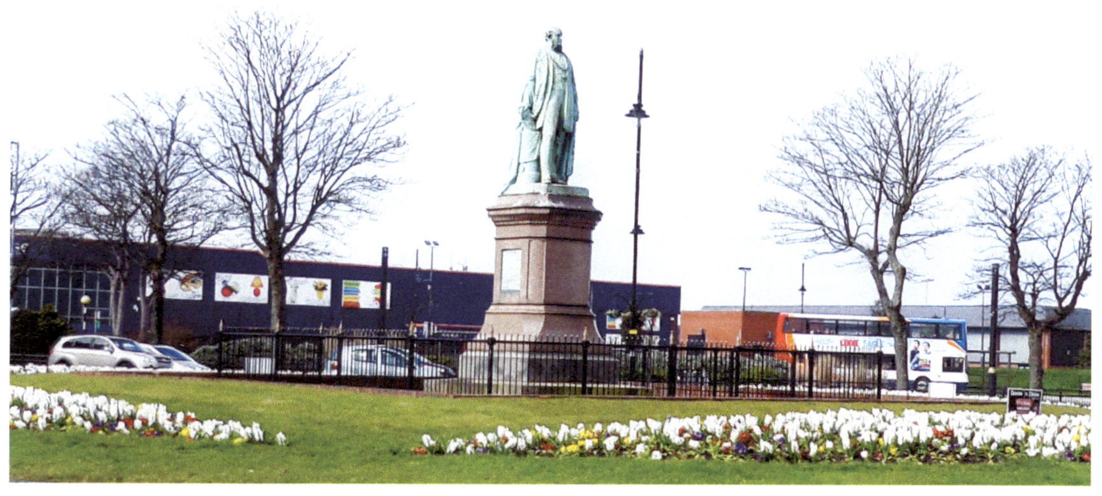

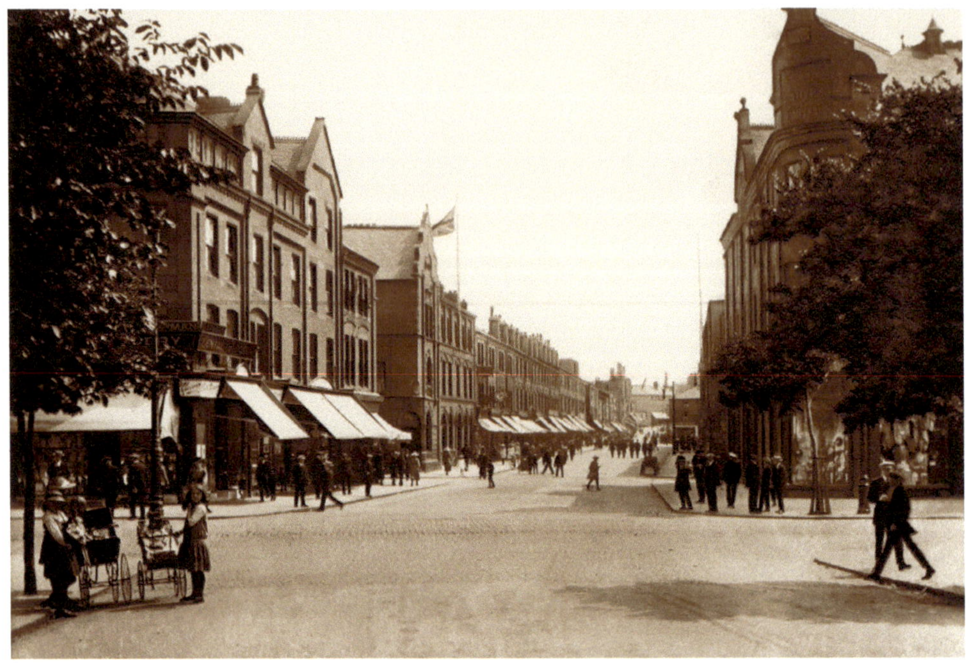

Dalton Road, North

The junction of Dalton Road and Abbey Road combines two of the oldest roads in Barrow. Dalton Lane, as it was called, followed the route to the original settlement of Barrow and, in Victorian times, became one the main shopping streets. It is a more organic route and is not one of the planned linear roads which are so representative of the town. The small shops all have awnings and, on the corner, the Barrow Cooperative Society store provided everything from clothing to furniture, as well the 'divi' – a scheme to reward the shoppers.

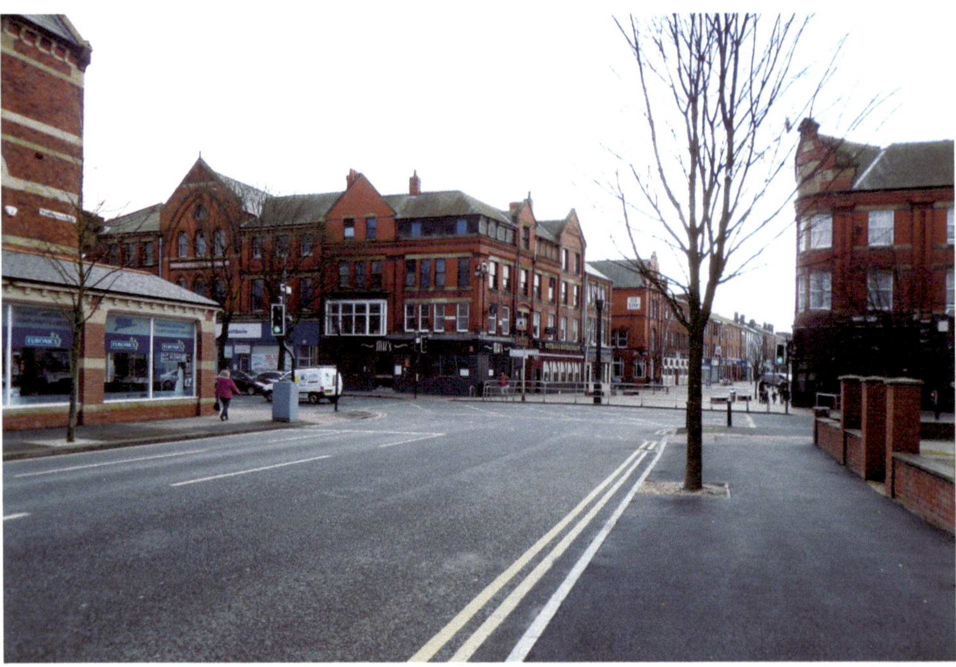

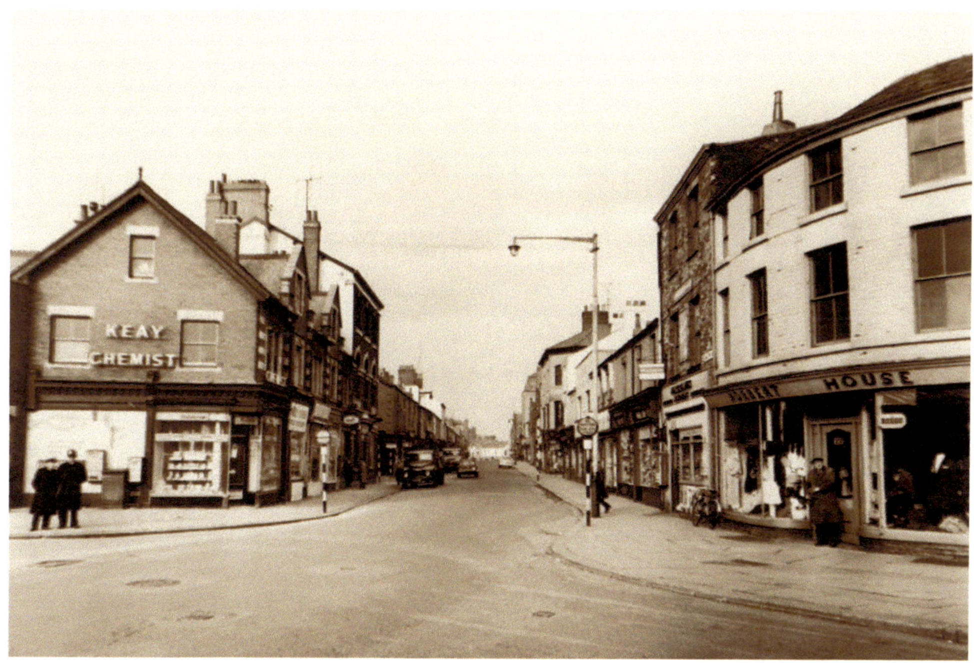

Dalton Road, South

The long Dalton Road culminated at the top of Schneider Square. There was a central statue of H. W. Schneider, the iron magnate who was instrumental in building Barrow's prosperity. By the 1960s the town was undergoing changes and, although many original shops were still there, new buildings and remodelling was taking place. One of the major changes to Dalton Road was when it was pedestrianised at the top and later extended along its full length.

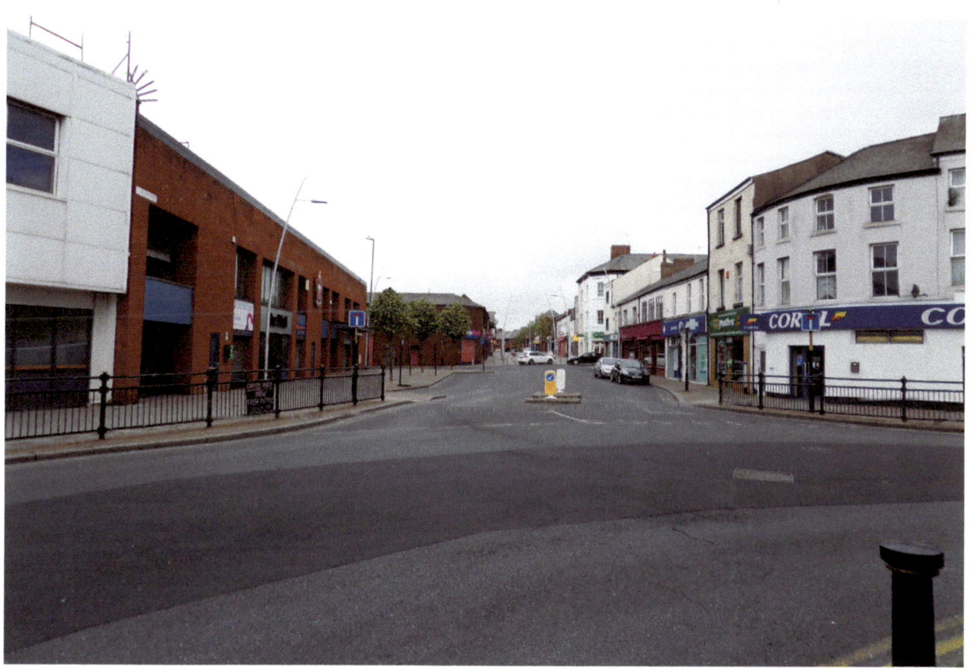

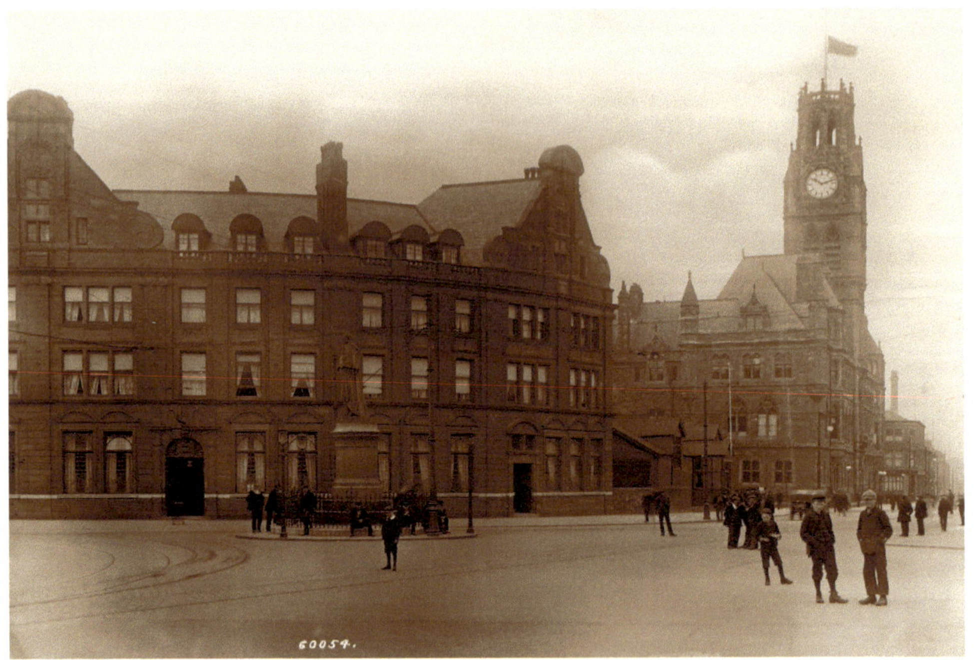

Schneider Square

Schneider Square celebrates another Victorian industrialist and town father, H. W. Schneider, who was responsible for the iron ore mines, later expanding into processing the ore as well. It is at the junction of Michaelson Road, Duke Street and Dalton Road, three important roads in the town. The location of the statue originally avoided the tramlines and was not centrally placed as it is today. Schneider's statue was erected in 1891 close to the town hall and in front of the Majestic Hotel.

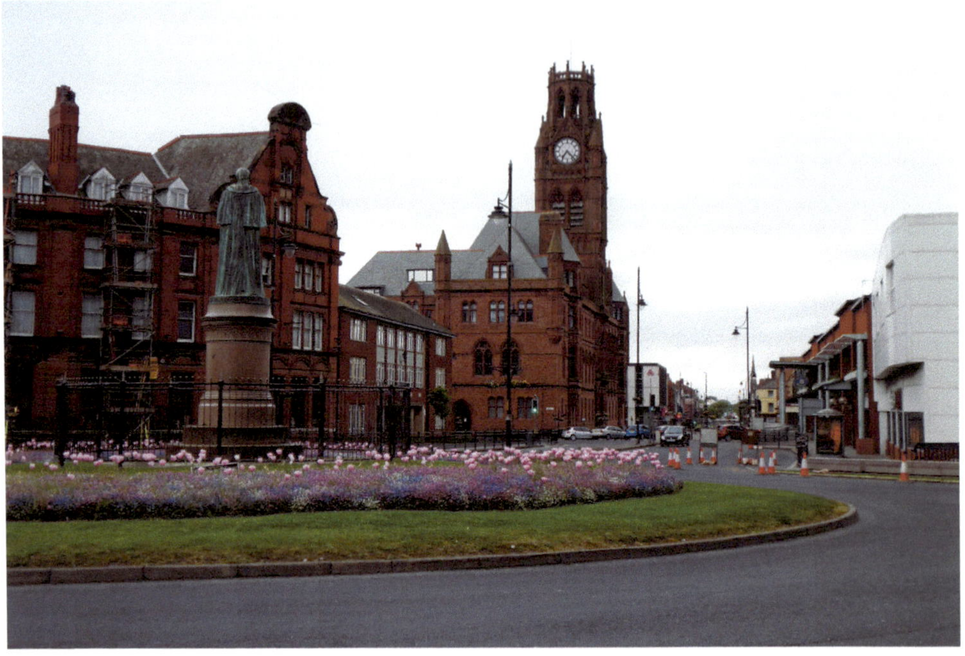

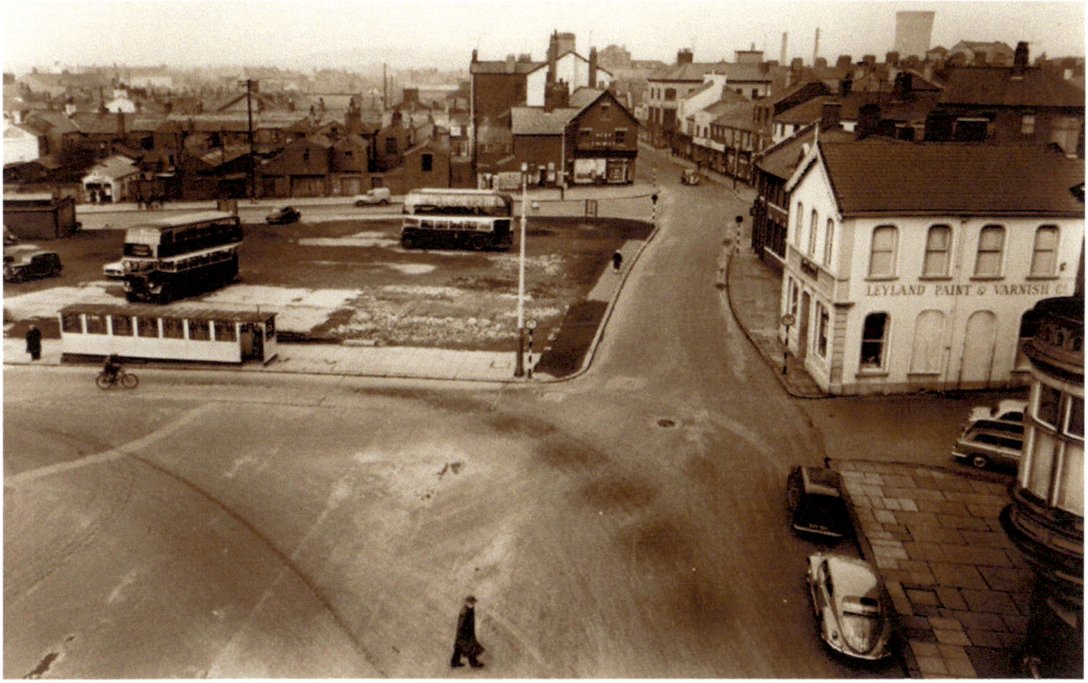

Schneider Square, 1950

The square was unimposing by the 1950s and housed a bus terminus, which was eventually replaced by the Market Hall and Arcade complex. This building has provoked many opinions – not all favourable. It is a concrete construction in typical 1960s style. This was adapted in recent years and the harsh and unforgiving architecture has been softened to blend in more acceptably with the surroundings.

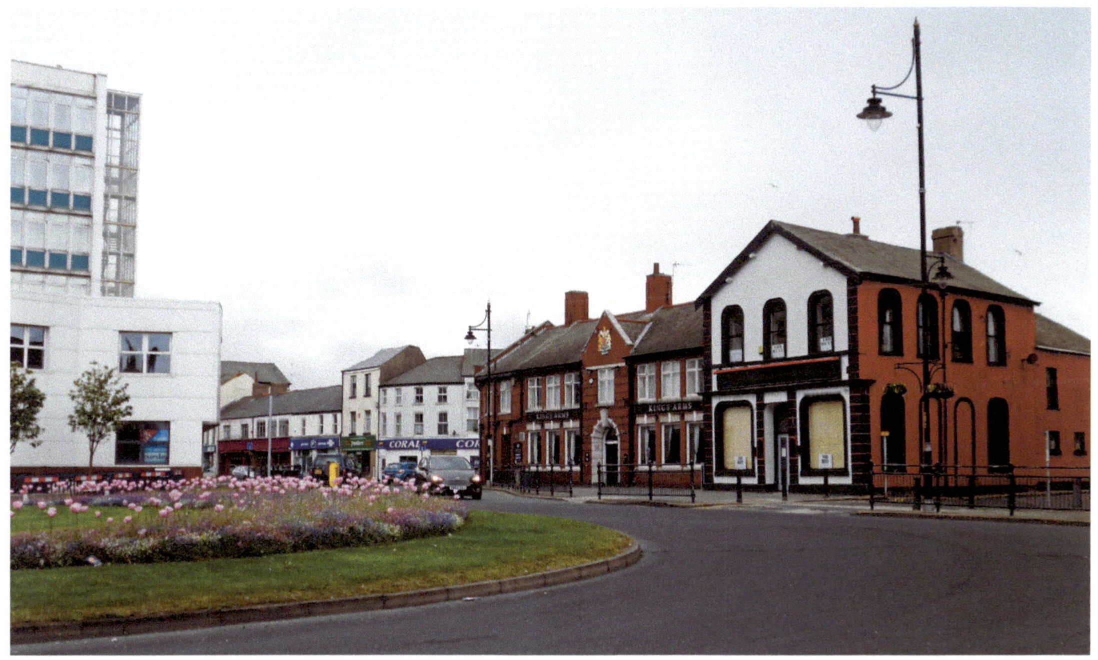

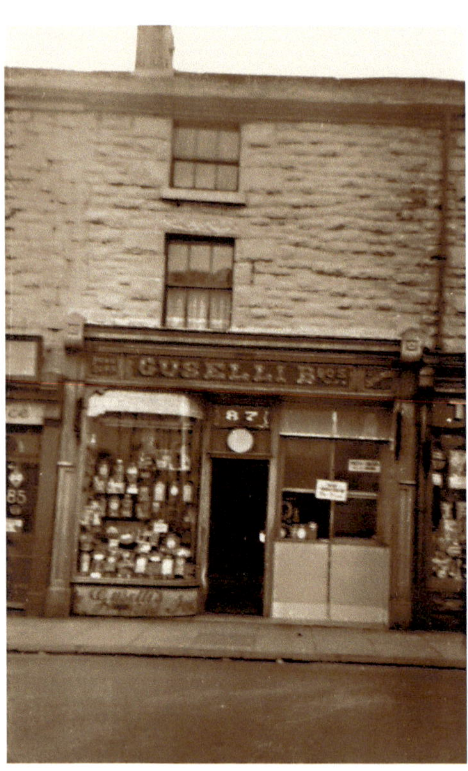

Guselli's, 87 Dalton Road

Louis Guselli opened his first ice cream parlour before 1900. It became a popular coffee and ice cream shop in the 1950s and was a modern 'American' diner with booths and a juke box. The distinctive ice cream and coffee produced unforgettable smells. Mary and Guido Guselli, brother and sister, remained at the Dalton Road coffee shop the longest. After Mary died Guido sold the shop to Mr and Mrs McGranthin. (Picture courtesy of Ray Guselli)

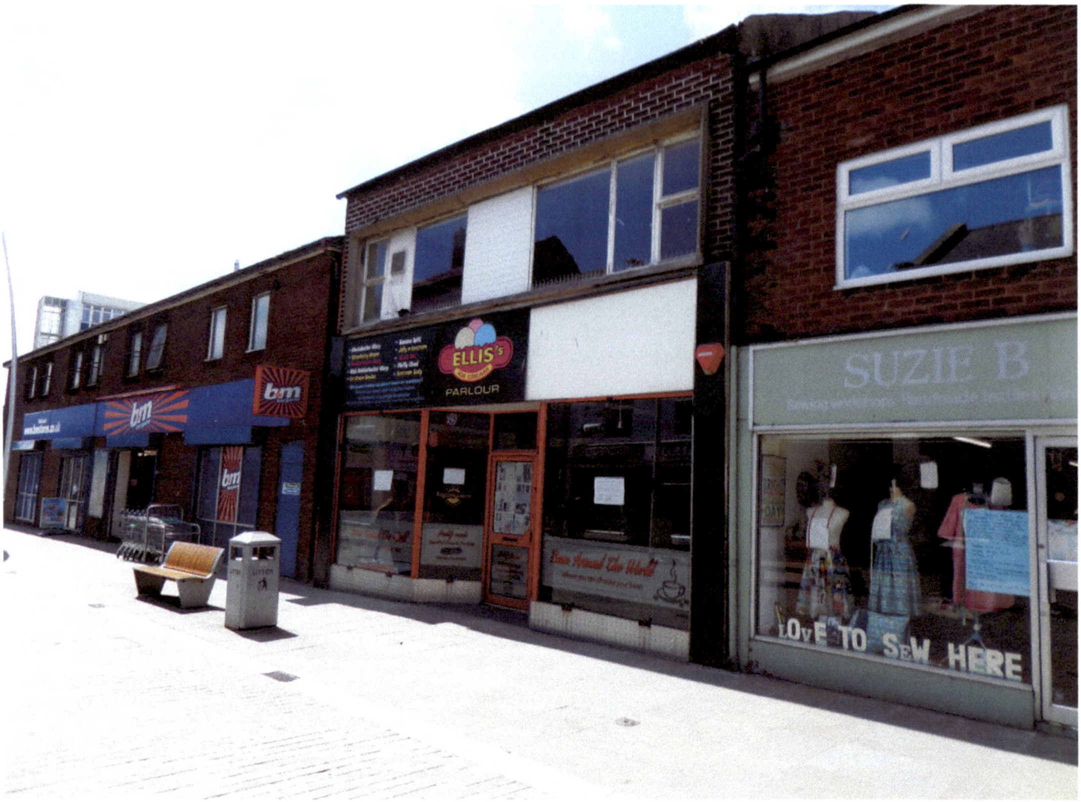

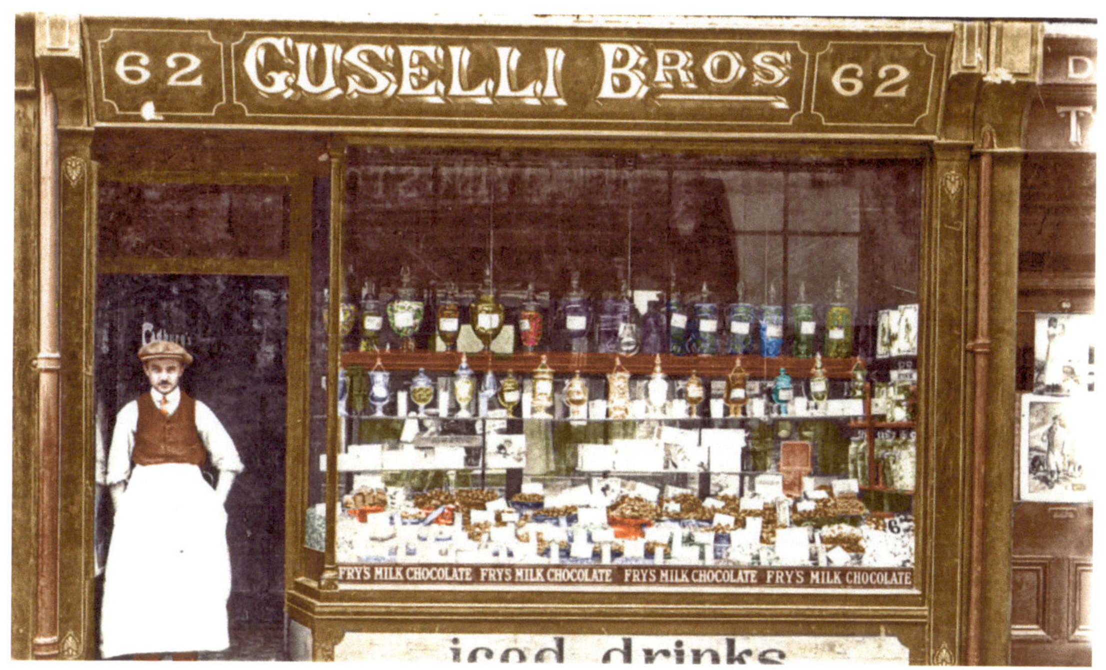

Guselli's Ice Cream Shop, 62 Cavendish Street

The Guselli brothers originated from Groparello, a small village near Milan, and had two shops selling ice cream, chocolate and iced drinks in Barrow. The family was one of a number of Italian immigrants who enriched and enhanced the culture of the town and who were well loved locally. Cavendish Street runs off the main shopping street and was a popular location for small businesses. Many of the shops and businesses are sadly closed now, becoming unviable against the supermarket culture of today. (Picture courtesy of Ray Guselli)

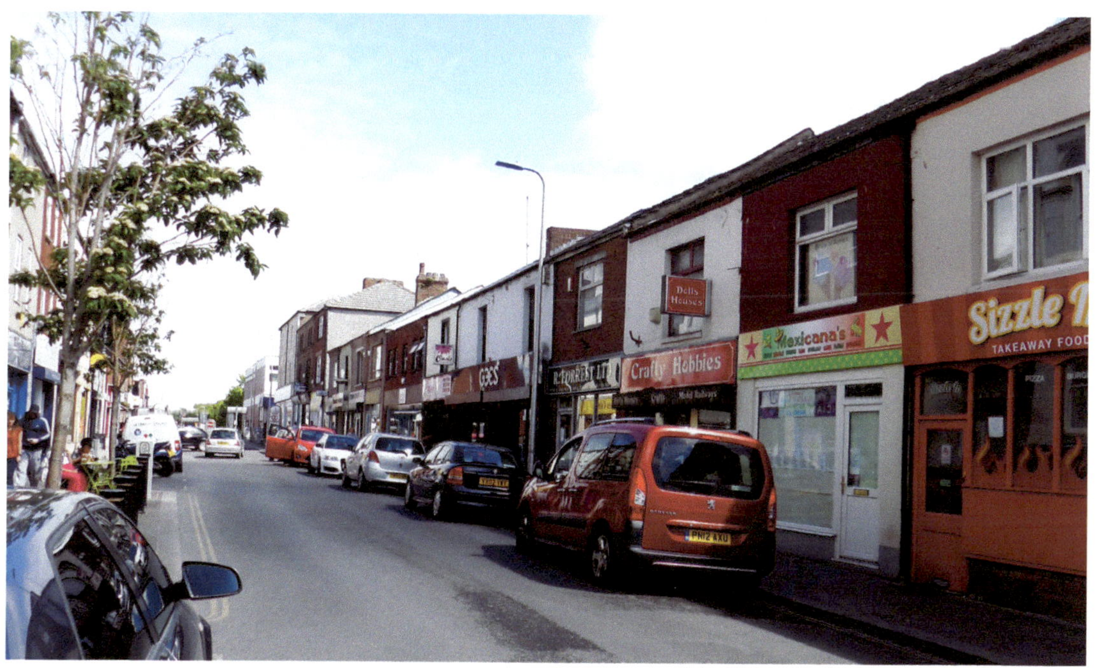

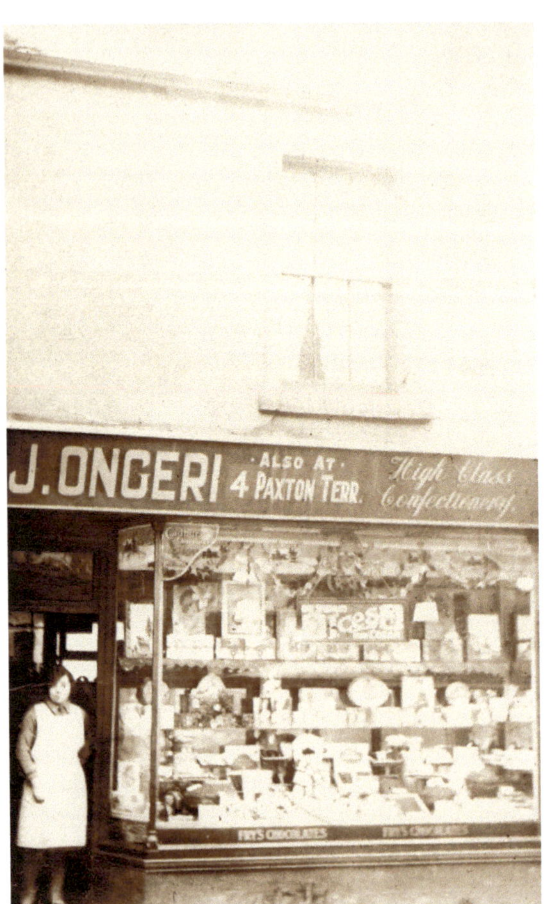

Ongeri's, Paxton Terrace

Ongeri's were another Italian family who chose to live and work in Barrow. They had a coffee and ice cream parlour in Paxton Terrace opposite the Town Hall. It was colourful, welcoming and always busy. Two more Italian families had similar businesses in the town, Brucciani and Franchi. These two prospered longer than the others; Brucciani had two shops on Dalton Road and Franchi's had an ice cream and freezer food outlet surviving into the 1980s.

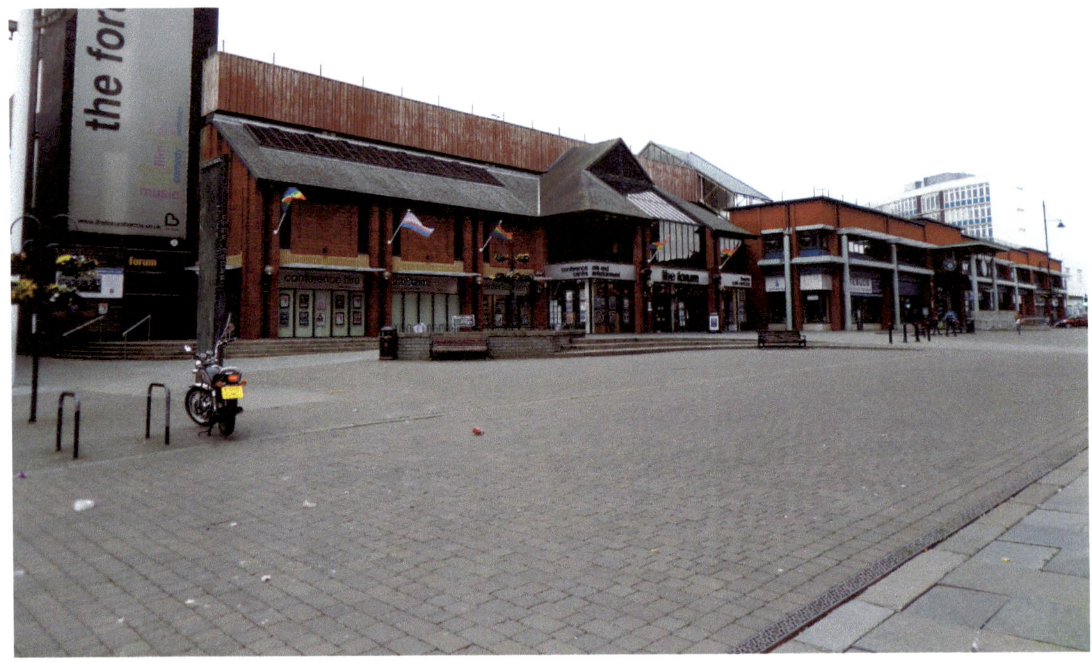

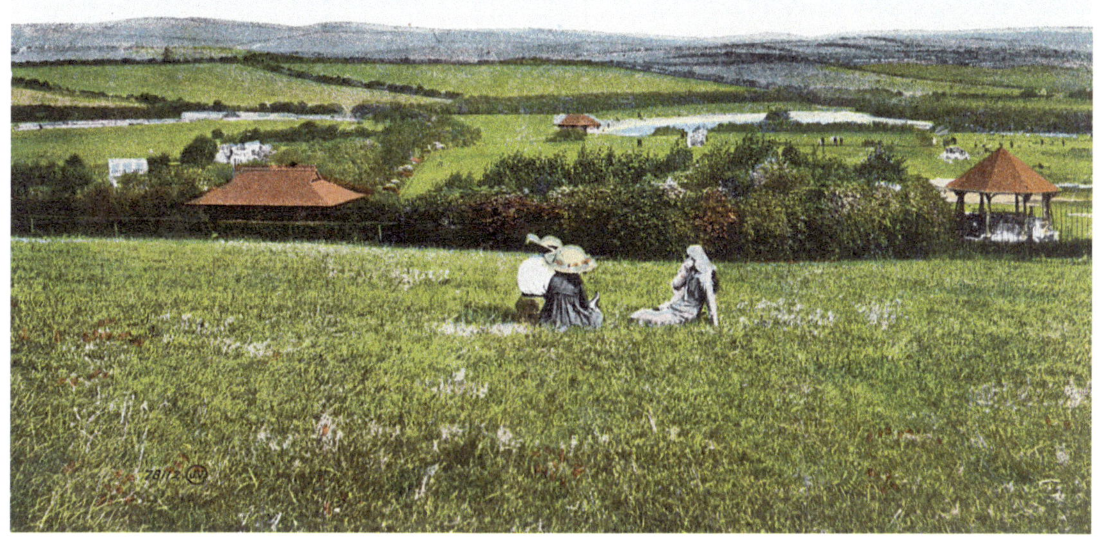

Barrow Park

The park was designed in 1908 by Thomas Mawson on the outskirts of Barrow. It sits in forty-five acres and has a lake, greenhouses, playground, café and a bandstand. The open views beyond the park that look east towards Yarlside have since been mostly obliterated by housing developments. The park has retained the sense of tranquillity and countryside but instead of being on the outskirts, as was originally intended, it now occupies a central position.

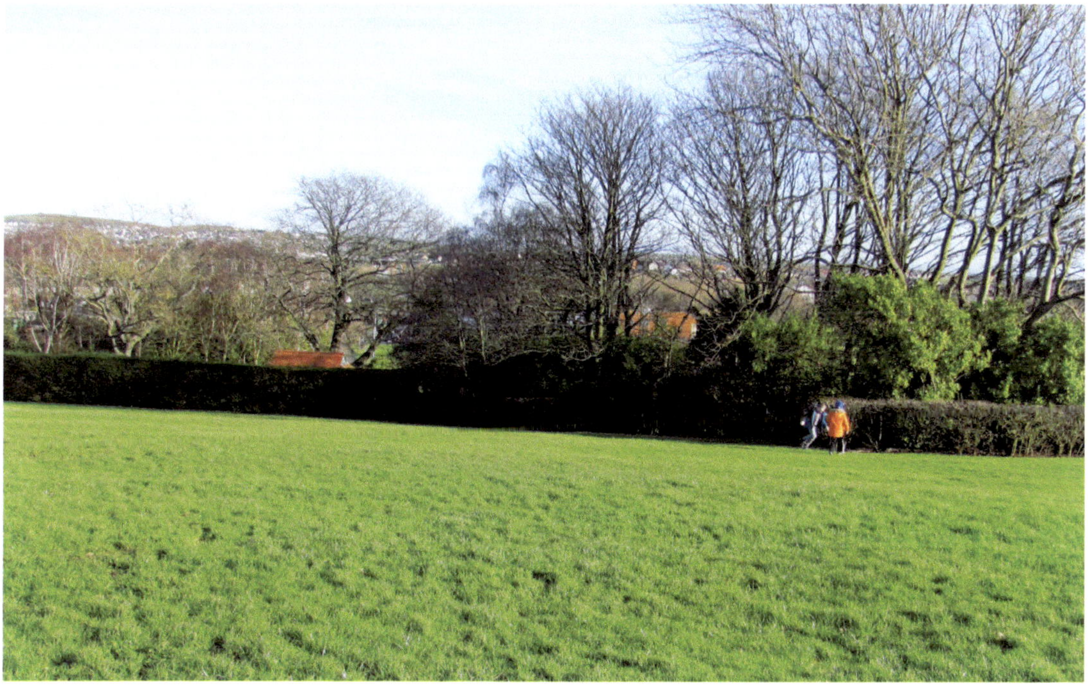

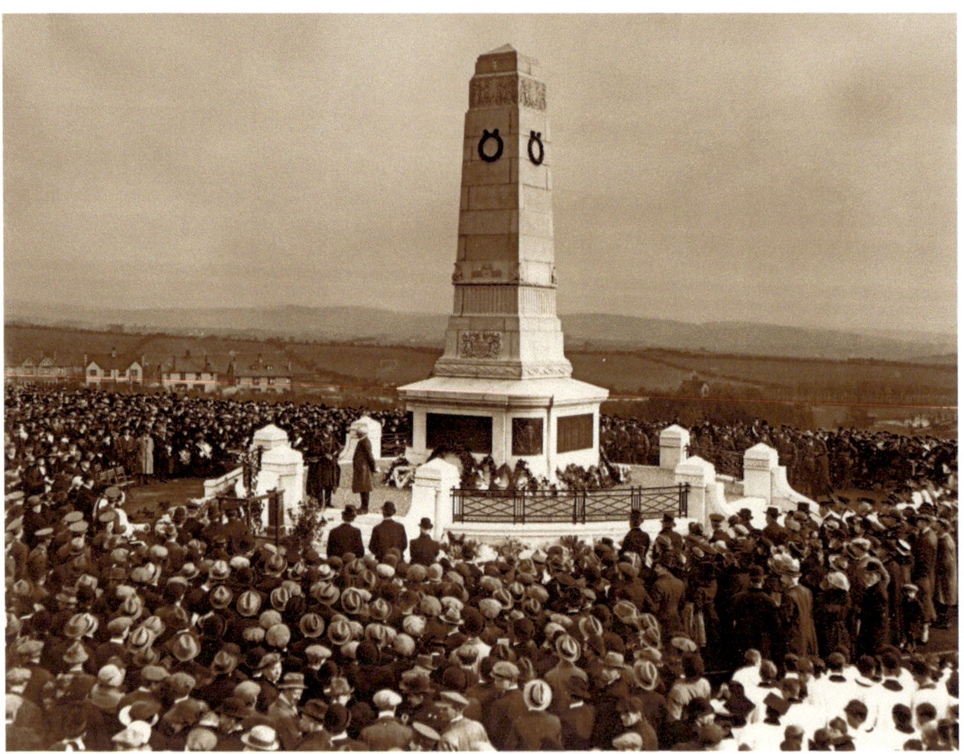

The Cenotaph

The Cenotaph was dedicated in 1921 to the war dead of Barrow from the First World War. It later incorporated the losses of the Second World War and other conflicts since. The picture shows the vast crowd attending the ceremony and emphasises how many families were affected. The service of remembrance is held each year in November and special benches were made in 2014 to commemorate the centenary of the start of the First World War.

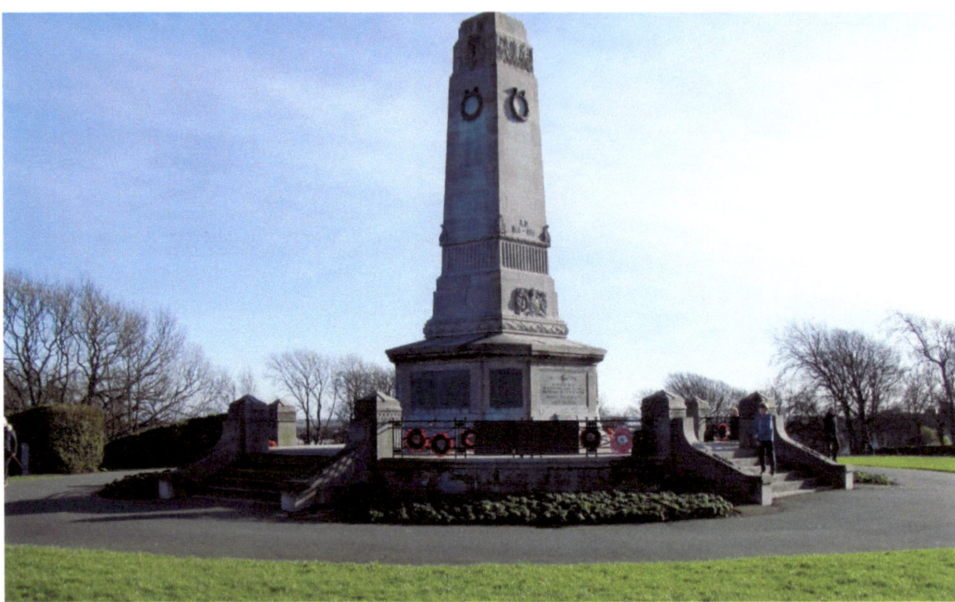

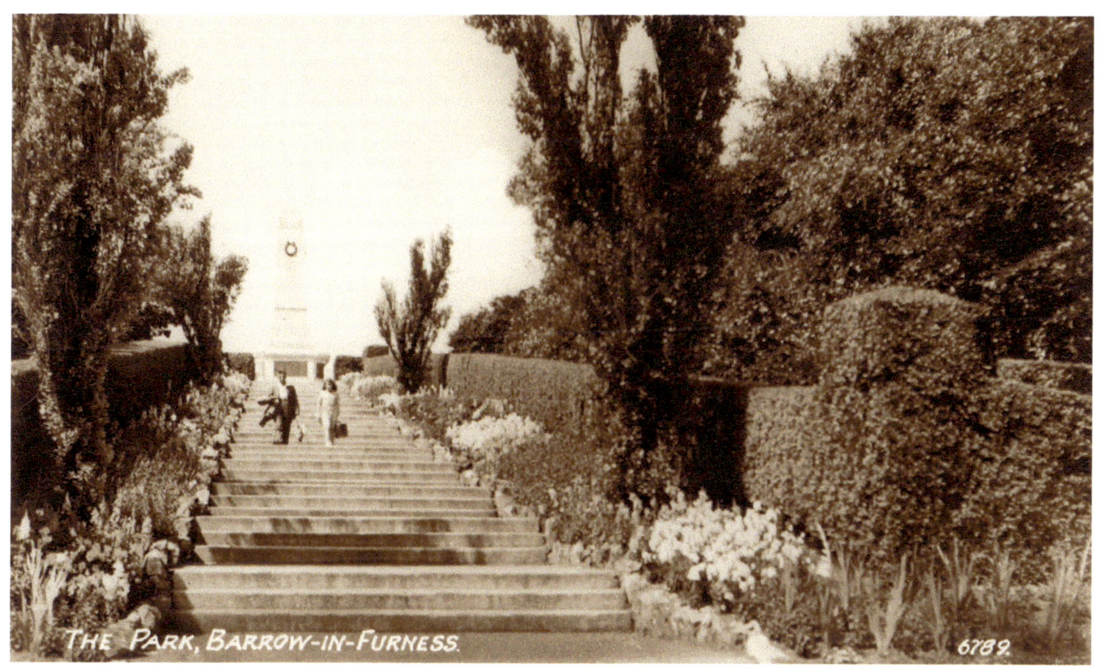

The Cenotaph Steps

The cenotaph stands proud on top of a hill previously known as Black Castle. It has been suggested that there was an Iron Age hill fort in this vicinity. This is as yet unsubstantiated but, if true, lends the site even more significance than it already holds. The imposing steps down from the cenotaph have always been a source of fun for local children and they still enjoy counting the ninety-nine steps. The view from the top remains impressive and the refurbished bandstand greets the visitor at the bottom.

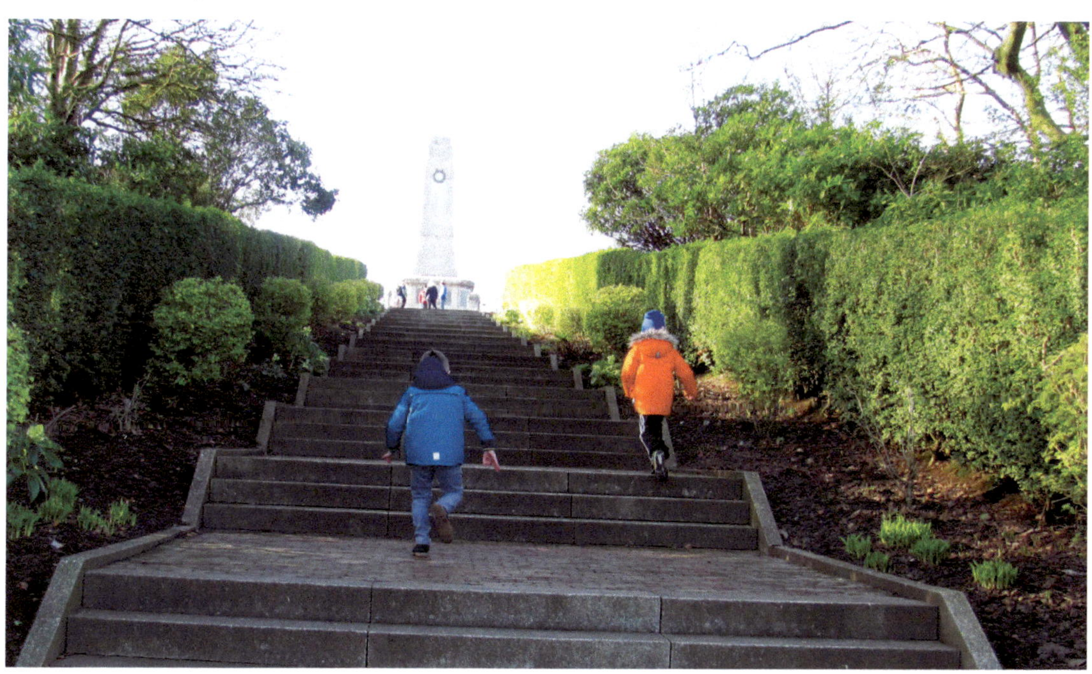

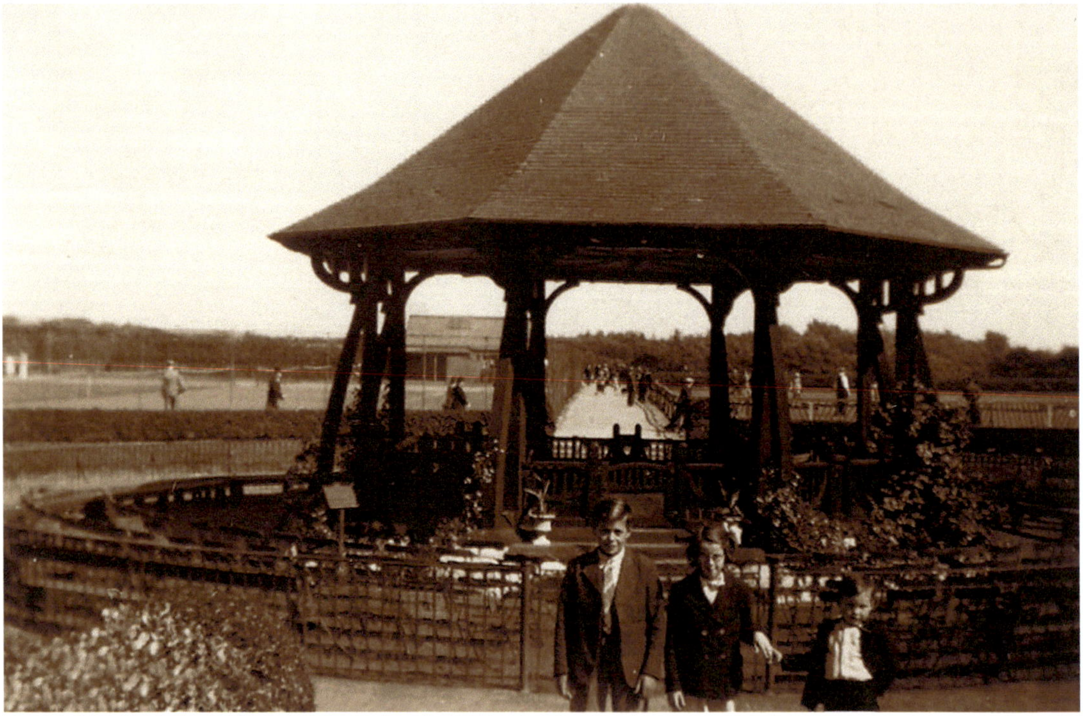

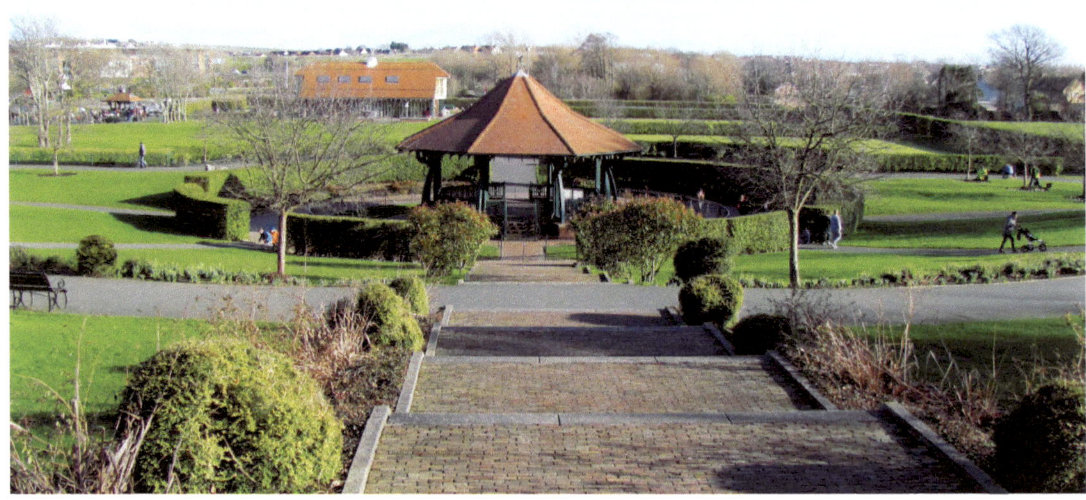

The Bandstand

Visible from the cenotaph, the bandstand is placed at the foot of the hill. Seating is provided for those who wished to linger and listen to the tunes of the day. The bandstand declined in its later years but has recently been renovated and is used for occasional concerts as before. Pictured are Johnnie, Norma and Tommy Turner in 1937 on a family outing to the park, a picture probably replicated many times by many people. (Picture courtesy of Keith Wallwork)

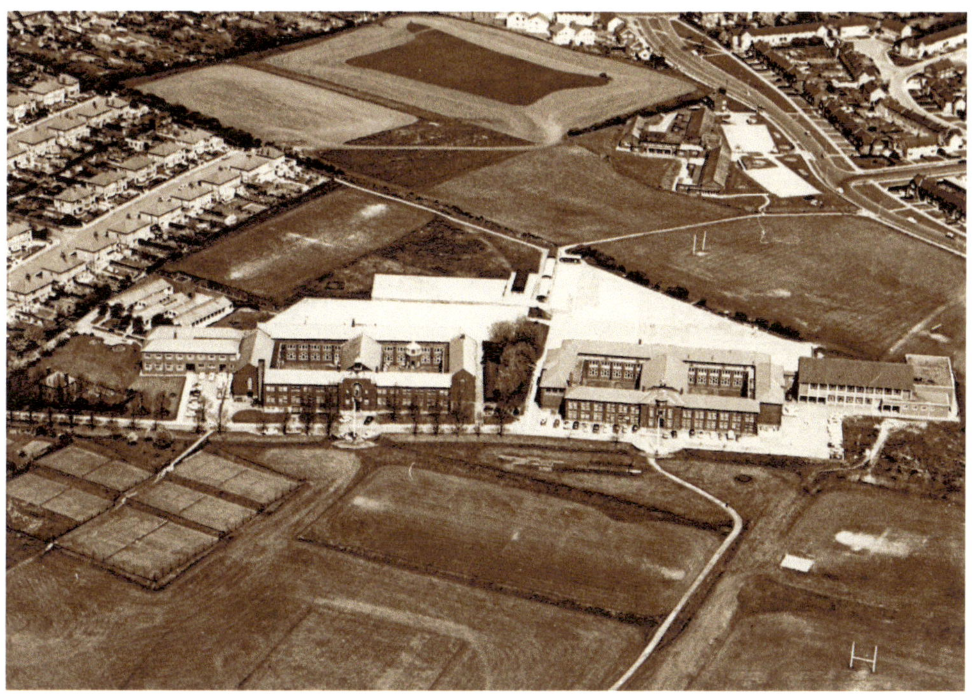

Barrow Grammar Schools, Parkview

The two imposing adjacent boys' and girls' grammar schools in this aerial view were built in 1930 and 1932 respectively. They were single-sex schools with traditional academic curricula. The schools were physically joined in 1975 with the opening of a new sports hall, later merging in 1979 to form the co-educational Parkview. This school amalgamated with Thorncliffe and Alfred Barrow Schools in 2012, forming Furness Academy. The buildings were demolished in 2014 despite massive public opposition and the land sold to a developer to build houses. (Picture courtesy of the *North West Evening Mail*/Ray Guselli)

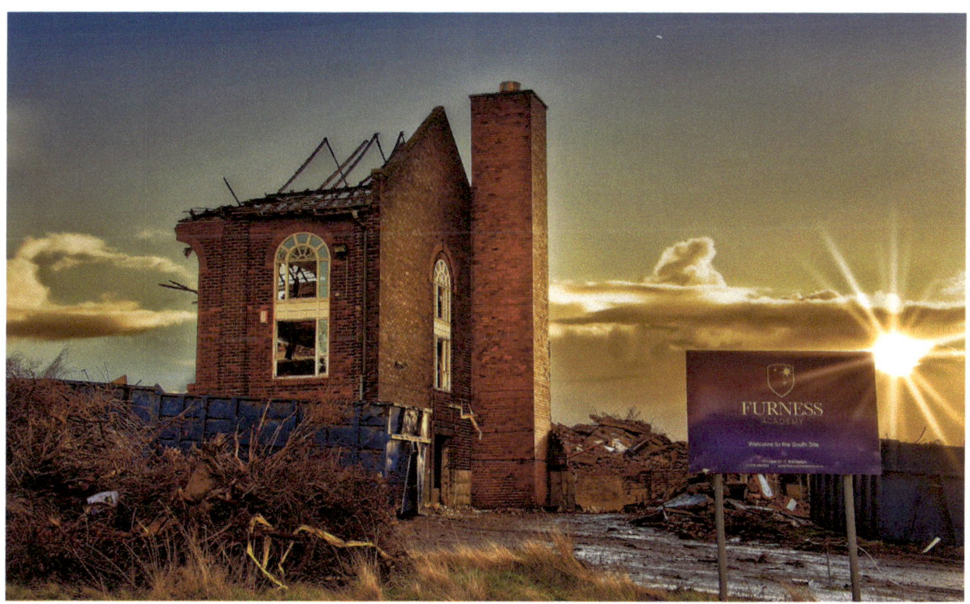

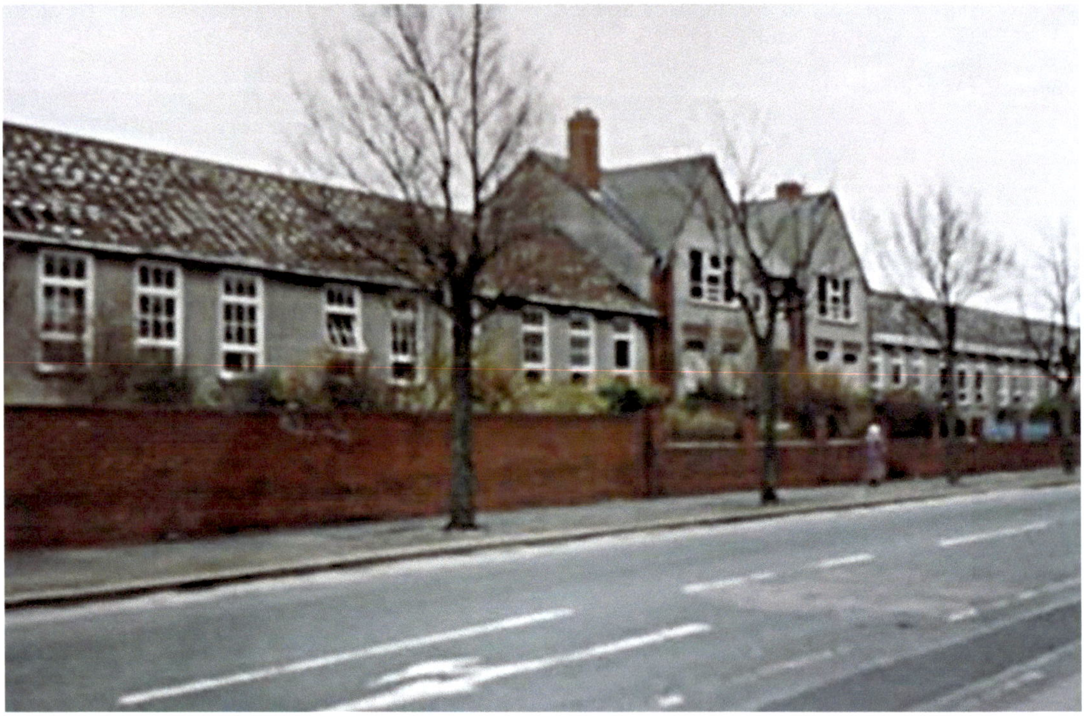

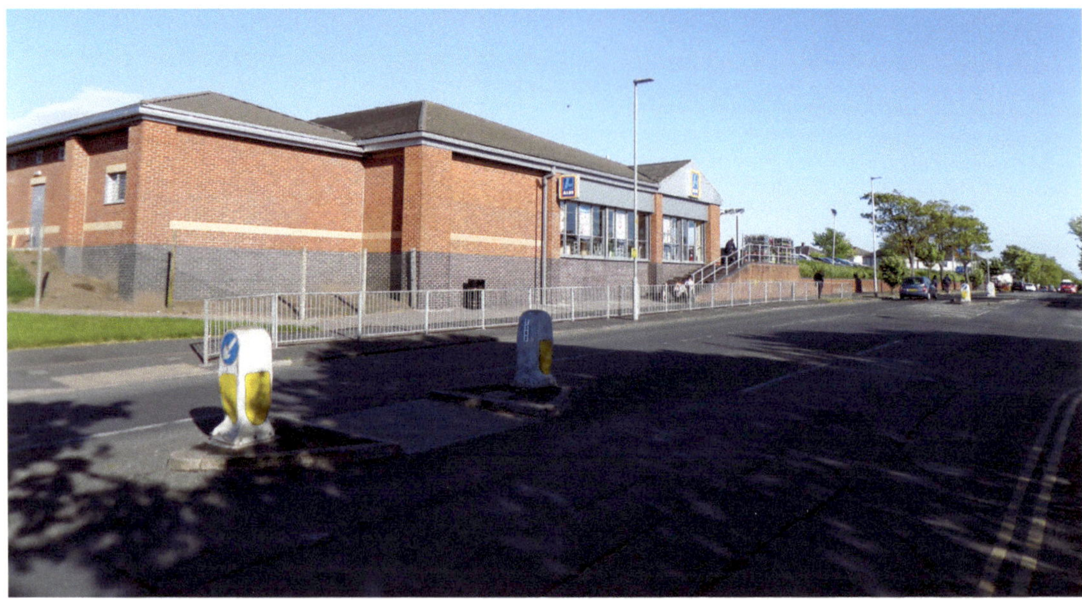

Risedale Secondary Modern School, Risedale Road

The Education Act of 1902 gave control of schools to the local authorities and this enabled the building of various schools. In 1926 Risedale School was built. This school became a secondary modern school after the Second World War and it specialised in commercial and secretarial skills as well as providing a general education. In 1979 it was closed and pupils transferred into other schools under the comprehensive system. A supermarket has subsequently been built on the site. (Picture courtesy of Jennifer Foote)

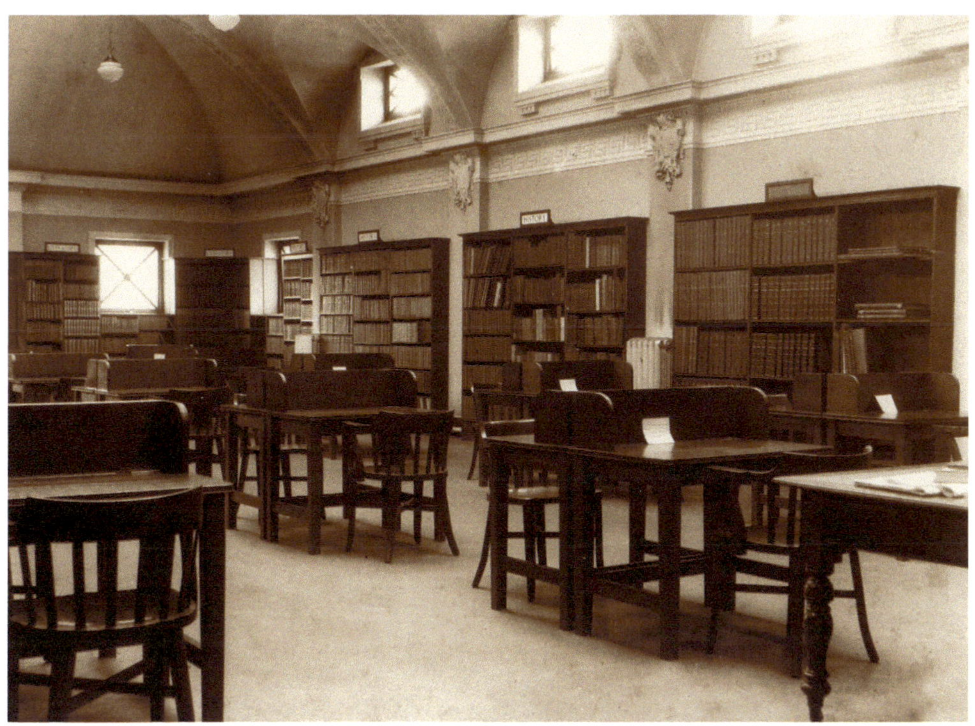

Barrow Public Library, Ramsden Square

Starting life in a tin hut in 1882, the library was later moved to the town hall. The growth of Barrow's population ensured a larger purpose-built library by 1915, although it was not fully completed until 1922. The library, built in the Beaux Arts style, is attractive; its reference library (shown here) has been replaced by a modern extension that houses the archives. Library services have been run by Cumbria County Council following the boundary changes in 1974.

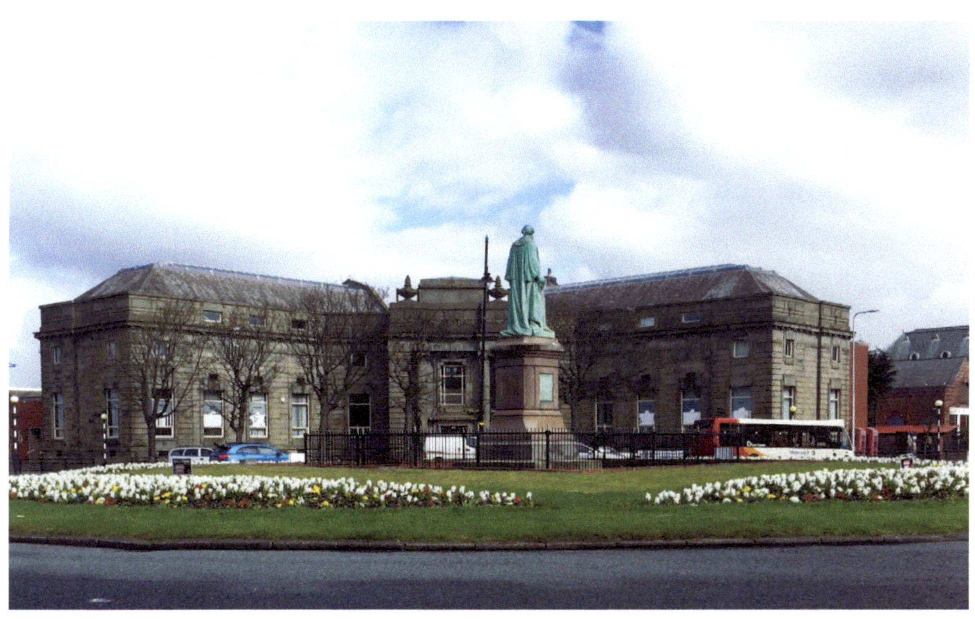

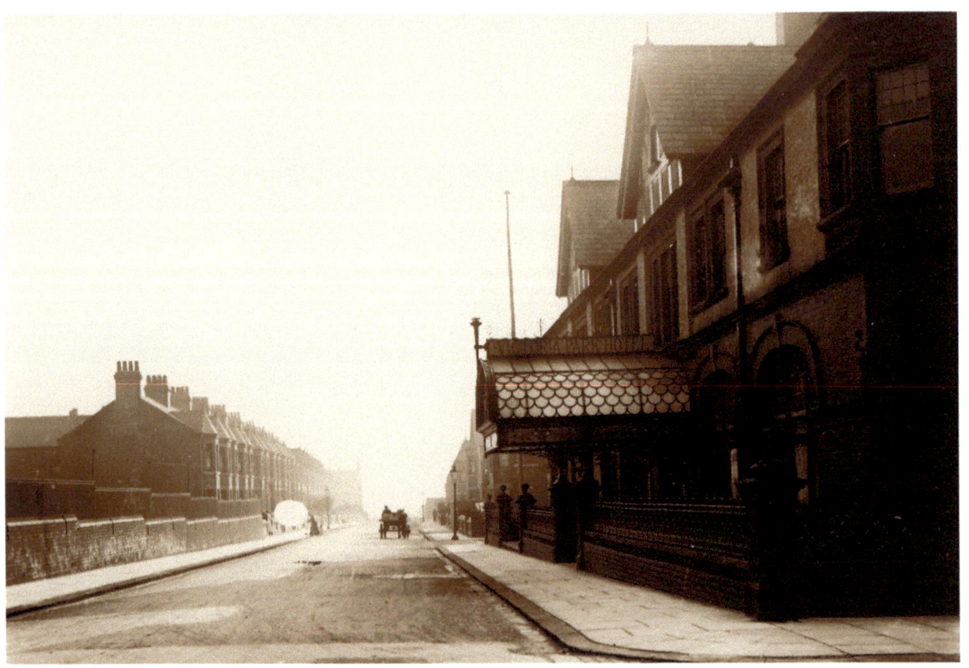

Victoria Park Hotel, Victoria Road

The Victoria Park Hotel was built around 1900 on the outskirts of town. It was a prestigious hotel built at the cost of £5,000. It had a bowling green, an ornate glass canopy above the entrance, a smoking room, ballroom, billiard room and stables. It was officially opened on Saturday 19 April 1902 and became a popular venue for weddings and dances. It endured through the years but is now about to be converted into apartments. Externally it has changed little, but there are new dwellings opposite.

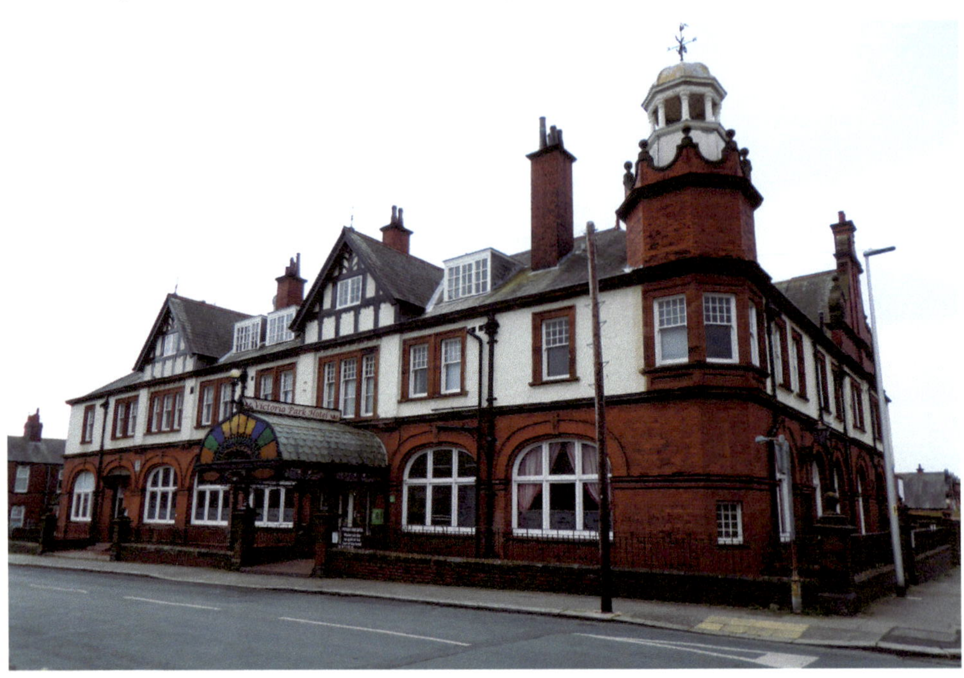

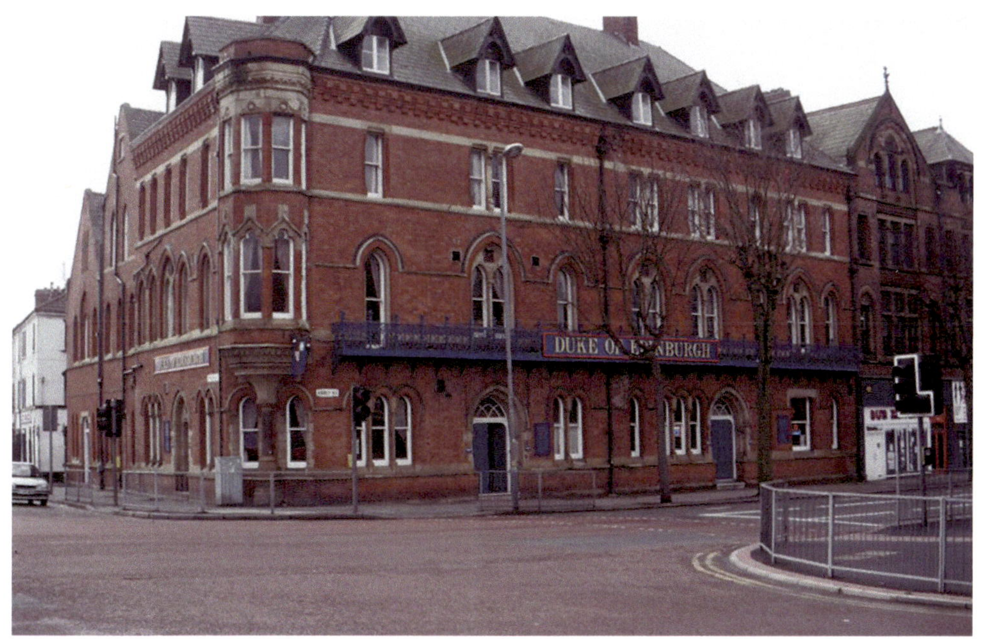

Duke of Edinburgh Hotel, Abbey Road

The Duke of Edinburgh Hotel was built in 1871 at the heyday of Barrow's growth and prosperity. It was positioned close to the railway station and within easy walking distance of the town. As the premier hotel it attracted many high-status guests like Charlie Chaplin, D. H. Lawrence, Clark Gable and many politicians. Its prospects faded after the Second World War and it gradually became dilapidated and under threat. Thankfully, Lancaster Brewery stepped in and in 2006 renovation began, finally returning to its former glory. (Picture courtesy of Peter Laird)

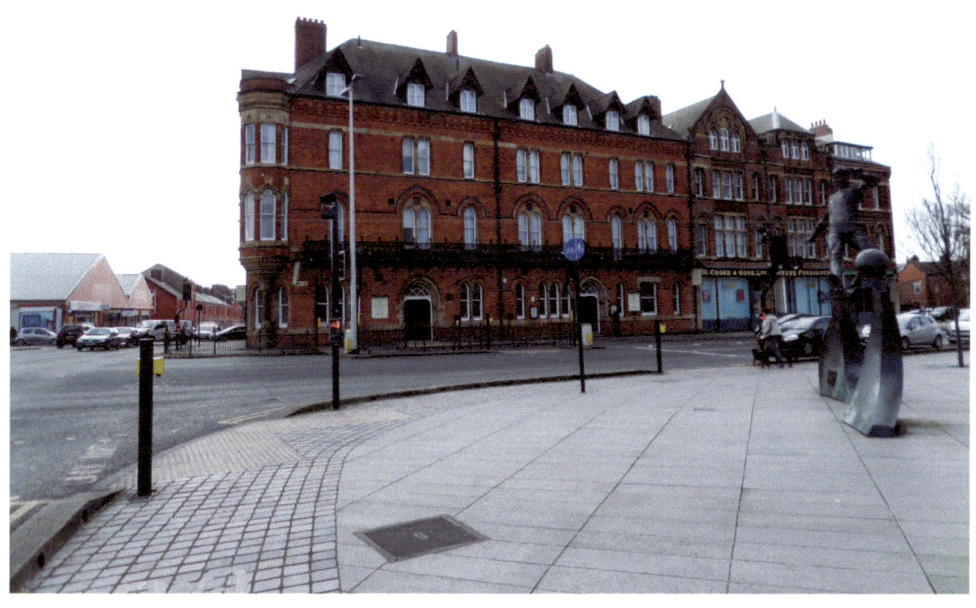

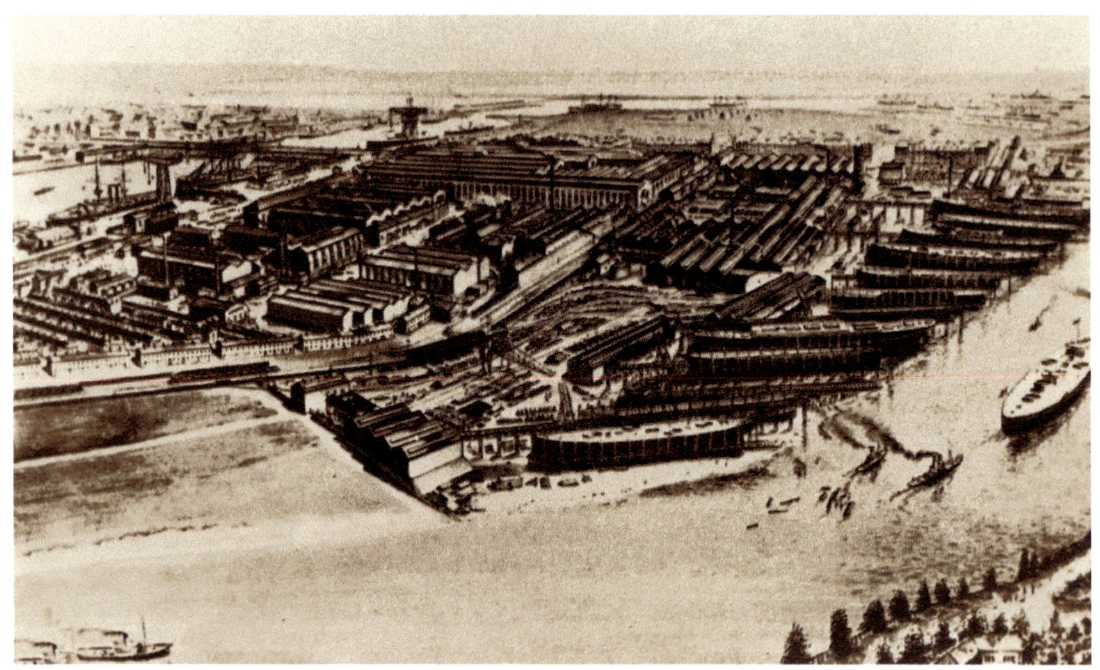

Barrow Island

Before the industrial revolution Barrow Island – or Old Barrow as it was known – was a distinct island separated from the mainland by the channel. The Michaelson family inherited the island and built a grand mansion, remaining in occupation until 1863 when it was bought by the Furness Railway Company. In 1870 the Barrow Iron Shipbuilding Company was founded and shipbuilding quickly expanded, gradually obliterating what remained of the Michaelson estate.

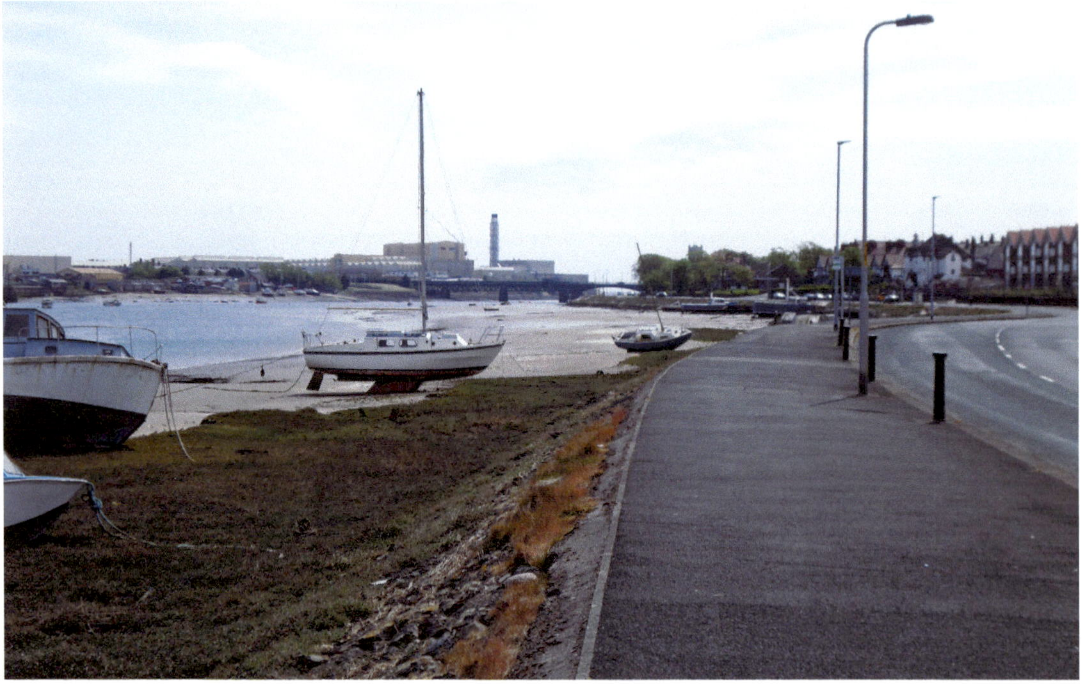

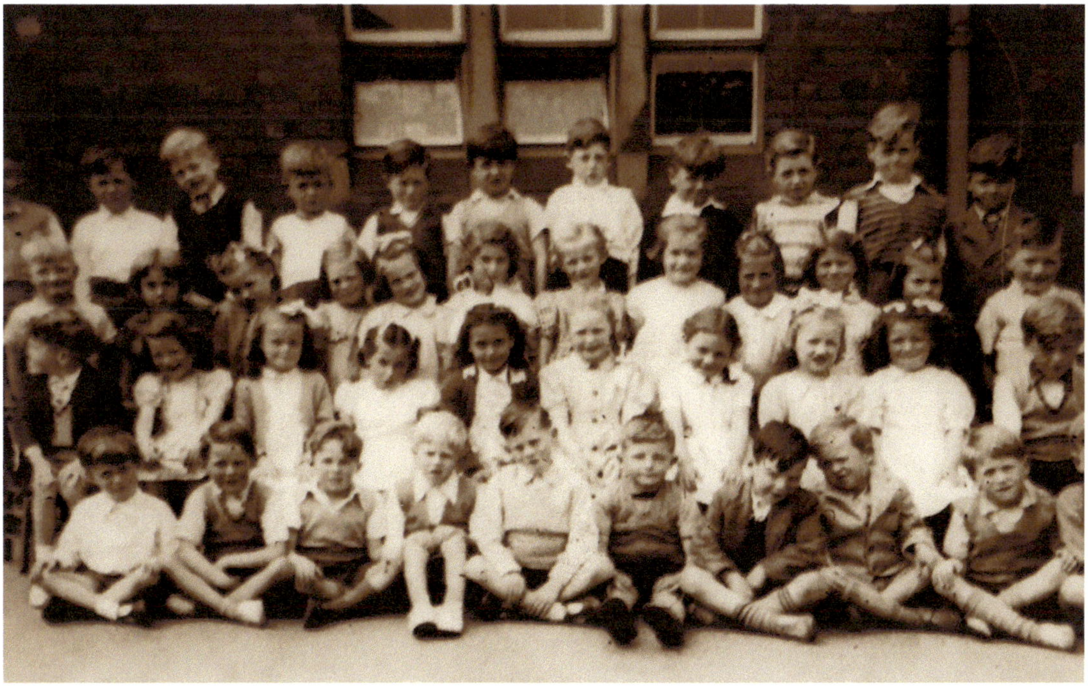

Barrow Island School, Trinity Street

There has been a school here since 1873 when a temporary National School was built. Much of the listed Victorian building survives, although with additions and alterations over the years that include the construction of a nursery and a Community Development Centre. The magnificent clock tower from the original school was demolished in 1959. The class shown smartly lined up outside are pictured from around this time. The school is a thriving community school and has adapted over time. (Picture courtesy of Sarah Taylor)

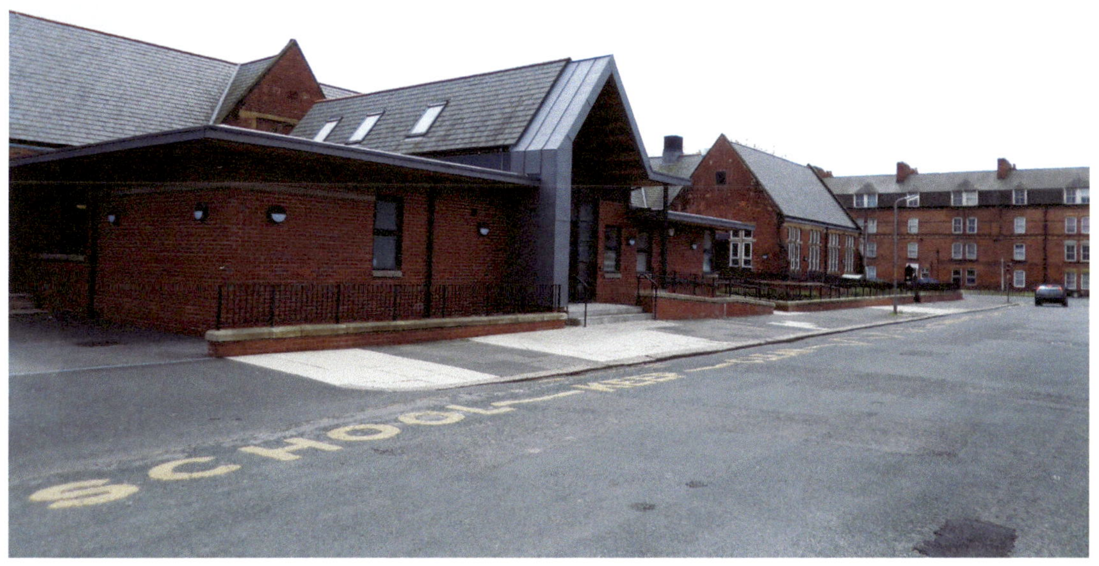

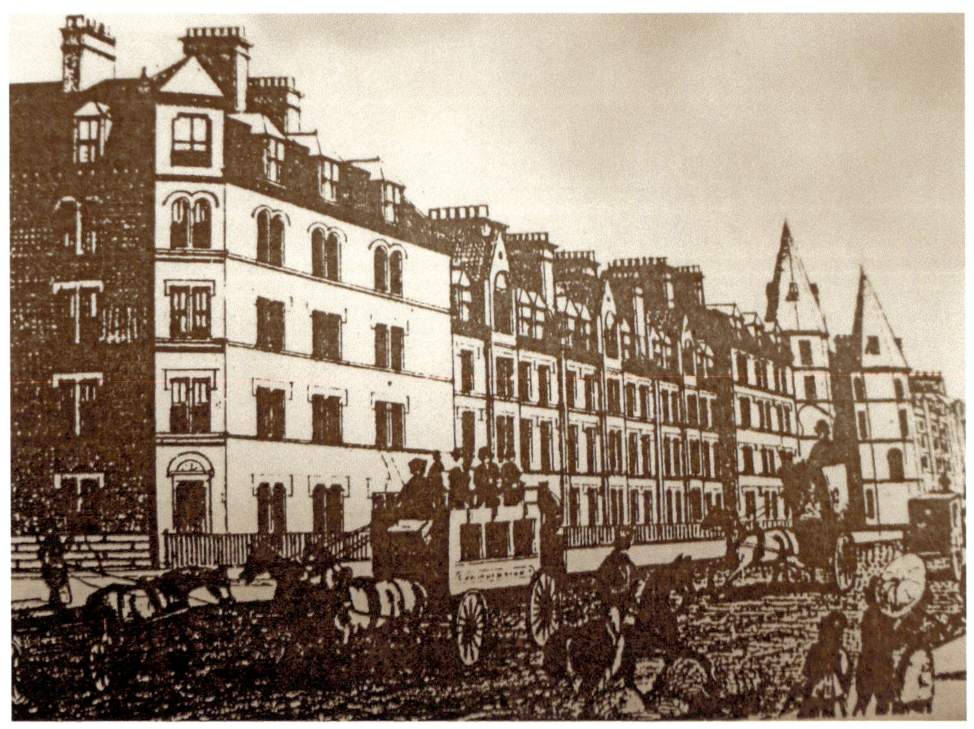

Built in response to a rapidly growing working population in the 1870s, Devonshire Buildings housed workers from Devonshire Docks and Barrow Iron Shipbuilding Company. They were designed by Paley and Austin and are Grade II listed. The design is similar to Glasgow tenements but with the addition of unusual octagonal towers at the ends of each block, where there was originally a bridge spanning Island Road. These apartments are currently being refurbished by Holker Estates to include all modern conveniences, a far cry from the functional accommodation of the past.

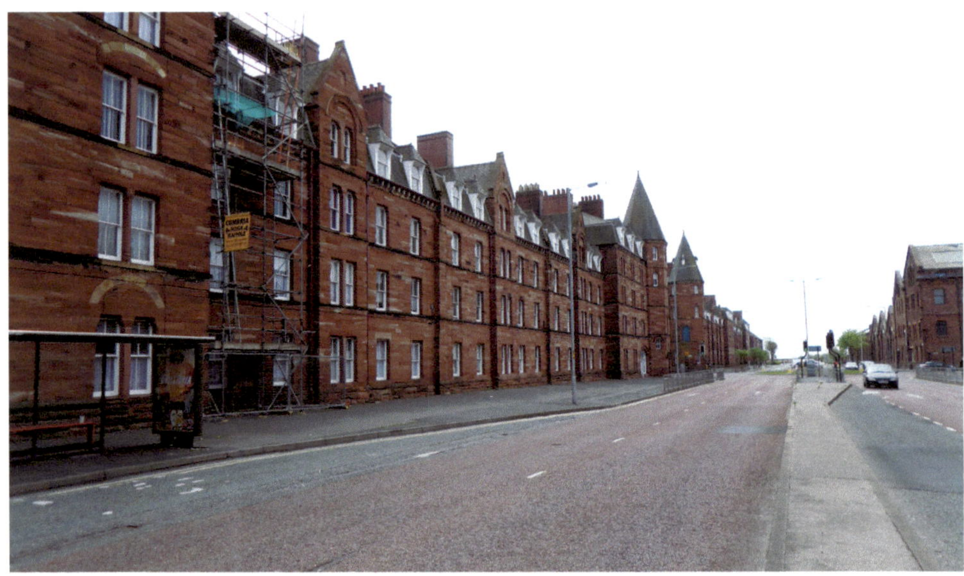

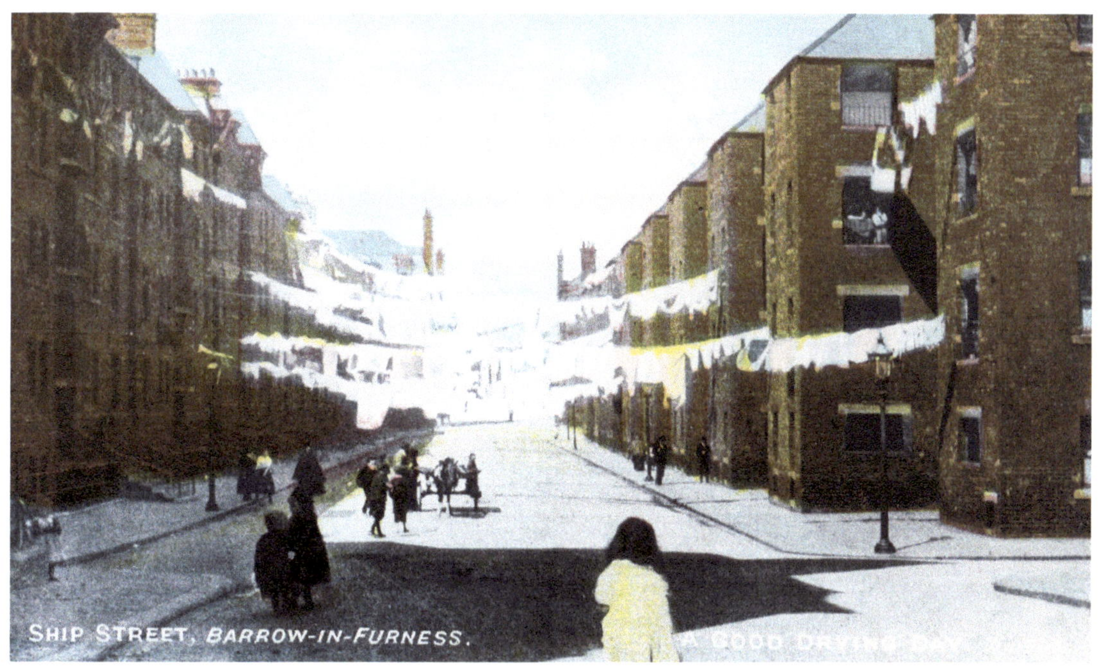

Ship Street, Barrow Island

This tenement block was built between 1881 and 1884 by Paley and Austin of Lancaster. They were created to house workers of Barrow Iron Shipbuilding Company. There are four identical blocks set behind the sandstone Devonshire Buildings on Michaelson Road. This model housing ensured workers were close to the workplace and that rents were returned to the employers, thus offsetting employee costs and being a fine example of Victorian 'paternalism'. The blocks are still inhabited and provide an iconic view of Barrow that is popular with the media.

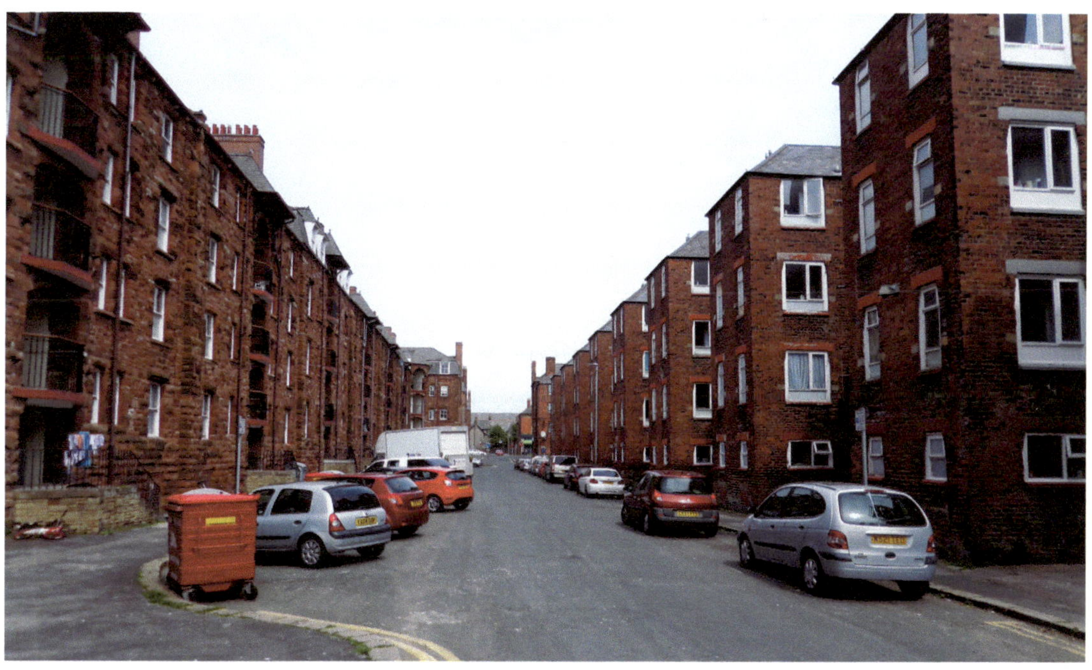

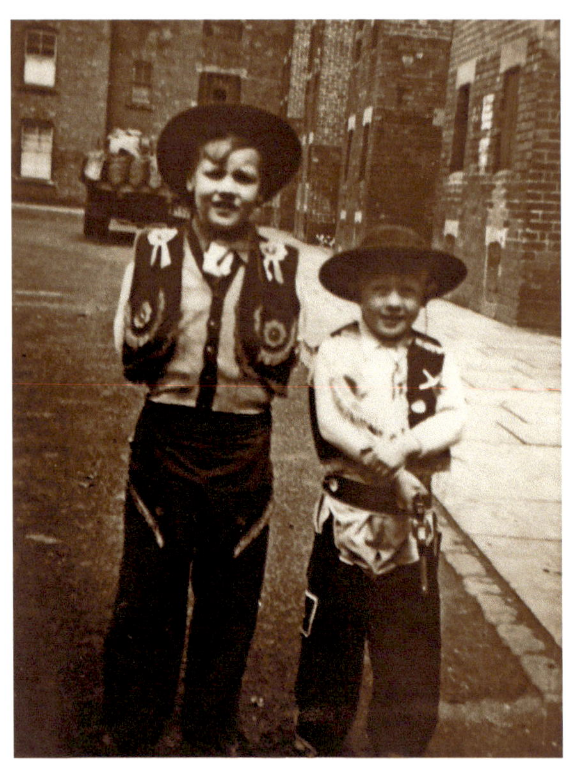

Egerton Buildings, Barrow Island
Again, Paley and Austin U-shaped
buildings were constructed for Furness
Railway Company workers between
1879 and 1884. The tenements have
been in continual use and have changed
little outside, though many of the
internal features have disappeared.
Generations of children like David and
Alan Dawes, pictured here in 1952,
played in the central areas within
a strong, safe community. (Picture
courtesy of Sarah Taylor)

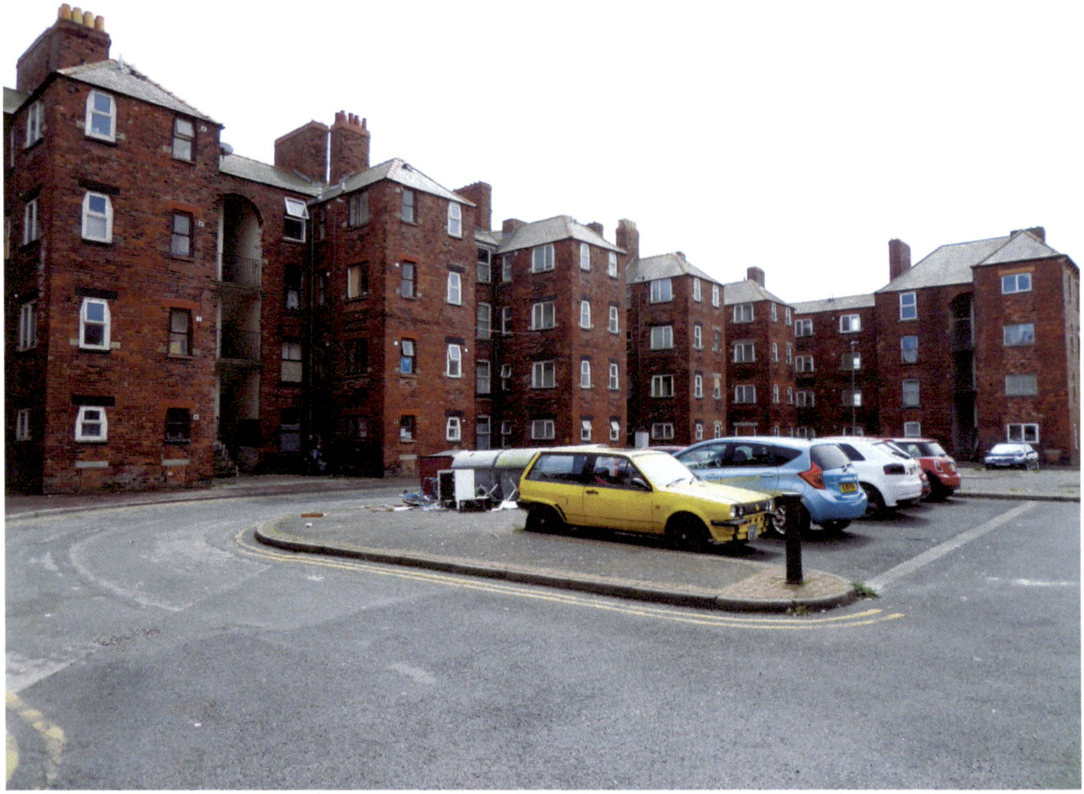

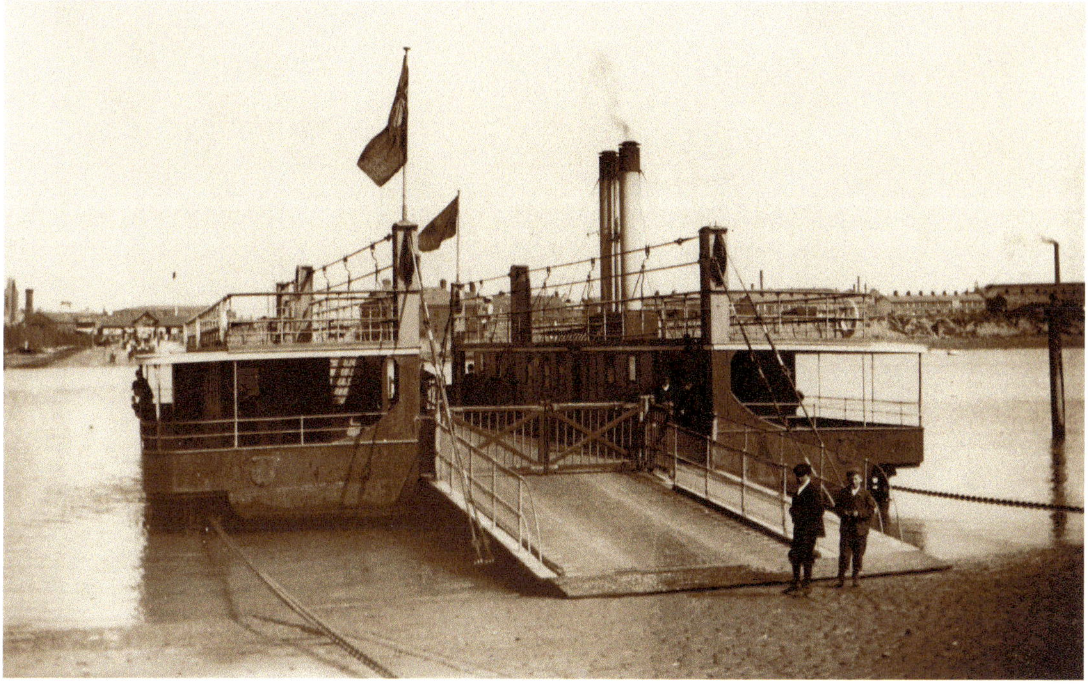

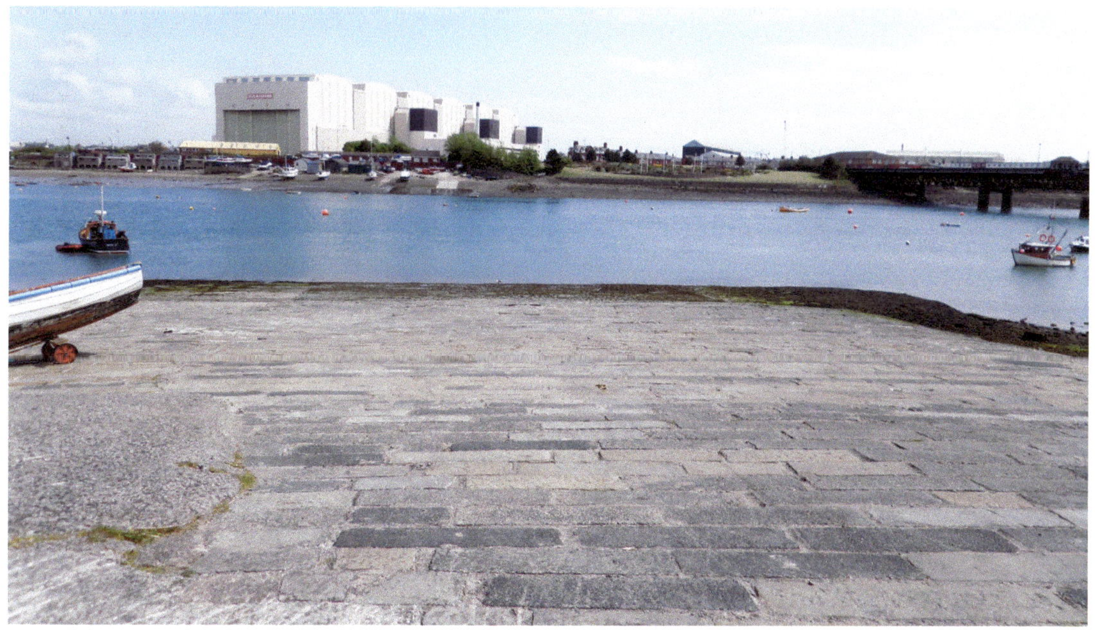

Walney Ferry

The ferry between the island and the mainland replaced the two earlier fords that had been dredged away during harbour improvements. Furness Railway established a steam ferry to take passengers across the channel. Other small ferry boats were commissioned by the corporation later as passenger numbers grew. Eventually, a bridge was built and opened in 1908 as a toll bridge and the ferry was no longer needed. The Ferry Hotel is still testament to the existence of the ferry, as are the cobbled ramps into the channel.

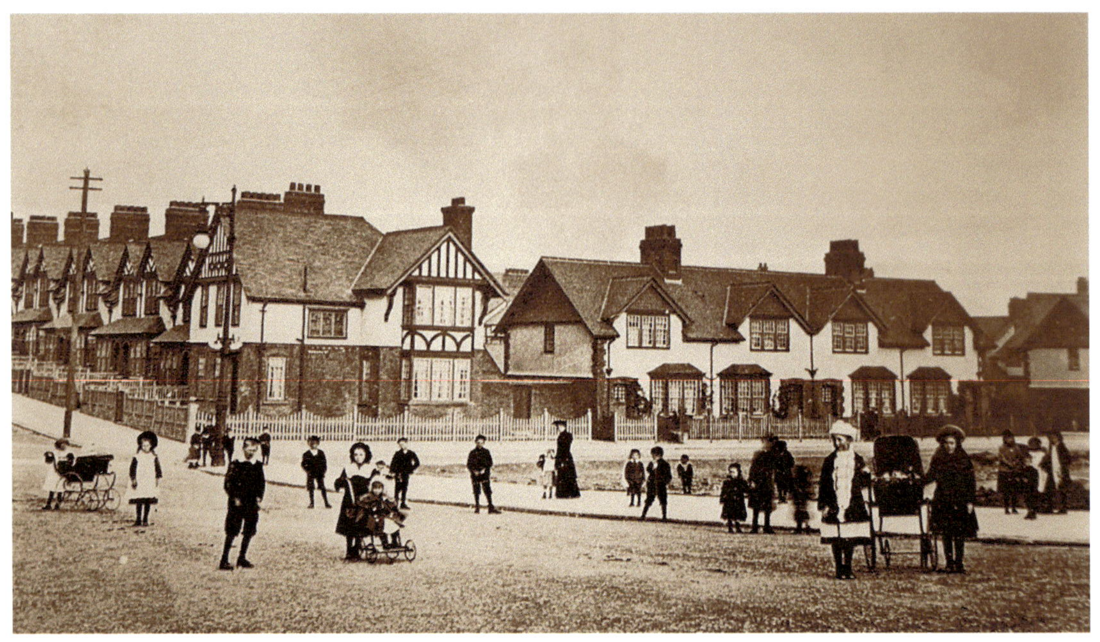

Vickerstown, Walney

With the rise in population, accommodation for workers was urgently needed. Vickers Ltd had acquired the Isle of Walney Estates Company in 1899 and purchased 341 acres of land on which they built housing. The 'Marine Garden City', or Vickerstown as it became known, was a model estate and included parks, sports fields and the King Alfred public house. It is distinctive in appearance with its mock-Tudor style houses and alleviated some of the housing need in the town.

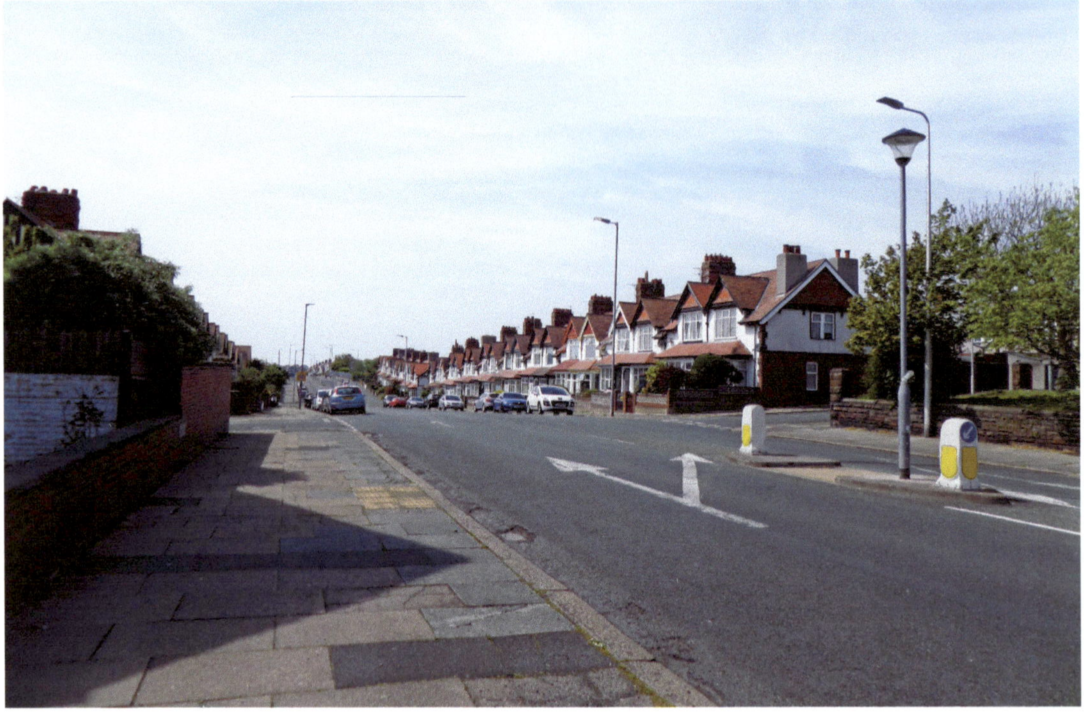

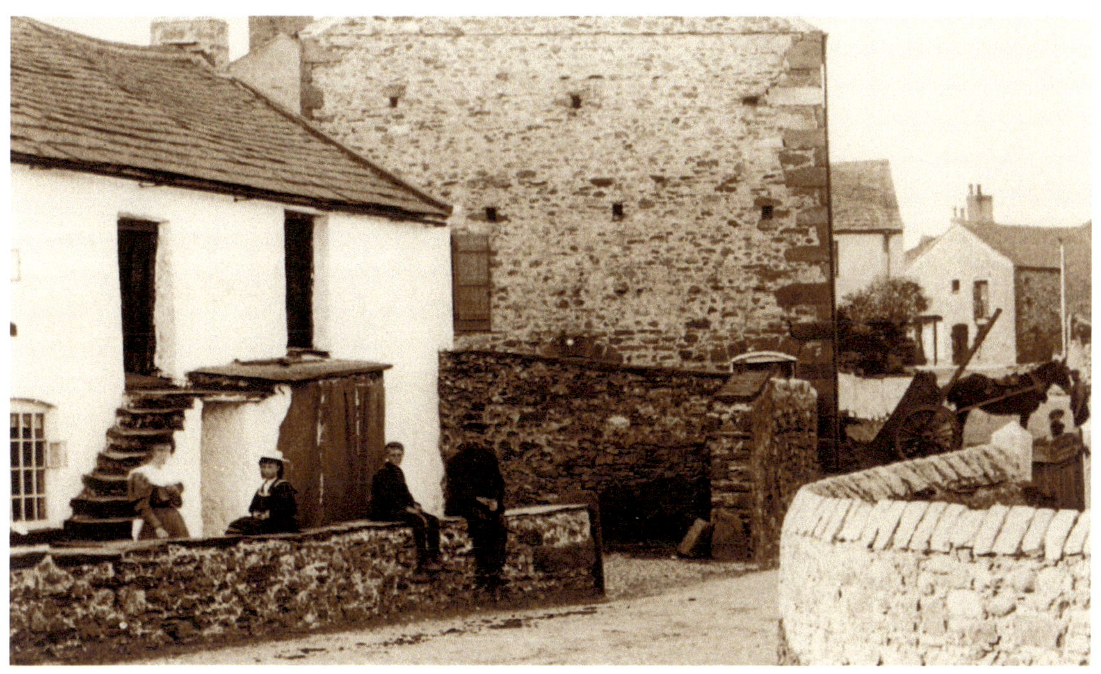

North Scale Village

This ancient settlement was once a Furness Abbey grange, mentioned in *Taxatio Furnesii* in 1292. The tenants were expected to offer work days in order to repair and maintain sea defences known as Biggar Dyke. This continued long after monastic times and tenants were fined by the Court Leet in 1722 for not performing these duties. In the Civil War a skirmish took place here after the Parliamentarians besieged the village. They abandoned it and reprisals followed – all except for the two Royalist houses the entire village was burned.

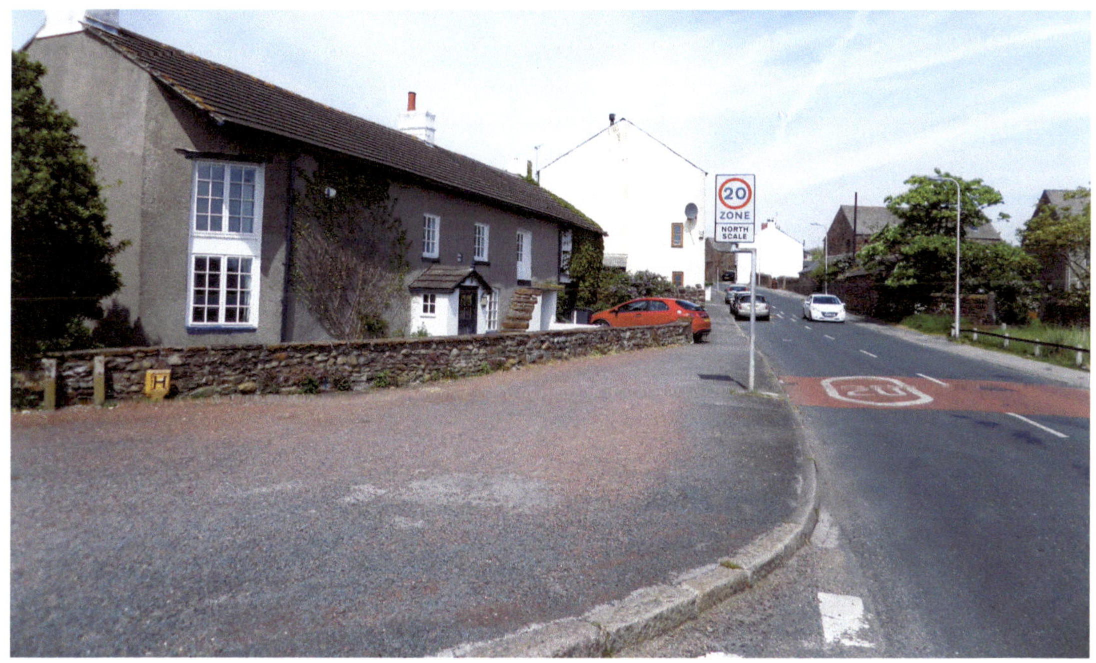

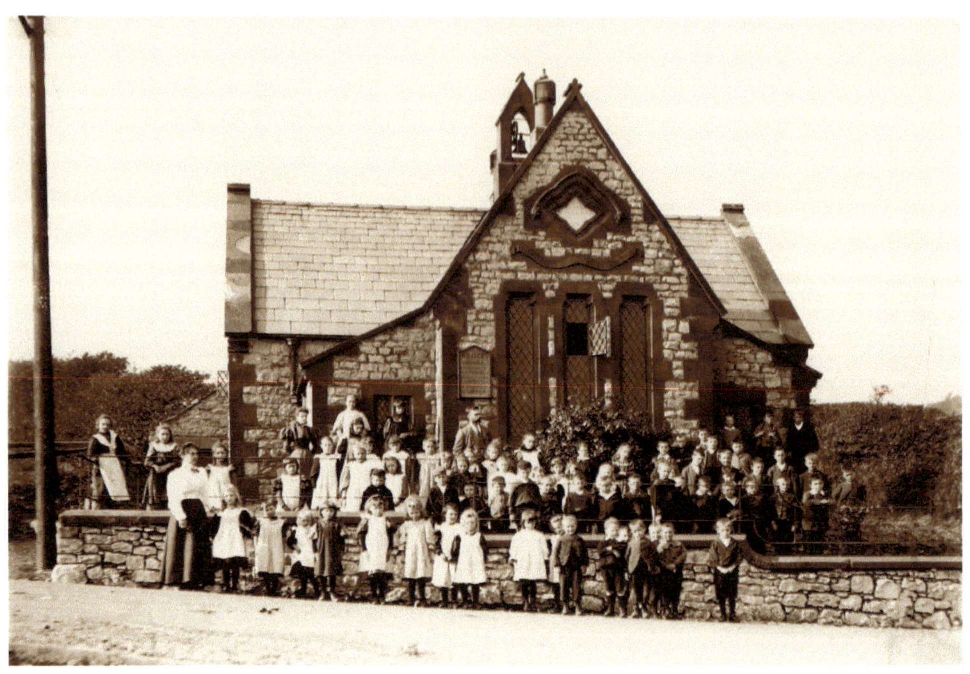

Walney School, 1898

The pupils are gathered in 1898 for a school photograph. The backdrop is very rural and has changed much over the intervening years. Following the 1870 Education Act, new schools were built across Barrow and on Walney – as the population grew so did the number of schools. Some of these have now disappeared due to falling numbers and the demand of the local authority to reduce costs. There are now three primary schools, one infant, one junior, a secondary and a special school on the island. This school is now a private house and looks much smaller.

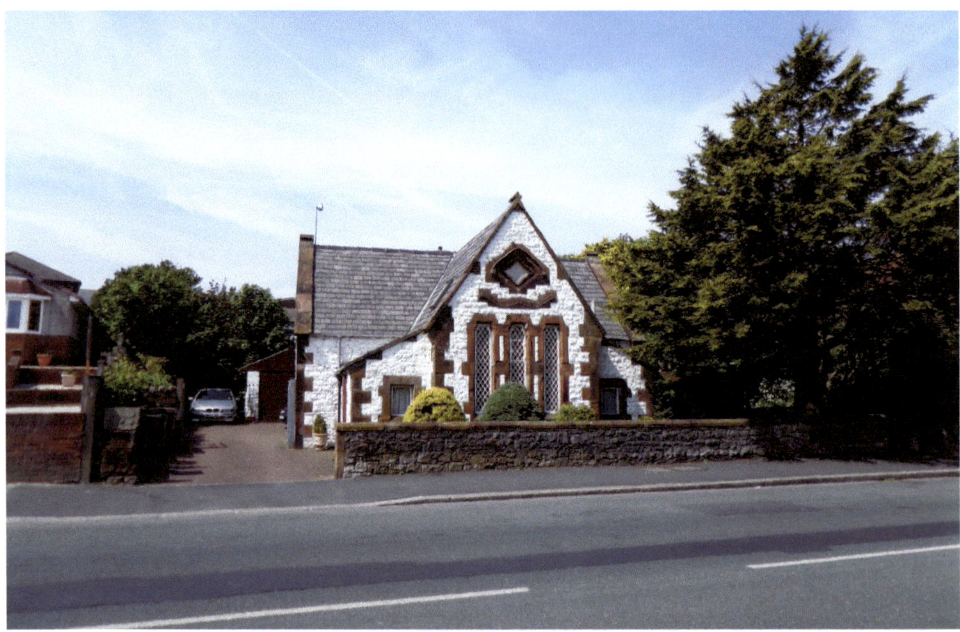

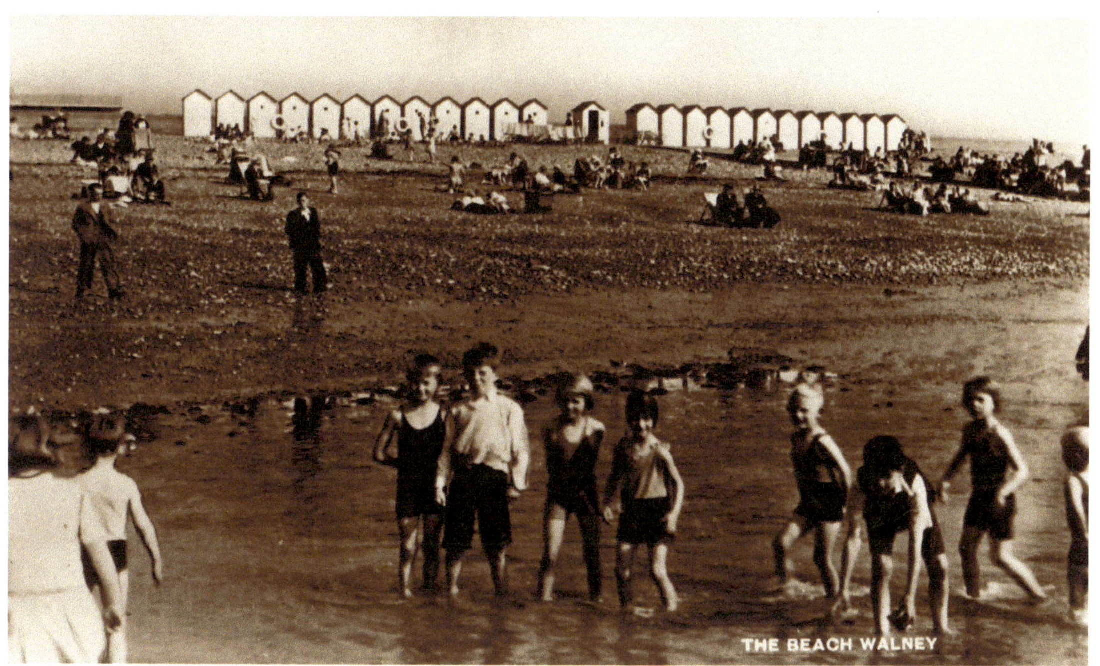

Biggar Bank, Walney

Walney has always provided a recreational area for Barrow people and is still popular today, though perhaps not attracting the same numbers of holidaymakers. Gone now are the beach huts and the pavilions but the scene here could be just as easily replicated today. Only the swimwear of the children gives away the time elapsed. Boys sport knitted bathing suits and parents watch on in full Sunday attire in this 1930s picture. The horizon is very different today, being peppered with wind turbines in the Irish Sea. (Picture loaned by Katy Millard)

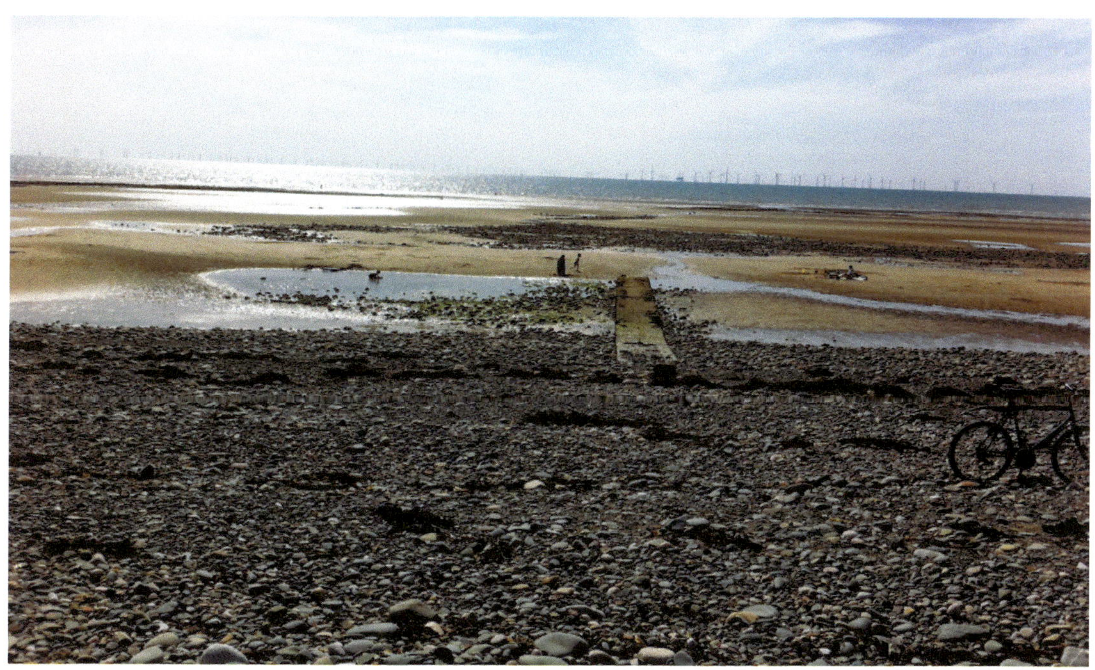

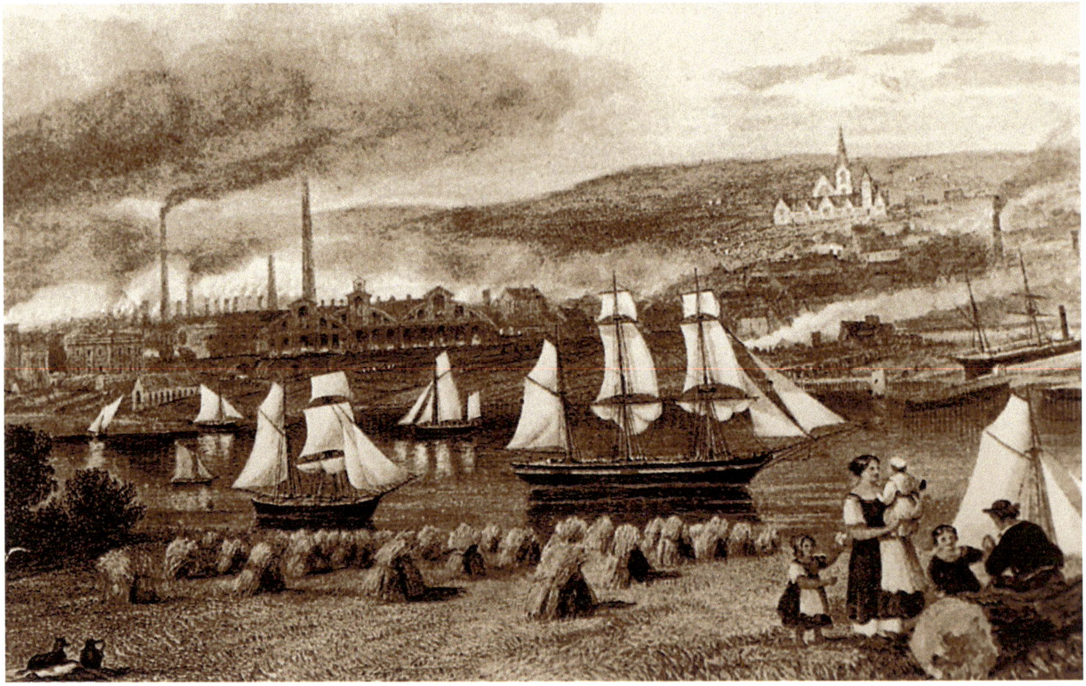

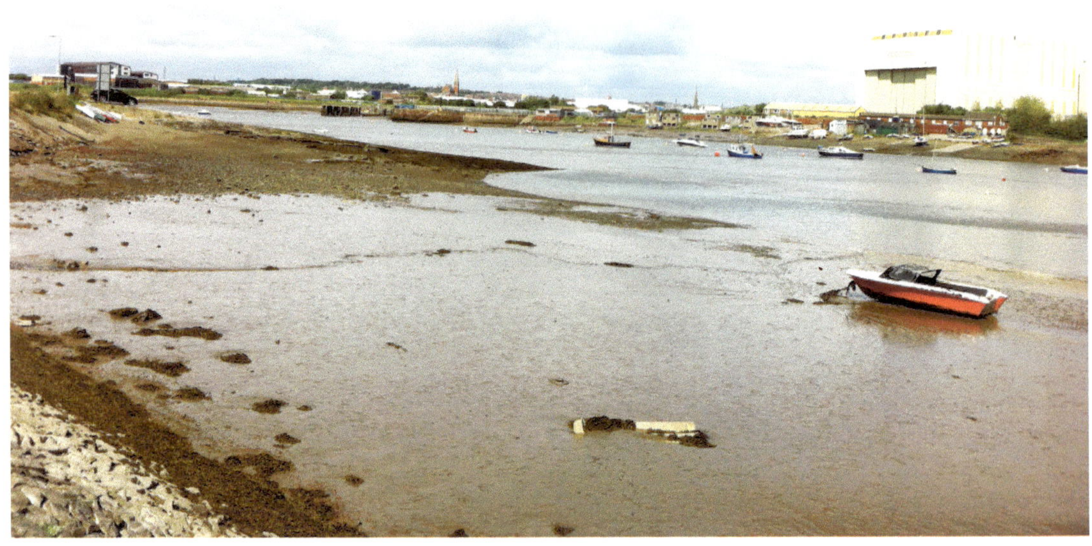

Hindpool from Walney Channel

A contrasting image of a pastoral scene against an industrial backdrop demonstrates the huge changes that were made to Barrow during the Industrial Revolution. The view is looking across Walney Channel towards Hindpool in the 1870s, at the peak of the industrial growth in Barrow. St James' church can be seen prominently in the distance, slightly out of proportion but easily recognisable. The pollution and industry has diminished now, but the importance of shipbuilding to the town is as important as ever and continues to have a highly visible impact on this view.

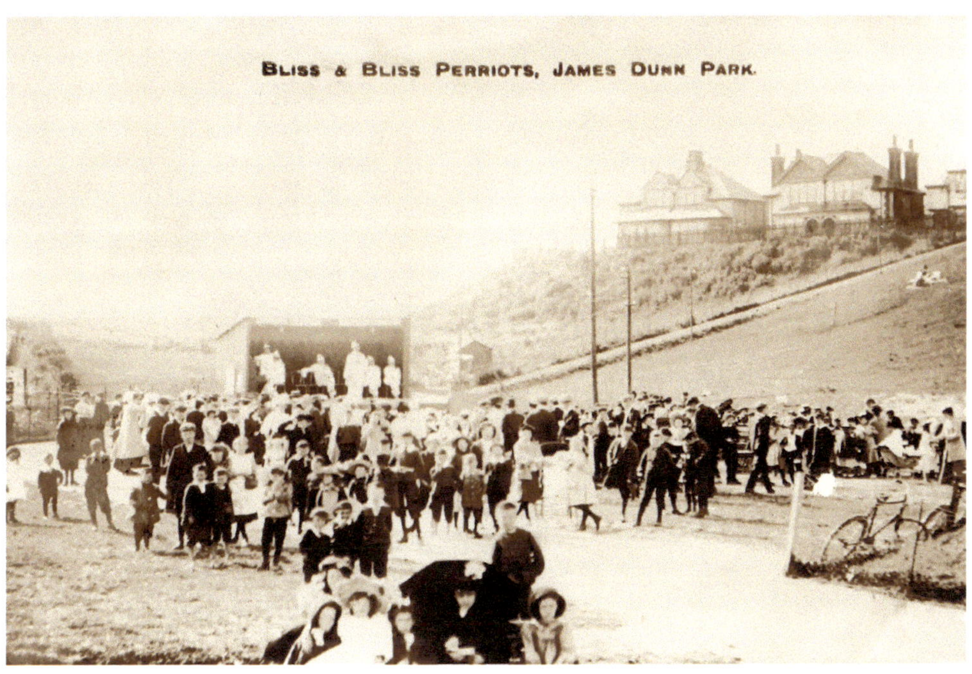

James Dunn Park, Walney

Walney Estates Company opened James Dunn Park in 1902. Additions such as the pond and bandstand were completed by 1904. Barrow Town Council took ownership of the park in 1915. The large boulder at the entrance is a glacial erratic brought down from Eskdale during the Ice Age. It commemorates the opening of Walney Bridge, which finally connected the island to the mainland. The park provided entertainment such as Pierrot shows and bands in its heyday, but nowadays there is a play area, bowling green and walks. (Picture loaned by Katy Millard)

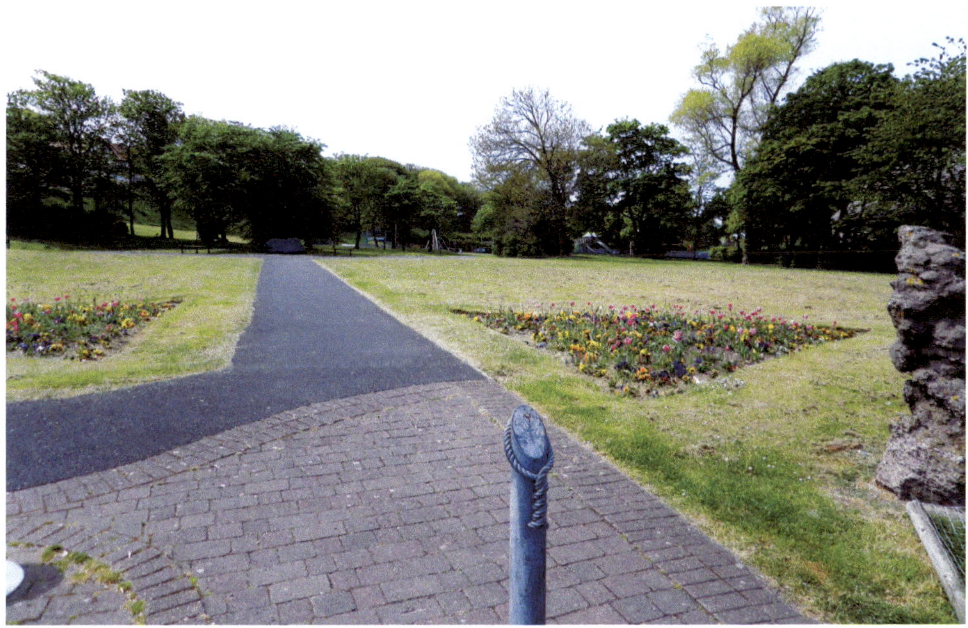

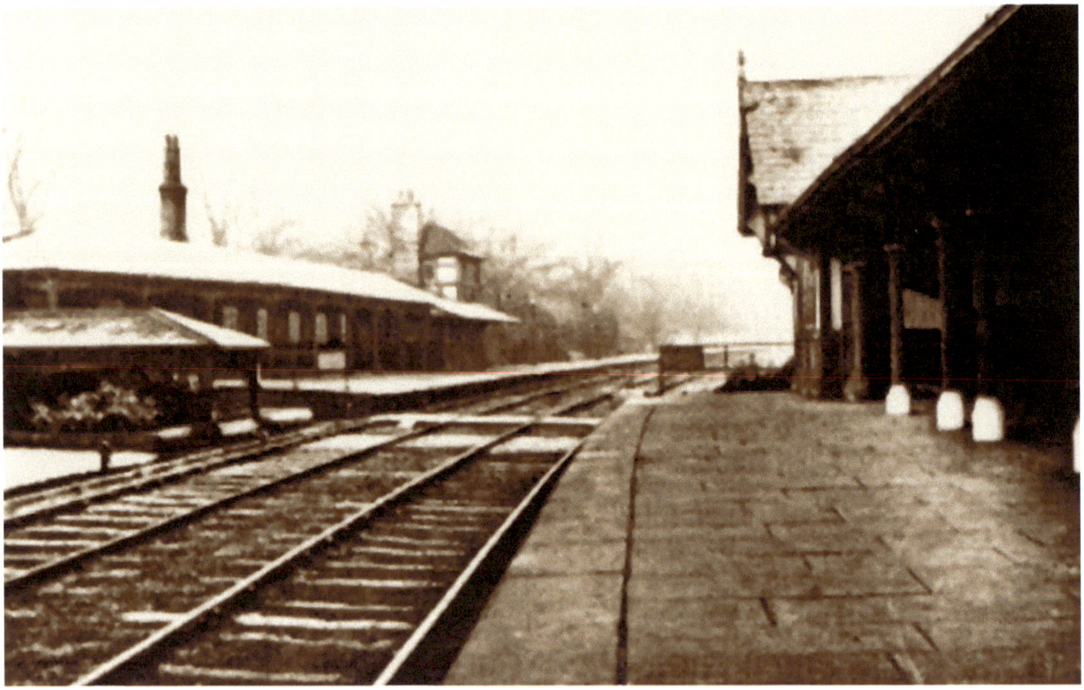

Furness Abbey Station

Furness Abbey station served the Furness Abbey Hotel and brought local visitors to the abbey itself. Its most significant customer was Sir James Ramsden, Managing Director of Furness Railway Company. Ramsden had a special siding from which to embark from his home at Abbotswood, causing complaints about delays on the line by passengers waiting for him to arrive. The station closed in 1950 and there is little visible evidence now of its existence.

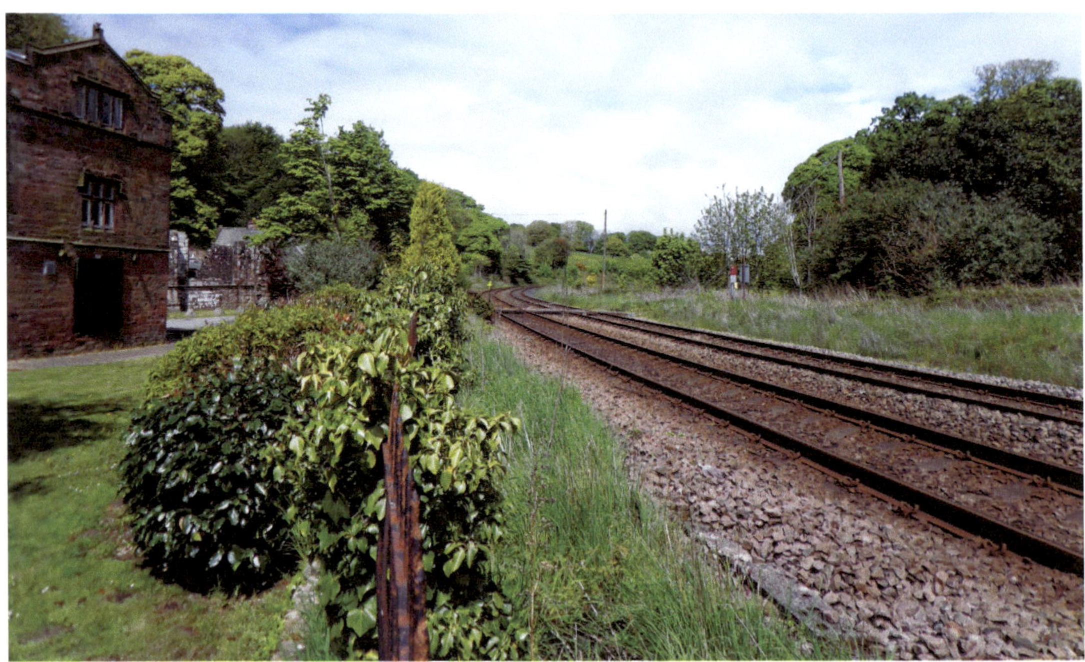

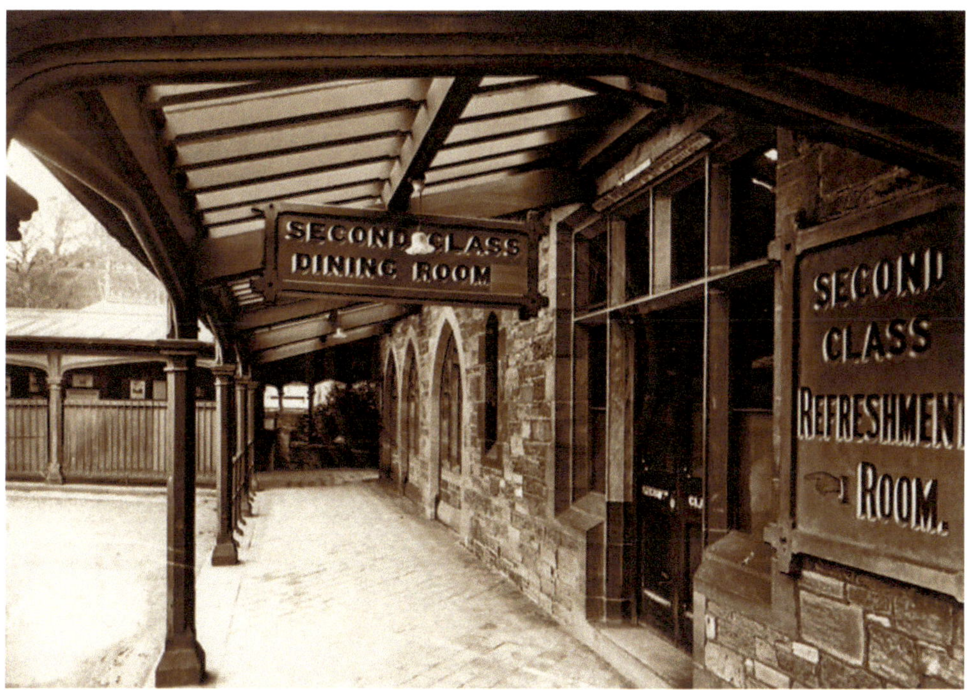

Abbey Tavern, Abbey Approach

This building was previously the second class refreshment room attached to Furness Railway's Abbey station. It was opened in 1846 and by 1862 passengers were coming from further afield. The station serviced Furness Abbey Hotel, which was owned by the railway company. It is all that remains of both the hotel and station and was more recently a pub and a bistro. It was empty and derelict for some years until English Heritage purchased it in 2015, protecting it for the future.

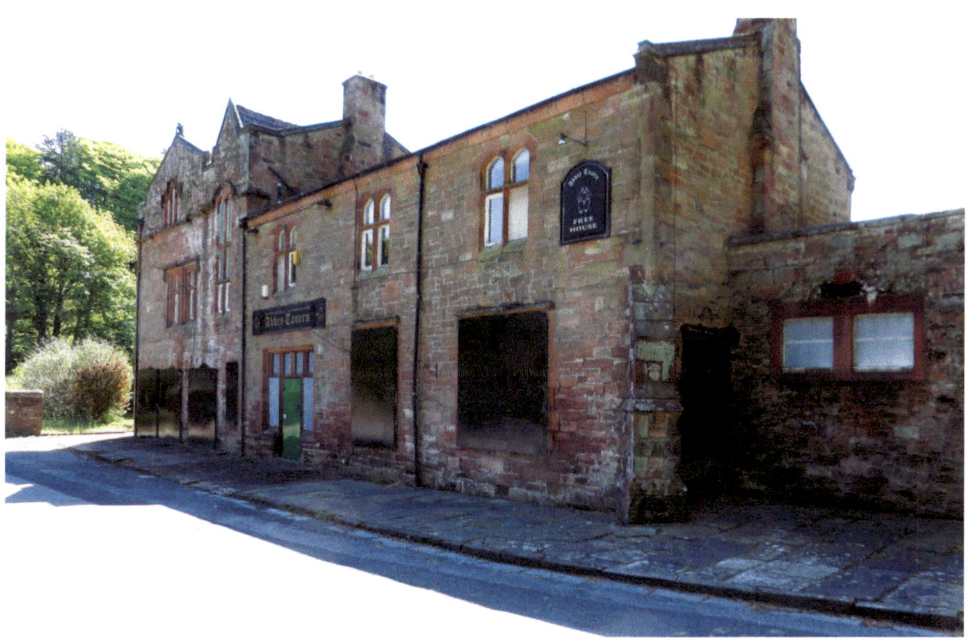

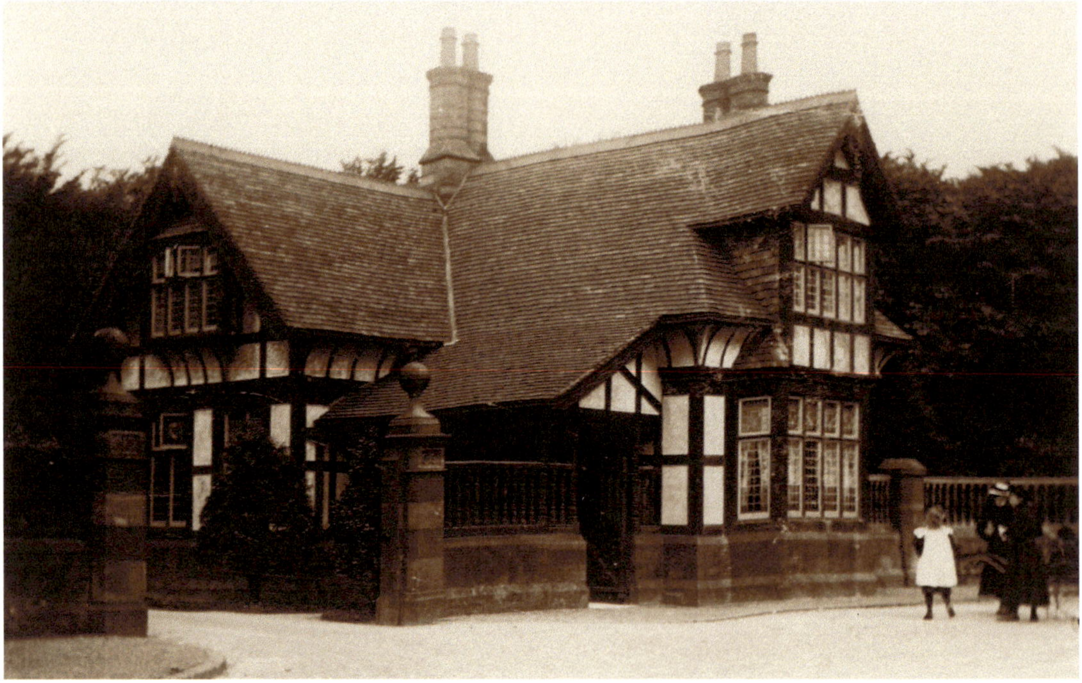

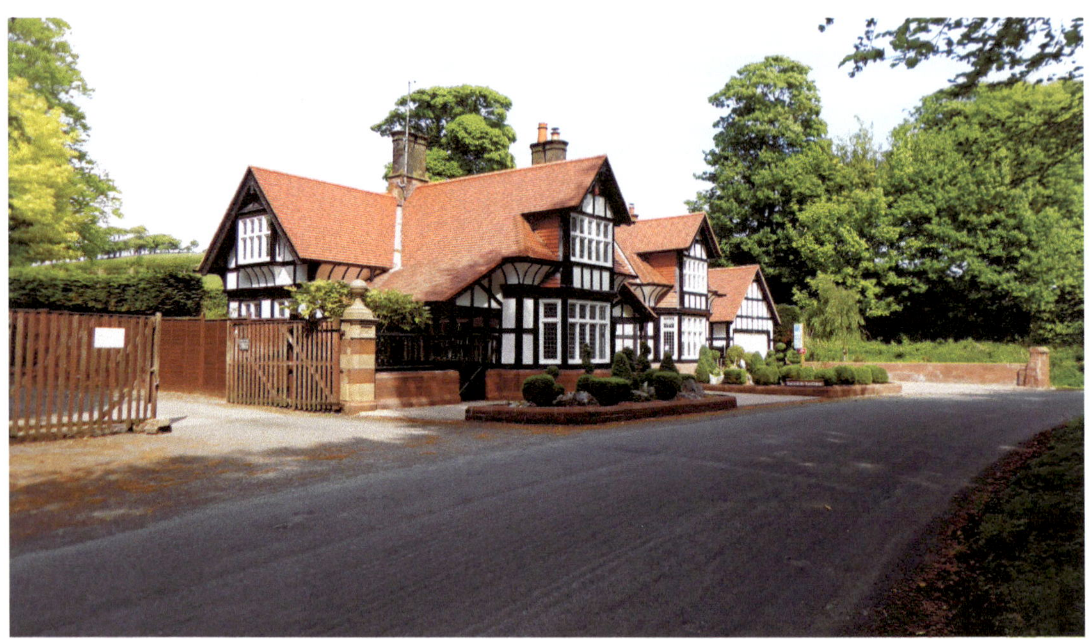

The South Lodge, Abbotswood

The Lodge was part of Abbotswood Estate, built for Sir James Ramsden by the railway company in 1873. It is next to one of the grand entrances leading to the mansion. The attractive half-timbered and sandstone style complimented the mansion and it was sympathetically extended in 1976. Its original function was to house the butler's family and they are recorded on the 1881 census, although the butler himself was marked as resident in the mansion. Although today the house is privately owned, there is public access to the woods through the large gated entrance.

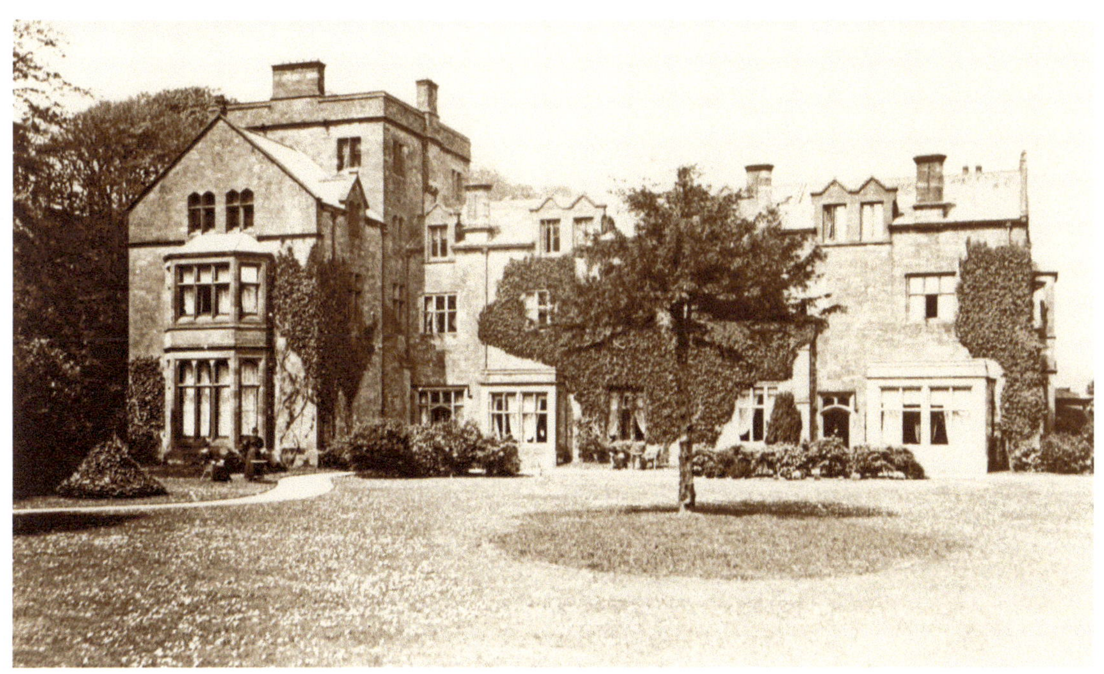

Furness Abbey Hotel

Furness Abbey Hotel was built by the Preston family on the site of the Manor House following the Dissolution. It was purchased by Furness Railway Company in 1847 and later converted into a hotel by Sharpe and Paley. In the 1860s it was extended, linking it to the railway station. It endured until the Second World War when it was damaged by bombing. The station was closed and it was demolished in 1953. The location of this building is roughly where the abbey visitor centre and car park is now.

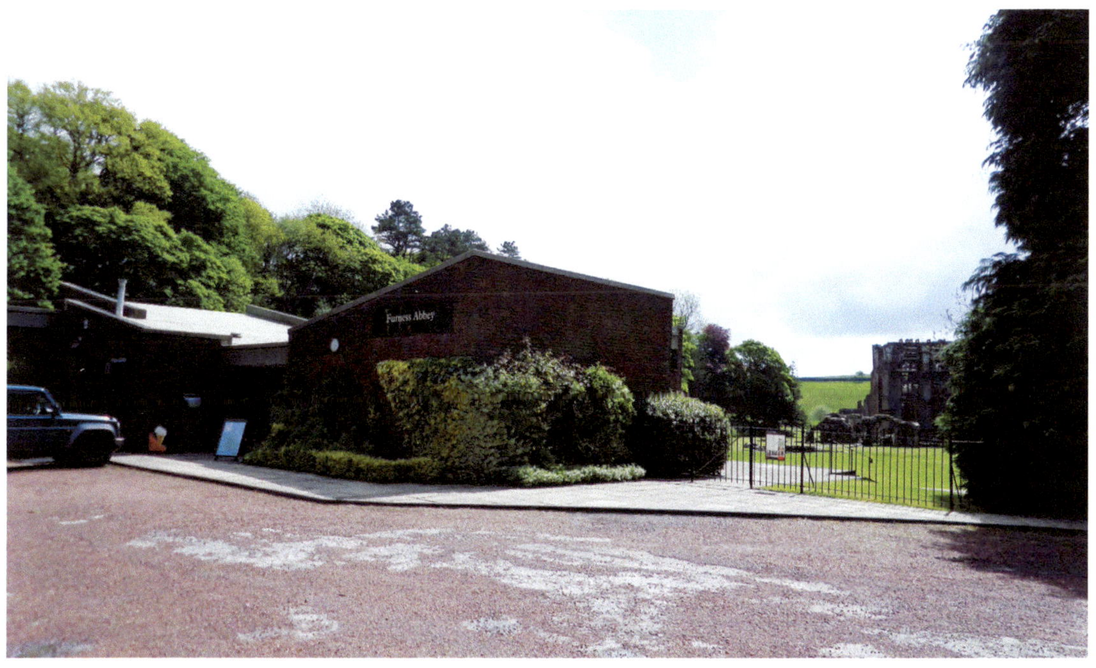

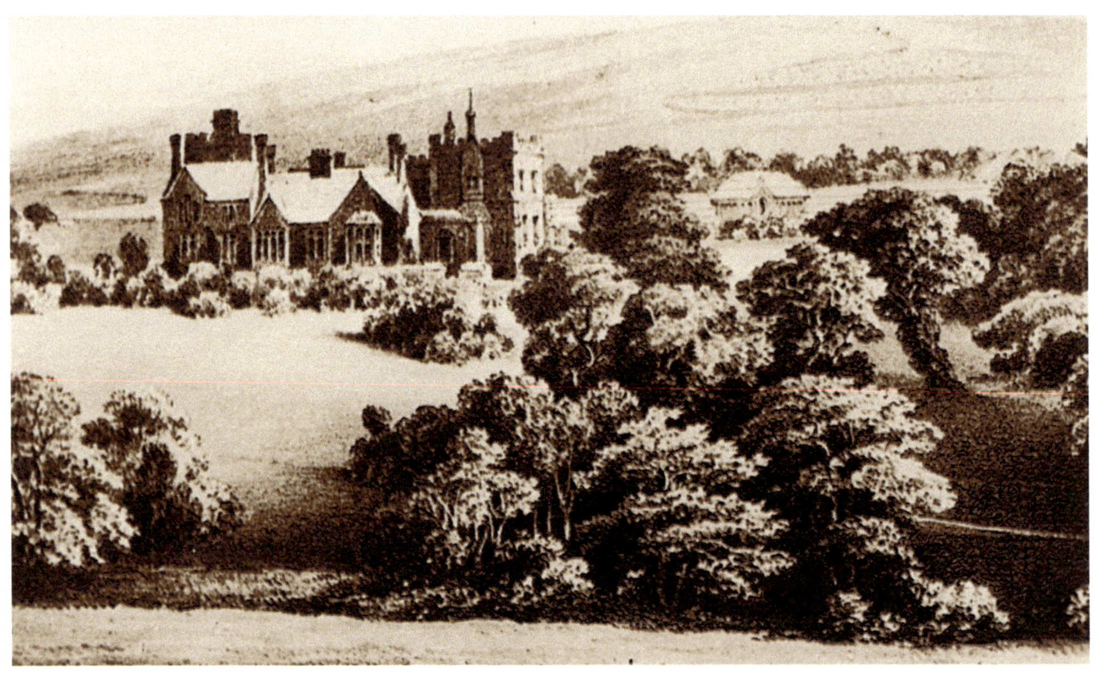

Abbotswood

Abbotswood was a gothic mansion built by Furness Railway Company for Sir James Ramsden at a cost of £2,000. After his son Frederic died, the estate reverted to the town and was later commandeered by the army. Incredibly, it was demolished with dynamite by the council in 1961, which seems an act of gross vandalism now. It briefly became a nuclear bunker but this too was demolished. The area is now a recreational space for the town but the gateway to the mansion remains as a memory of grander days.

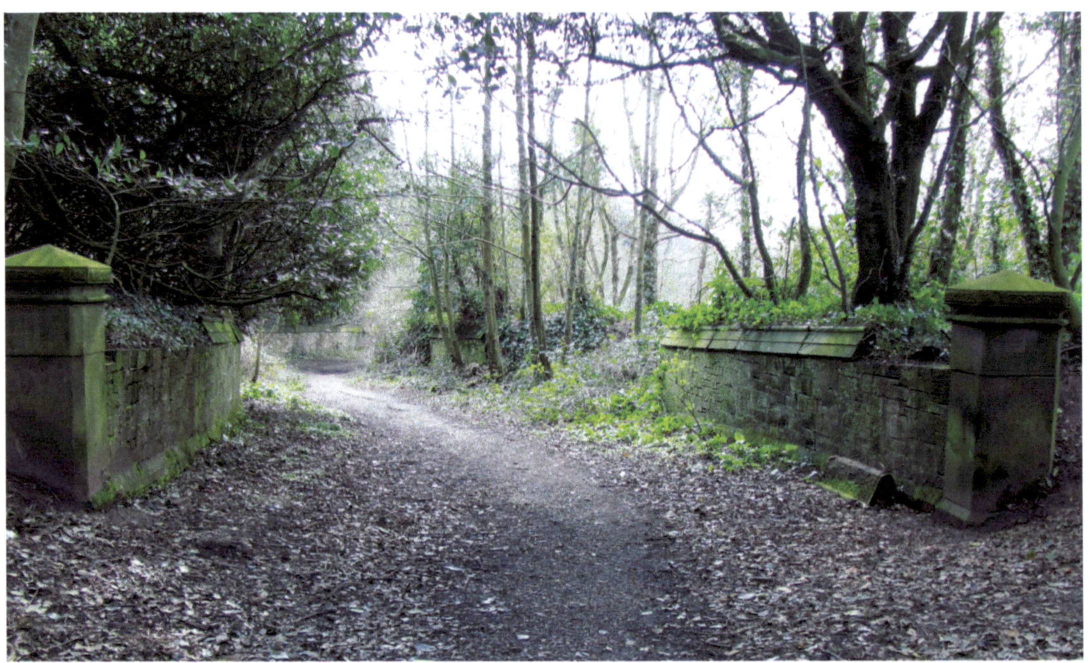

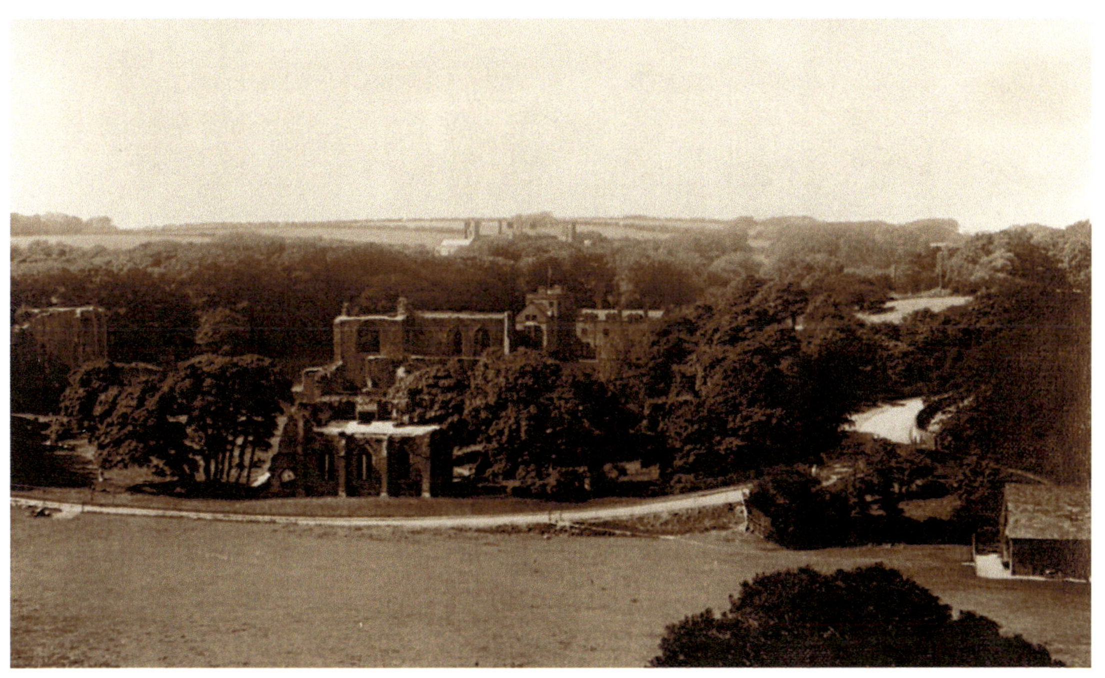

The Abbey of St Mary of Furness

Built in 1127 by monks from Savigny, the abbey later became Cistercian. It was the second richest abbey after Fountains Abbey. Its influence stretched across the north of England and included the Isle of Man and Ireland. It had numerous granges and became prosperous from the wool trade. It was the first large abbey to be dissolved and the Deed of Surrender was signed on 9 April 1537. It is now under the control of English Heritage and is a Grade I listed building of national importance.

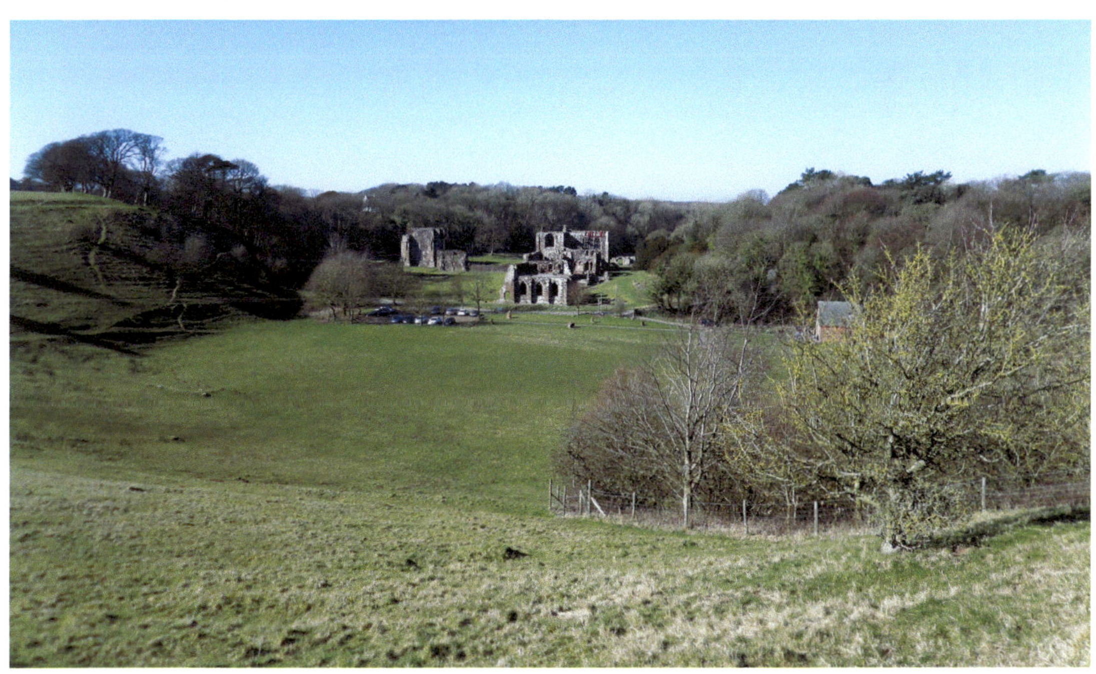

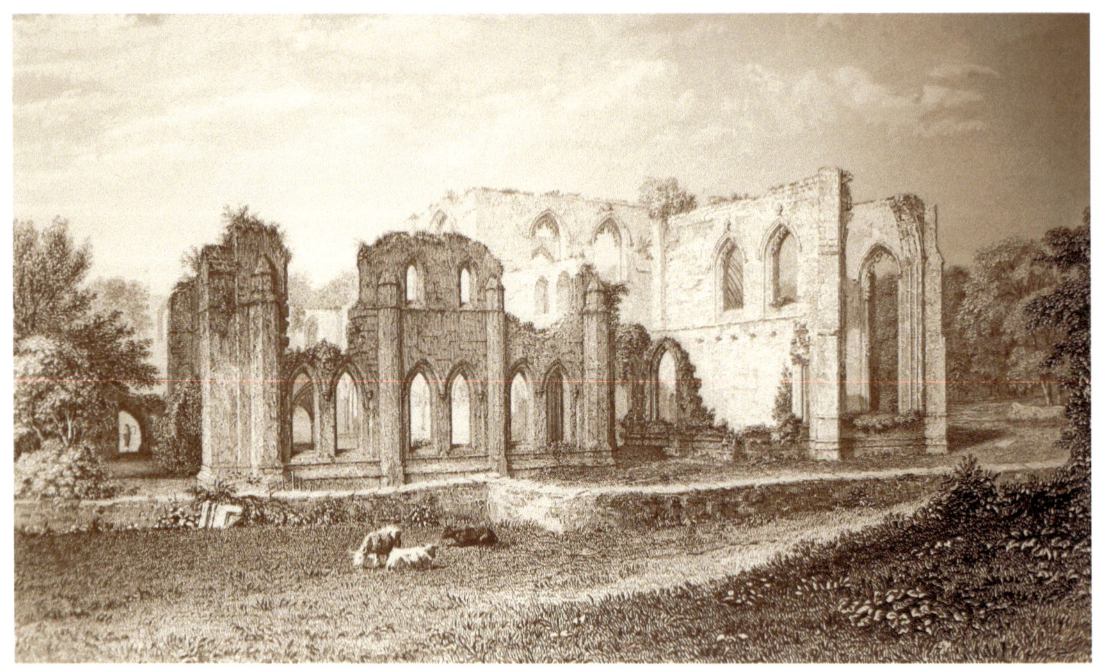

Turner sketched it and Wordsworth included it in his poem *The Prelude*. He objected strongly when the railway was constructed so close to the ruins. It became a tourist venue, thriving because of the railway being cut through the valley. Sir Richard Cavendish donated it to the nation in 1923 and it is now administered by English Heritage. In 2010, during work to stabilise the presbytery, an abbot's skeleton, his crosier and ring were found. These rare finds are now housed in the abbey museum.

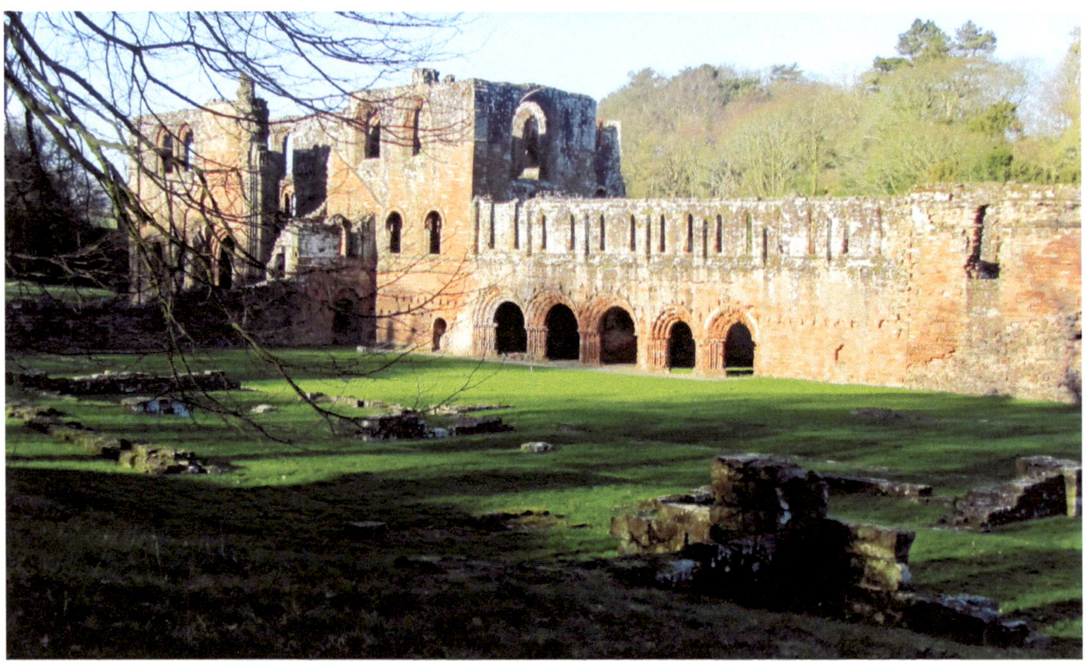

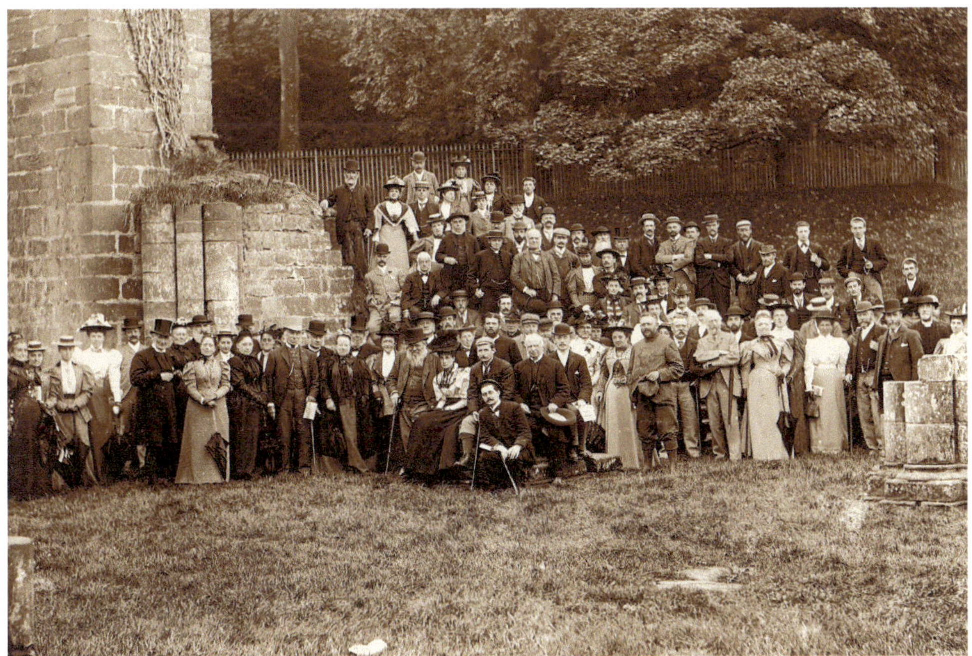

Furness Abbey Bell Tower

During the late Victorian and early Edwardian period, Furness Abbey attracted the attention of amateur antiquarians. Historian Harper Gaythorpe investigated much of Furness heritage, including Furness Abbey. The Cumberland and Westmorland Archaeological Society used the Bell Tower (the final building addition was in 1500) as a location for the photograph recording a visit in the 1890s. The abbey continues to draw local heritage groups and the latest one, Furness Abbey Fellowship, which was set up in 2012, supports the abbey with a Medieval Fair, welcoming over 1,000 visitors annually. (Picture courtesy of the Harper Gaythorpe Collection)

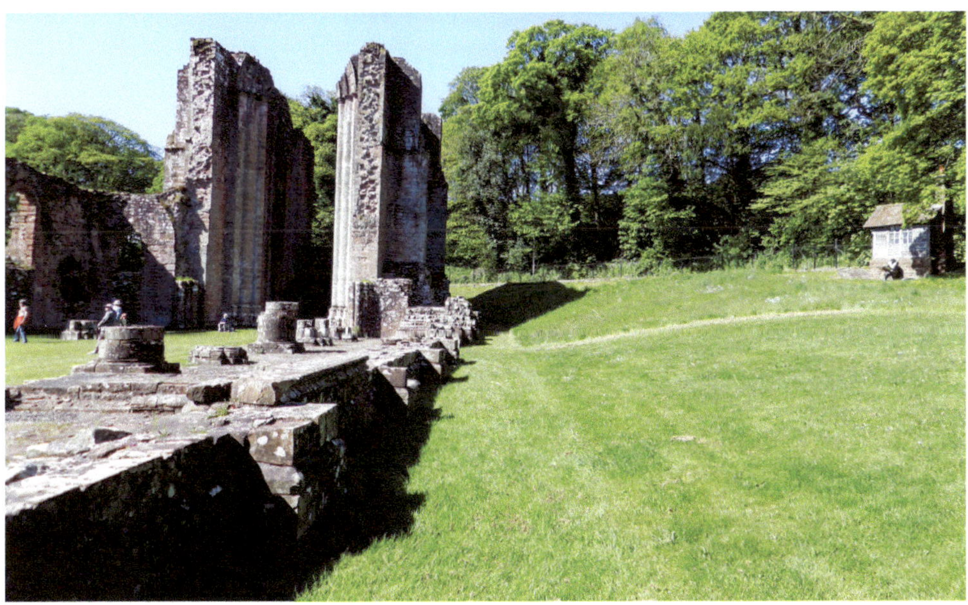

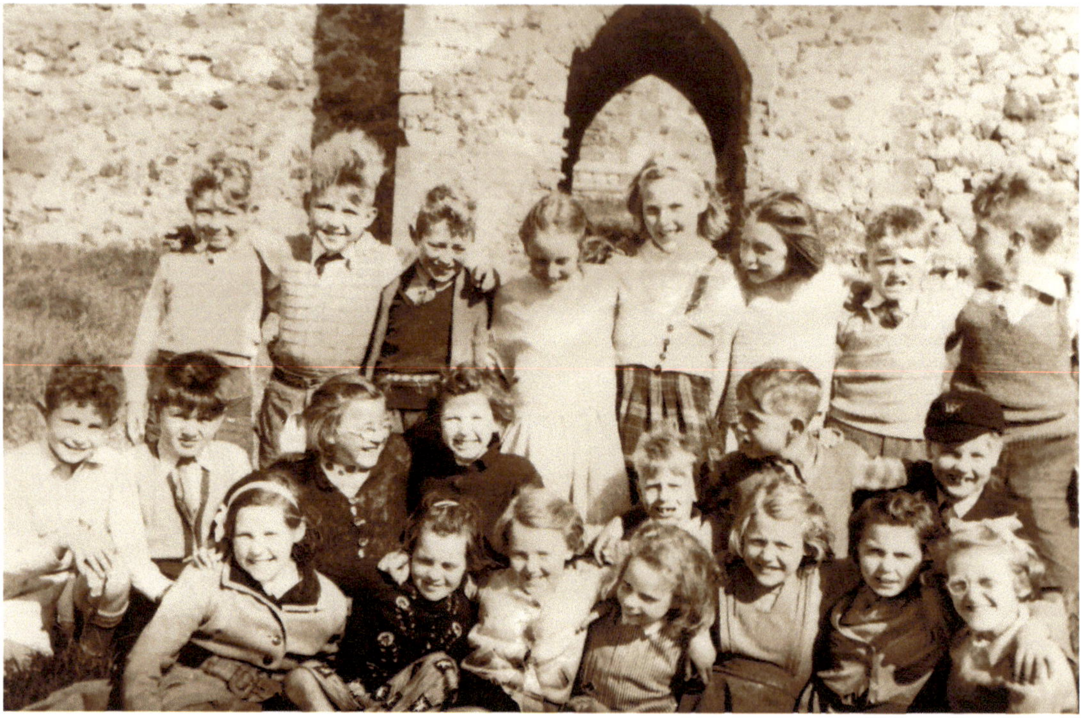

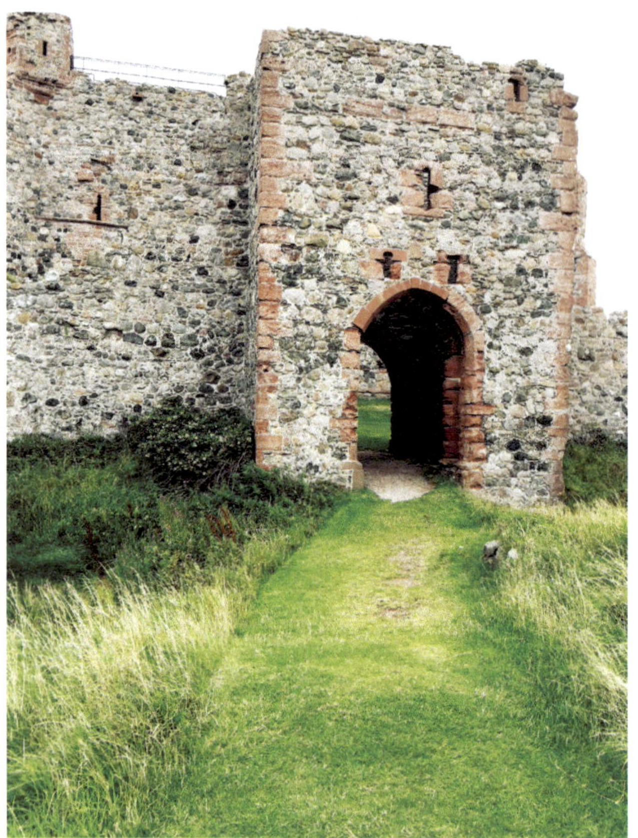

Piel Castle

This popular destination for school trips has always captured the imagination. The castle was built for Furness Abbey and in 1327 John Cockerham was given permission to crenellate. Its purpose was two-fold: to provide safe refuge and to monitor traffic along the Irish Sea. In 1487 the pretender Lambert Simnel landed here before being defeated at Newark by Henry VII. It was given as a war memorial to the town by the Duke of Buccleuch in 1920 and is now under the protection of English Heritage. (Picture courtesy of Sarah Taylor)

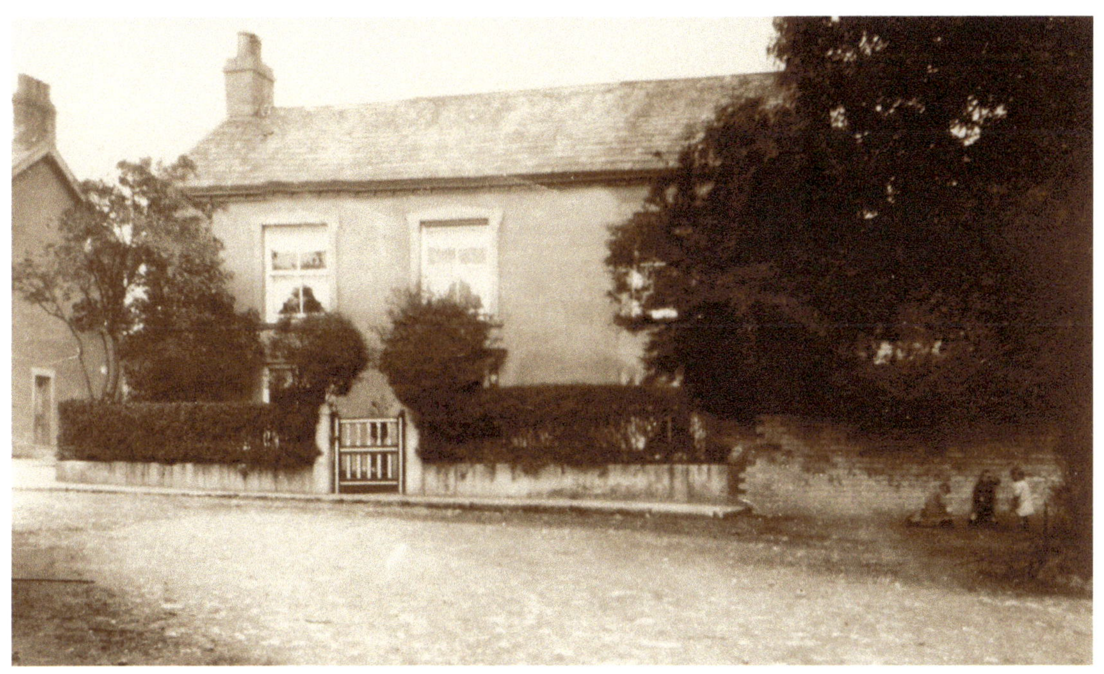

Hector House, Newbarns

The origins of this house's name is unknown, but seems to have classical connotations. The Greek theme continues with streets such as Athens Drive and Dorcas Avenue. Hector House is an eighteenth-century listed building marking the location of the original Newbarns village. Nearby, an even older building, Sandylands Farmhouse, dates from 1623. This village was originally created when tenants of Furness Abbey were turned out of their homes at Sellergarth by the abbot Alexander Bankes in order to extend his deer park and they relocated to 'new barns'.

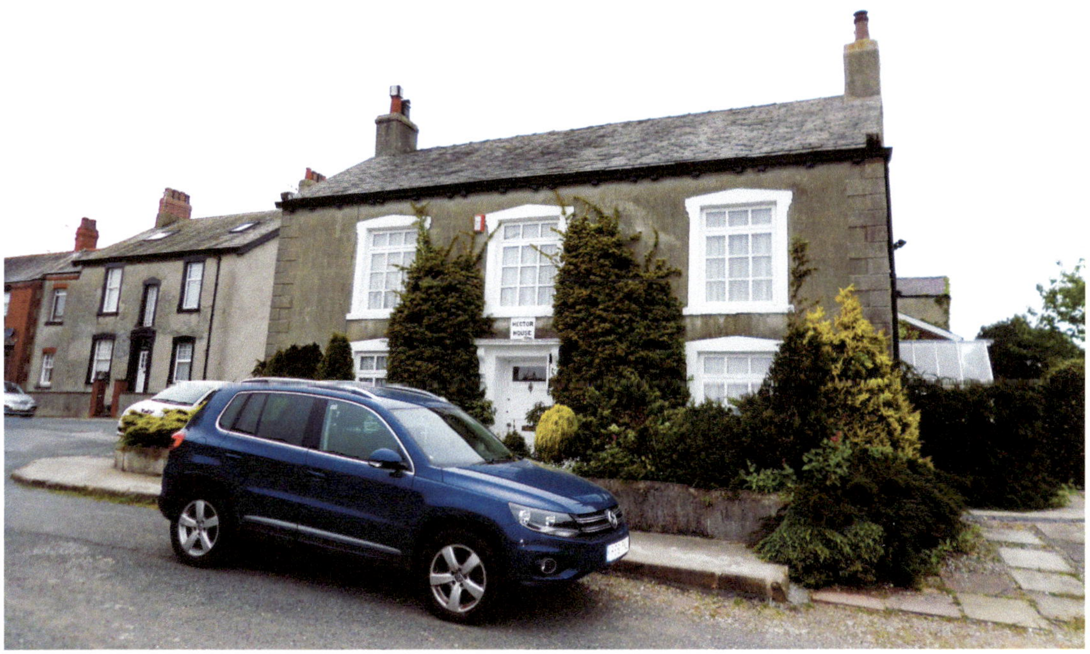

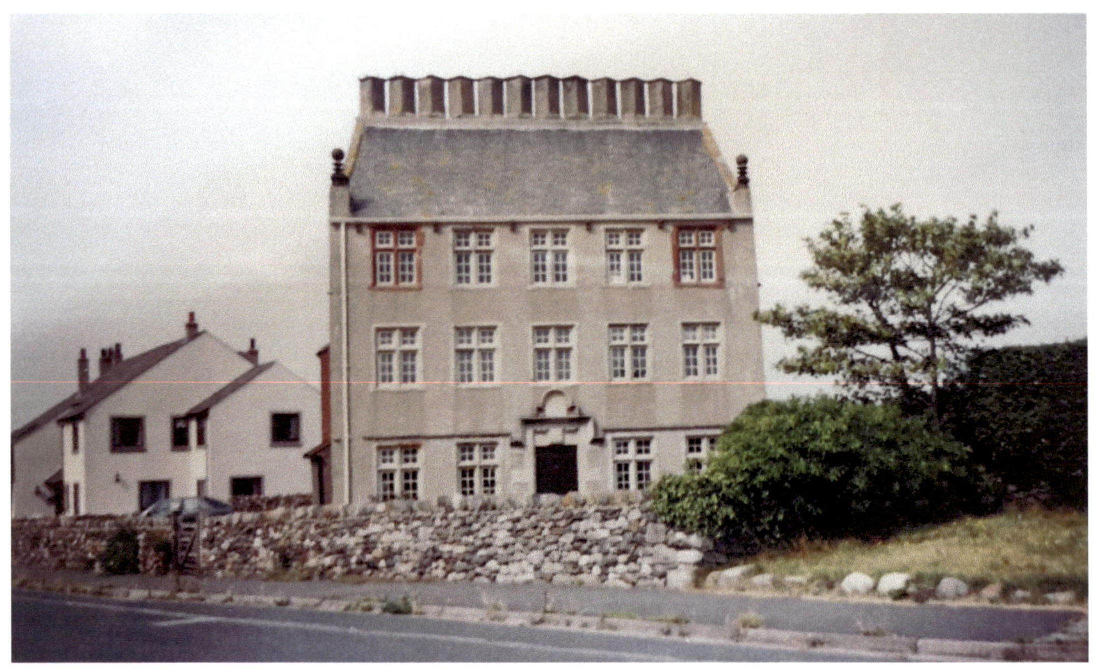

Rampside Hall

Rampside Hall has survived with few exterior changes. It was built in the seventeenth century for the Knype family and is a Grade I listed building. It is a well-known landmark because of its twelve chimneys, earning the nickname 'the twelve apostles'. Three chimneys were displaced in an earthquake in 1865, but the damage was repaired and the building retains its integrity. However, modern developments now engulf it and the fields have disappeared beneath modern housing, which does nothing to enhance the heritage of this lovely building.

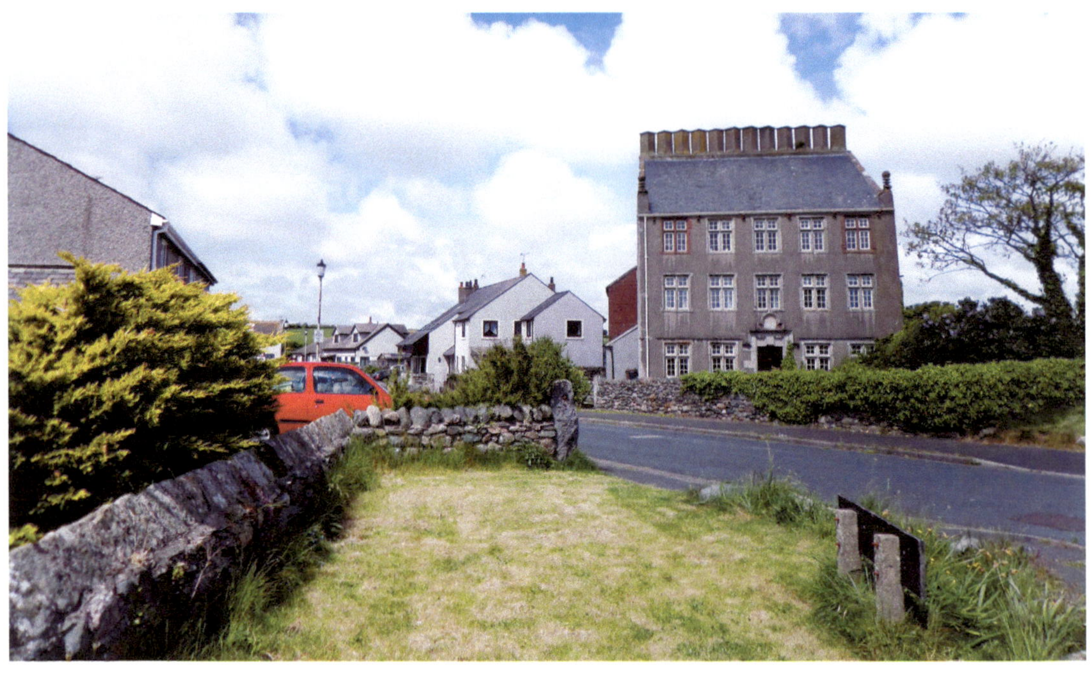

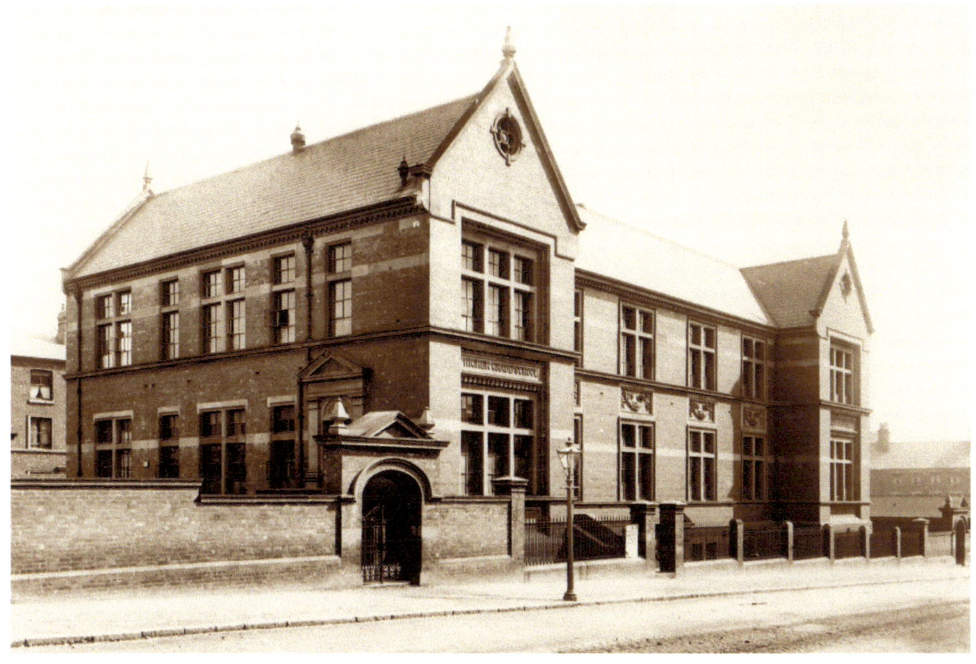

Alfred Barrow Higher Grade School

The higher grade school was built in the late 1890s and was the only high school at the time. A new wing was built in 1930, providing a girls' school. Eventually, the boys' school moved to a new site at Holker Street. Extensions followed and it became a mixed comprehensive in the 1970s. Following negative reports, the school was threatened with closure by the Department for Education, despite a public outcry. The school was absorbed into the new Furness Academy in 2009, again after a vehement public protest.

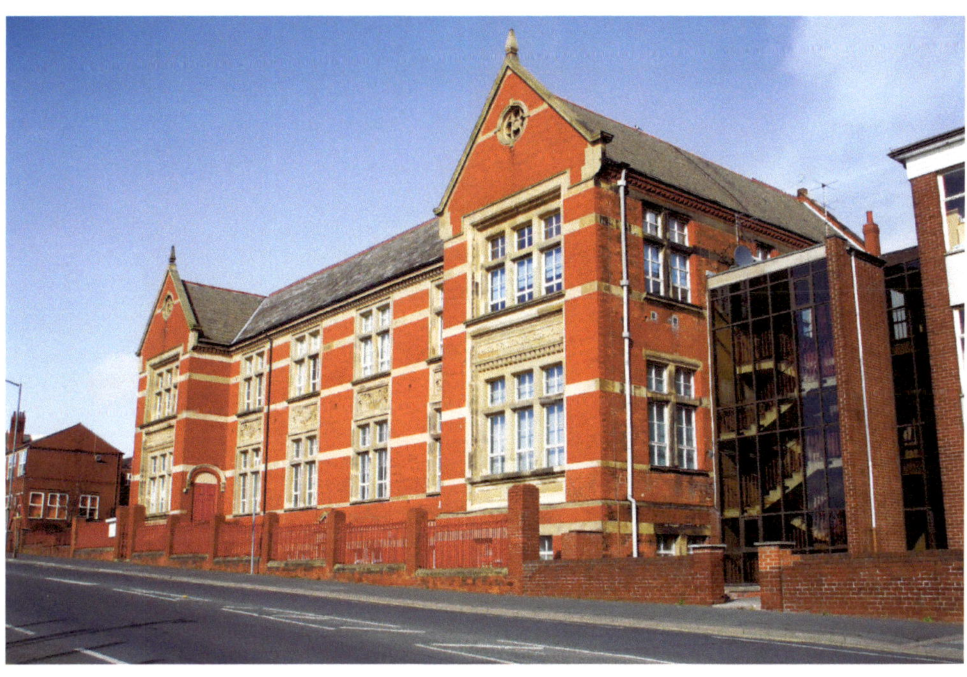

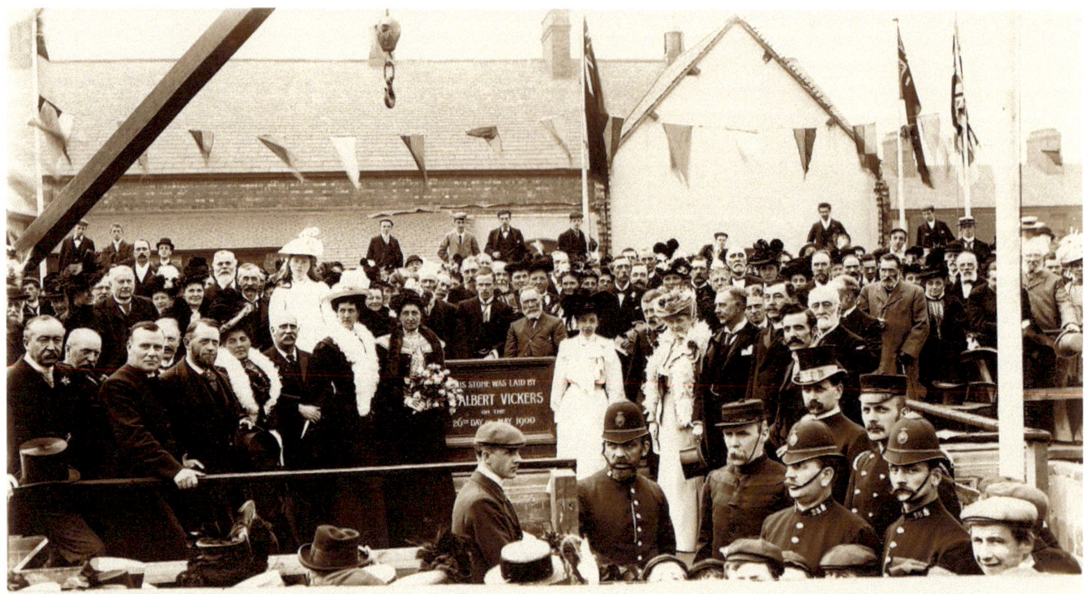

E, LAID BY MRS ALBERT VICKERS, 26 MAY, 1900

Technical School, Abbey Road

The foundation stone of Barrow Technical School was laid by Mrs Albert Vickers on 26 May 1900. The school was a training ground for the workforce of the shipyard and the pupils were channelled into apprenticeships and higher education from here. The school endured until the 1950s when Thorncliffe Technical School and Howard Street College replaced it. The building fell into neglect for many years and was under threat of demolition, but it was rescued in 2000 when it was refurbished.

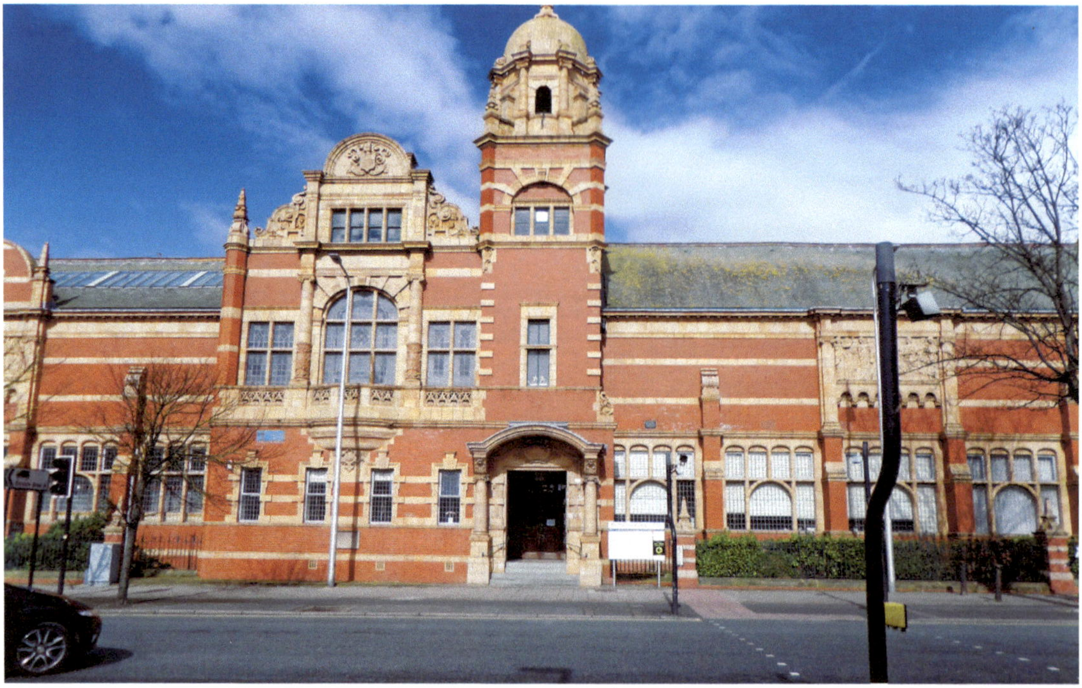

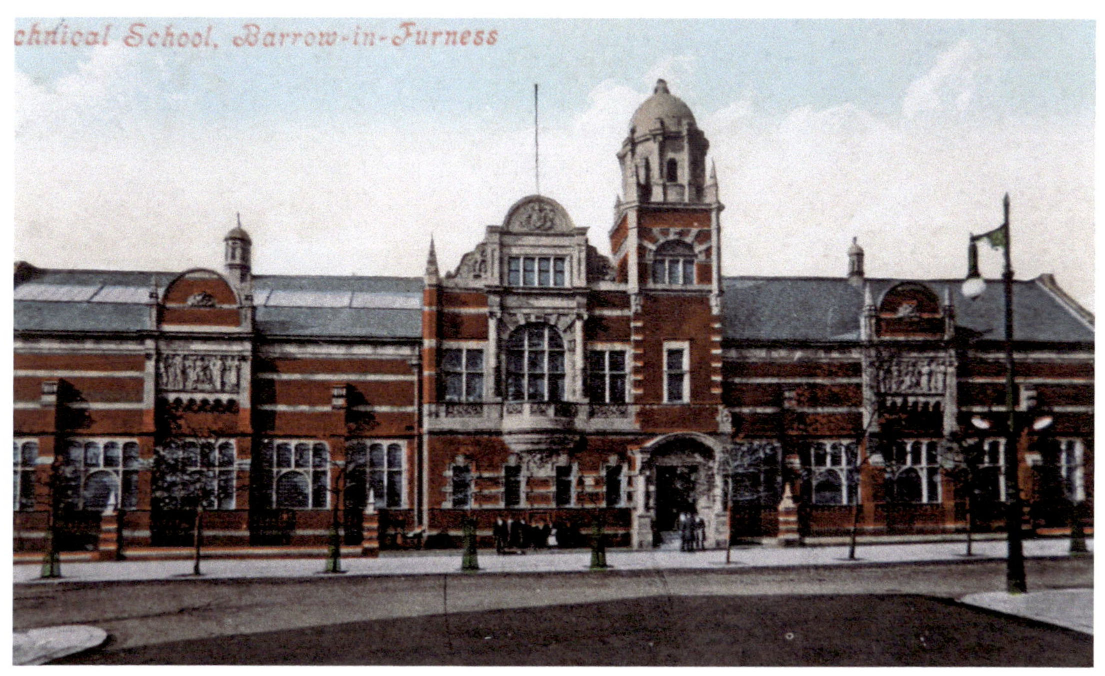

Barrow Technical School

This beautiful building has become a Cumbria County Council office, registrars and arts centre and is known as the 'Nan Tait Centre', named after the mayor who served between 1959 and 1960. It remains an iconic building and one which was reinvented to make it fit for purpose in the twenty-first century. Howard Street, which replaced it, is office space. A statue to another famous Barrow sportsman, Willie Horne the rugby league player for Barrow and Great Britain, graces the frontage. Thorncliffe has been demolished for yet more housing.

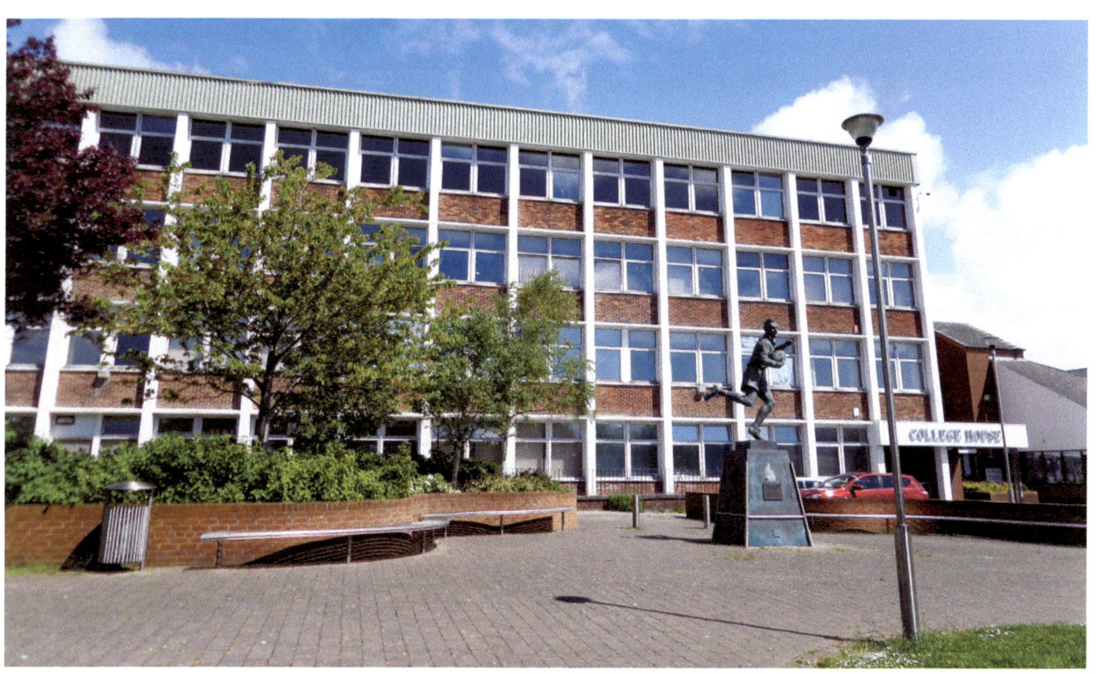

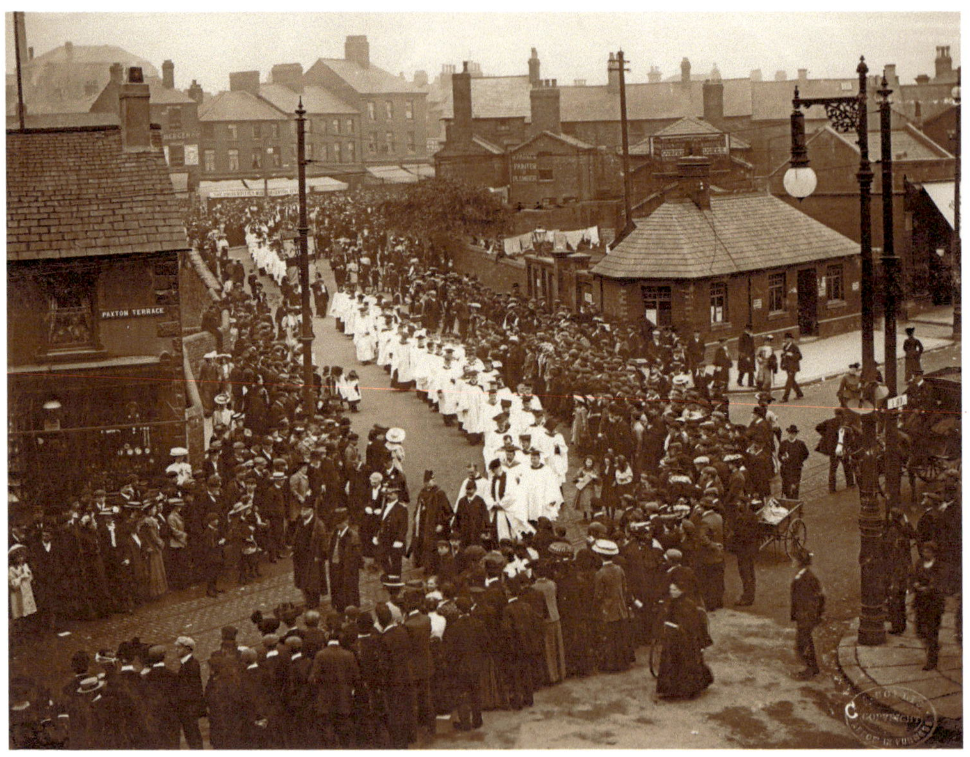

Paxton Terrace

In 1906 the Church Congress Procession went down Paxton Street into Paxton Terrace (built on land belonging to the Paxton family of Dalton) and there to the Town Hall. The picture shows a gathering of the great and the good watched by local residents who line the street. Tram lines and modern gas street lighting are visible and demonstrate how up to date the town was at this time. This area was demolished in the 1960s and completely concealed by the current Market Hall and Forum Theatre complex.

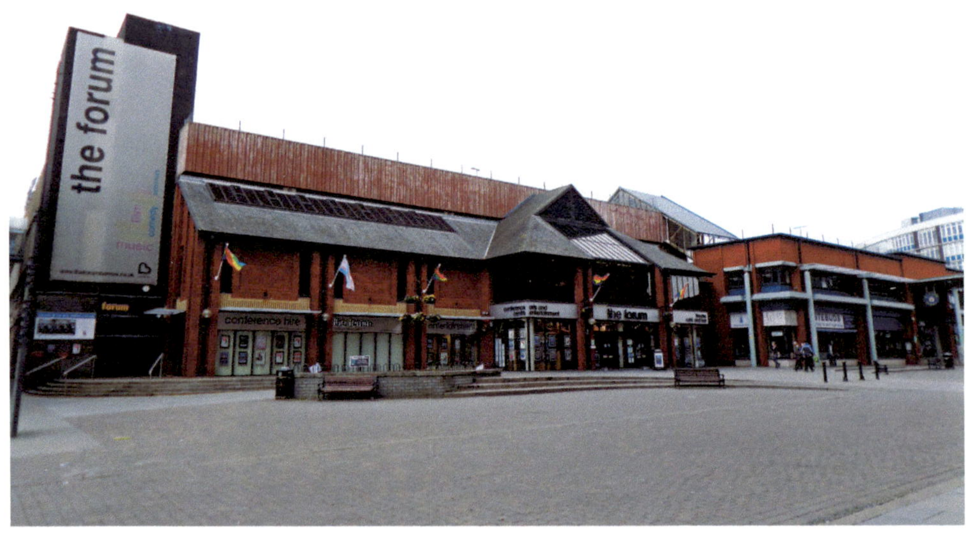

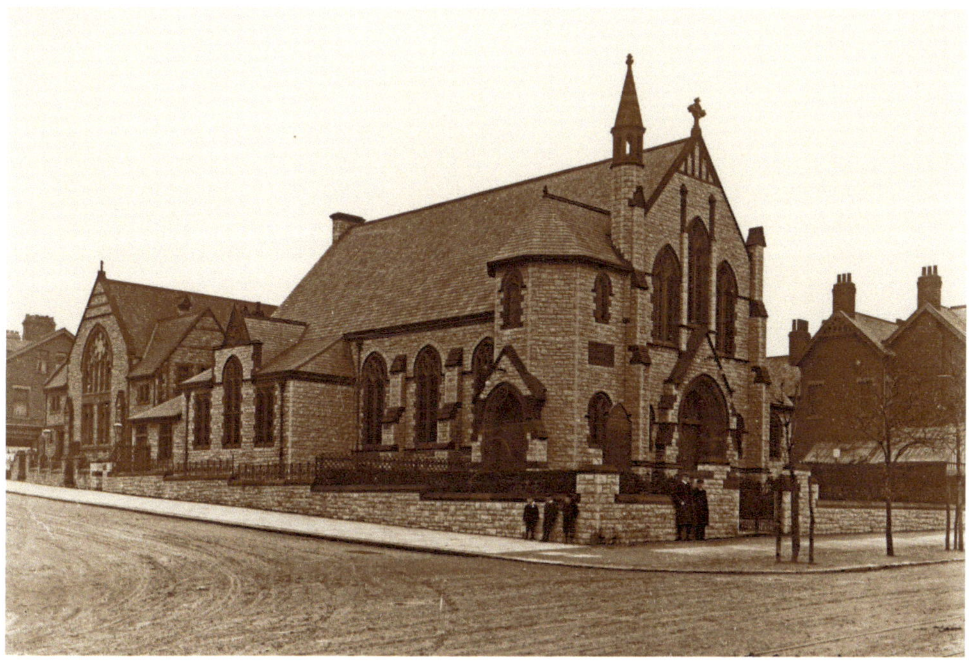

Emmanuel Church, Abbey Road

Emmanuel Congregational church was on the corner of Abbey Road and Ainslie Street and was the second congregational church. Built in 1876 from local limestone, it was extended in 1900. It became part of the United Reform church in 1972 and continued to dominate the corner of Ainslie Street. The building deteriorated and by 1991 repair costs were so prohibitive that the congregation moved to the Methodist church, becoming part of Trinity churches. The church was demolished in 1993 and a retirement home has replaced it.

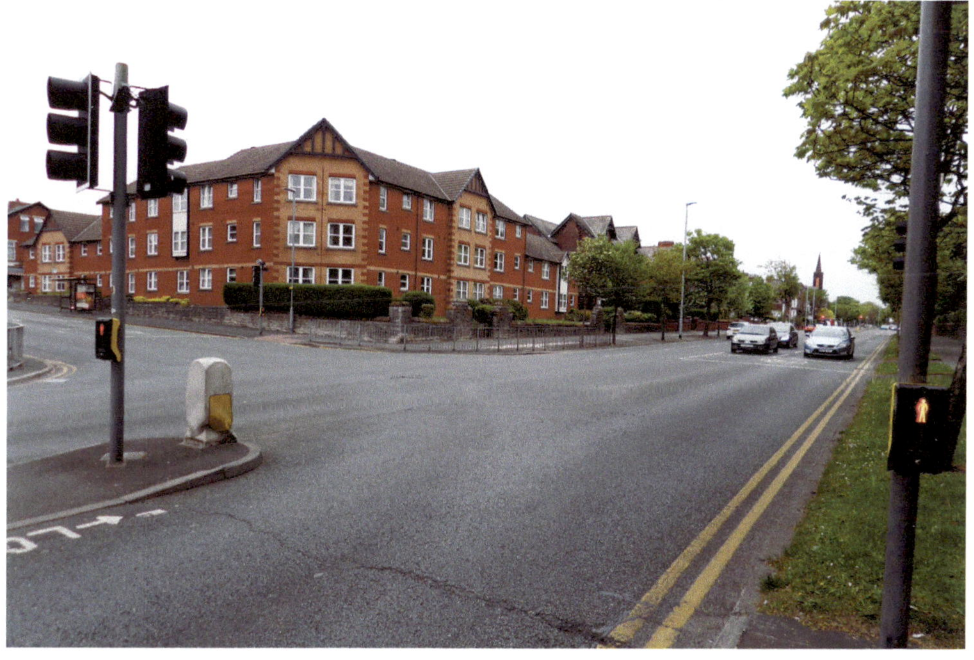

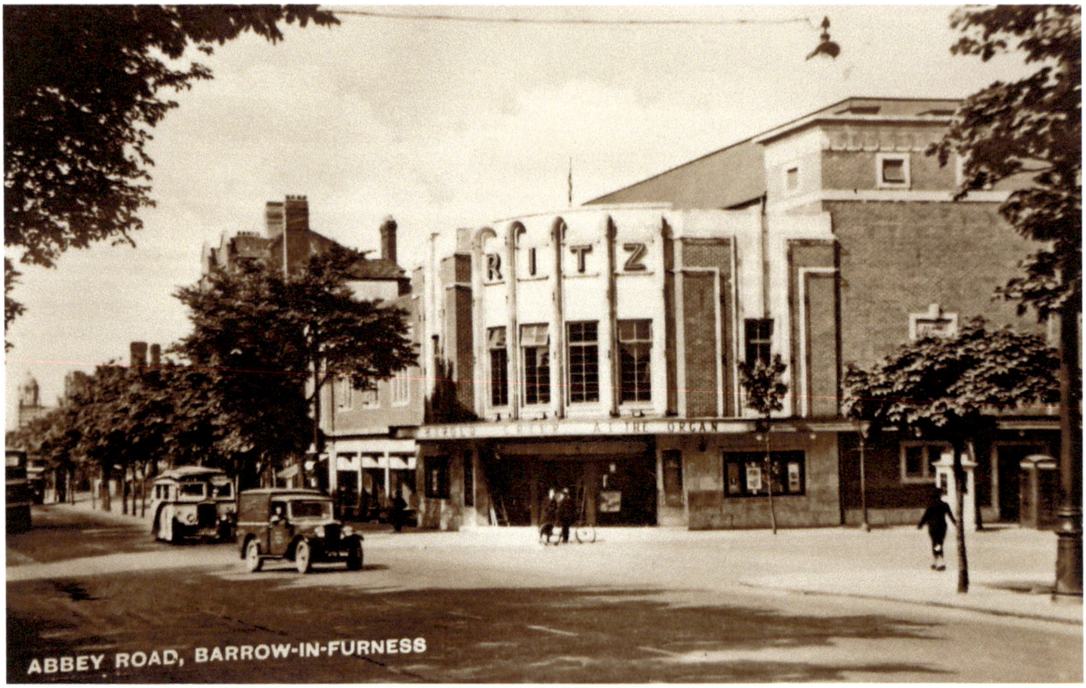

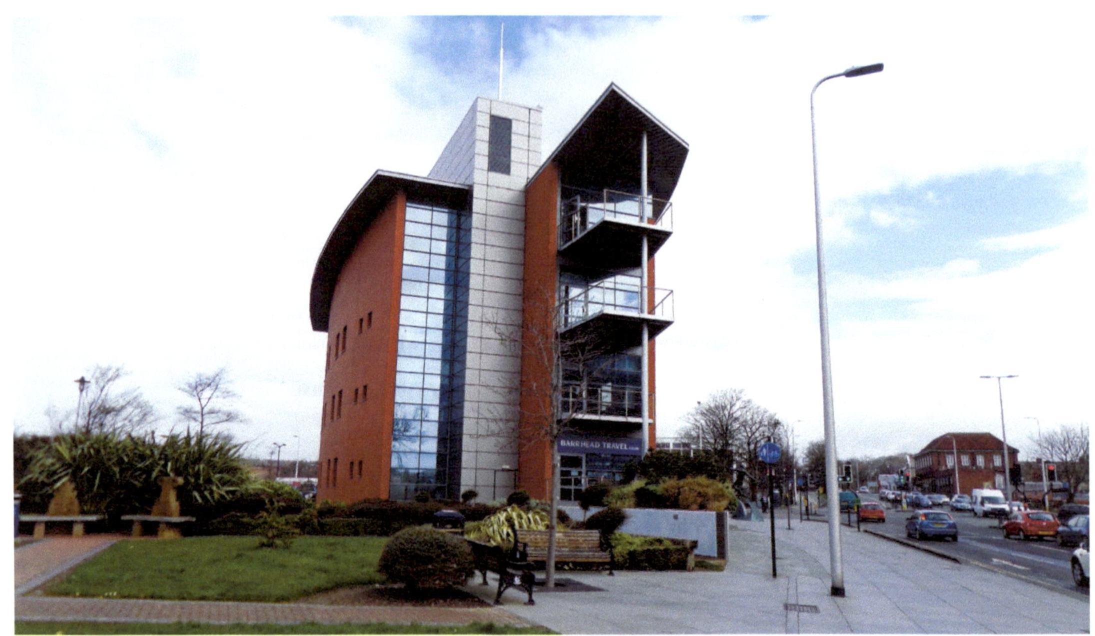

The Ritz, Abbey Road

Barrow had many cinemas and theatres, all of them now demolished. The Ritz was a high-class picture house built in the art deco style in 1936. It had a restaurant and gave its patrons a classy night out. Generations of children attended Saturday morning 'Minors Club' and it was not unusual to see queues around the corner. It fell into disrepair after the new multiplex was built and it was demolished in 2003. Emlyn Hughes House replaced it and a statue to the Barrow-born England and Liverpool player is at the front.

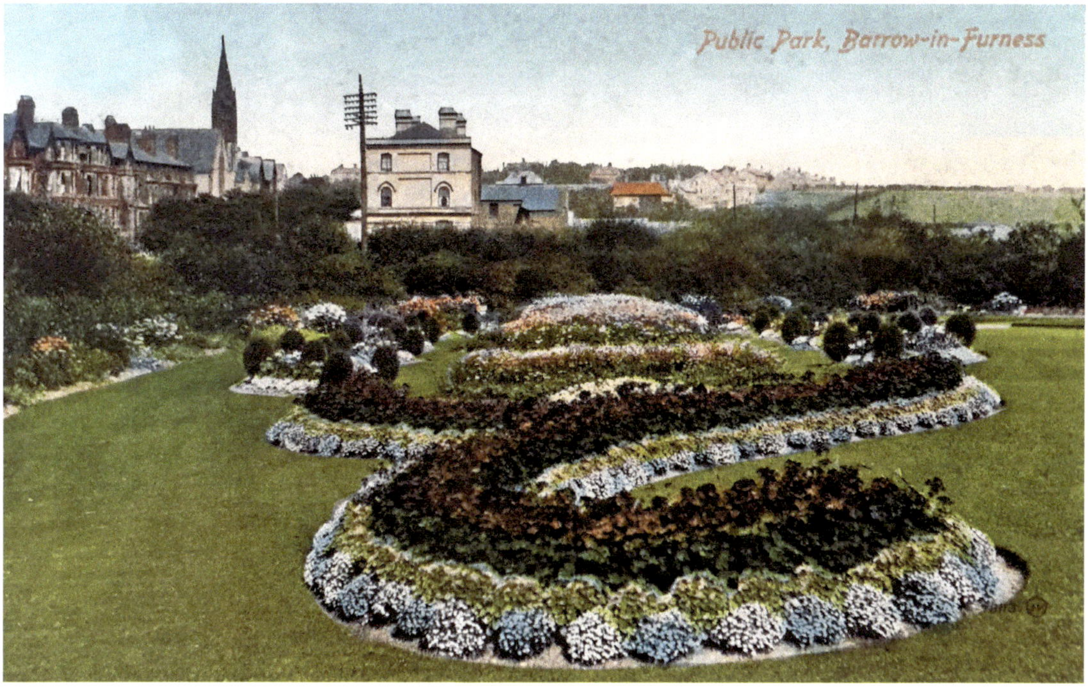

Barrow Park, Abbey Road

A lovely open view across the north side of the park shows the limit of urban growth in 1918. The fields in the distance are Risedale and Greengate. On the left is Abbey Road Methodist Church, now Trinity Churches, and opposite is the original White House Hotel. The urban development is clear along the route of Abbey Road towards the Strawberry. This is an early picture of the park as can be seen by the extent of the vegetation and trees visible; it is quite a different view today. (Picture loaned by Katy Millard)

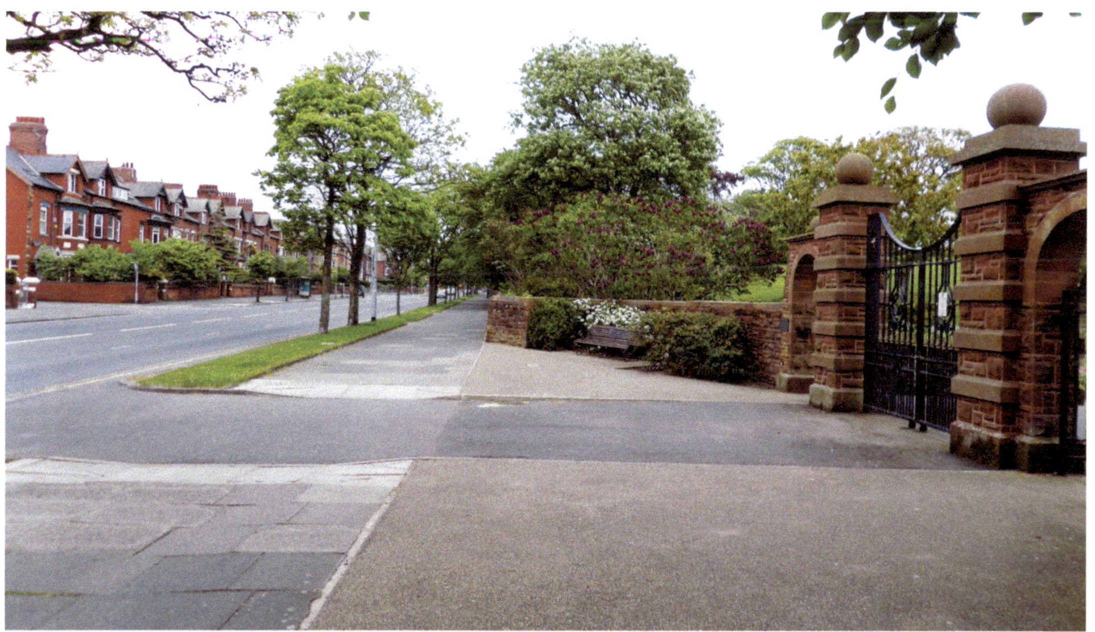

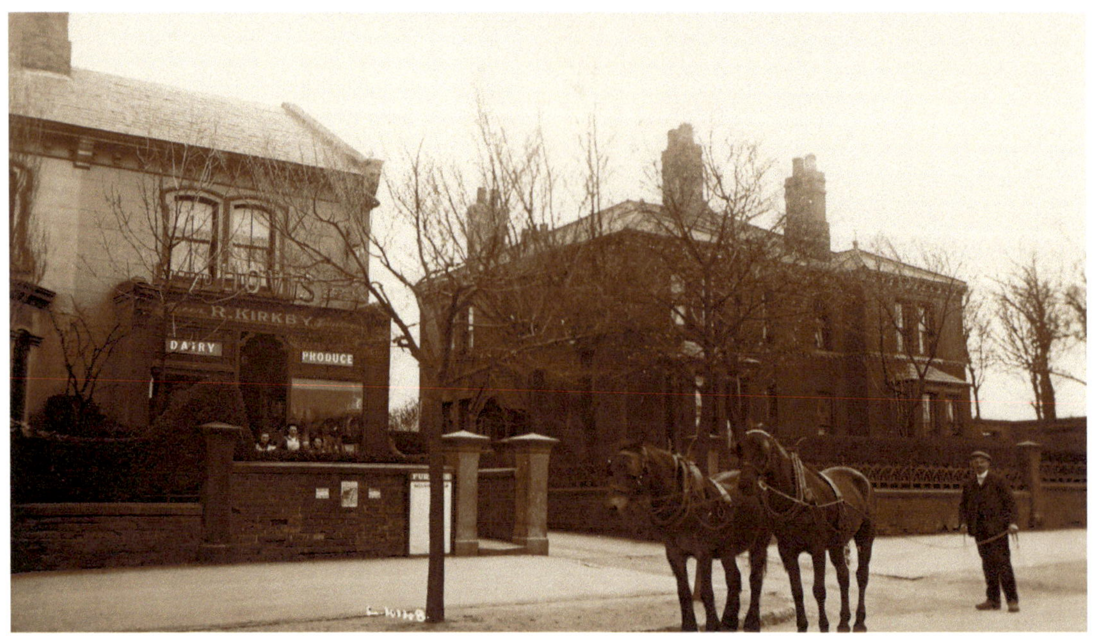

Alexandra Villas

The urban spread ran along the main arterial road, once known as Barrow Lane. It was widened and straightened as Barrow grew and became Abbey Road. Different builders made their mark along it and Alexandra Villas, built in the 1870s, is one example. The shop in the photograph 'R. Kirkby' is a dairy and grocers, typical of local shops serving the community at this time. It is now a photographer's studio. The trees are mature and the frontage has been opened up to accommodate parking for cars.

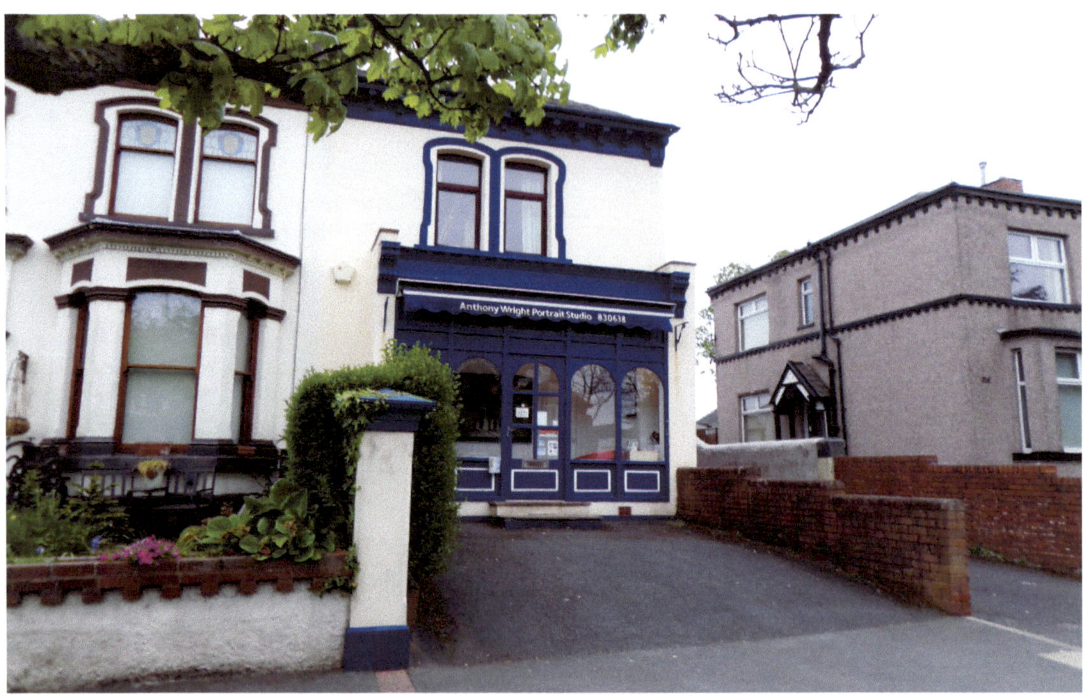

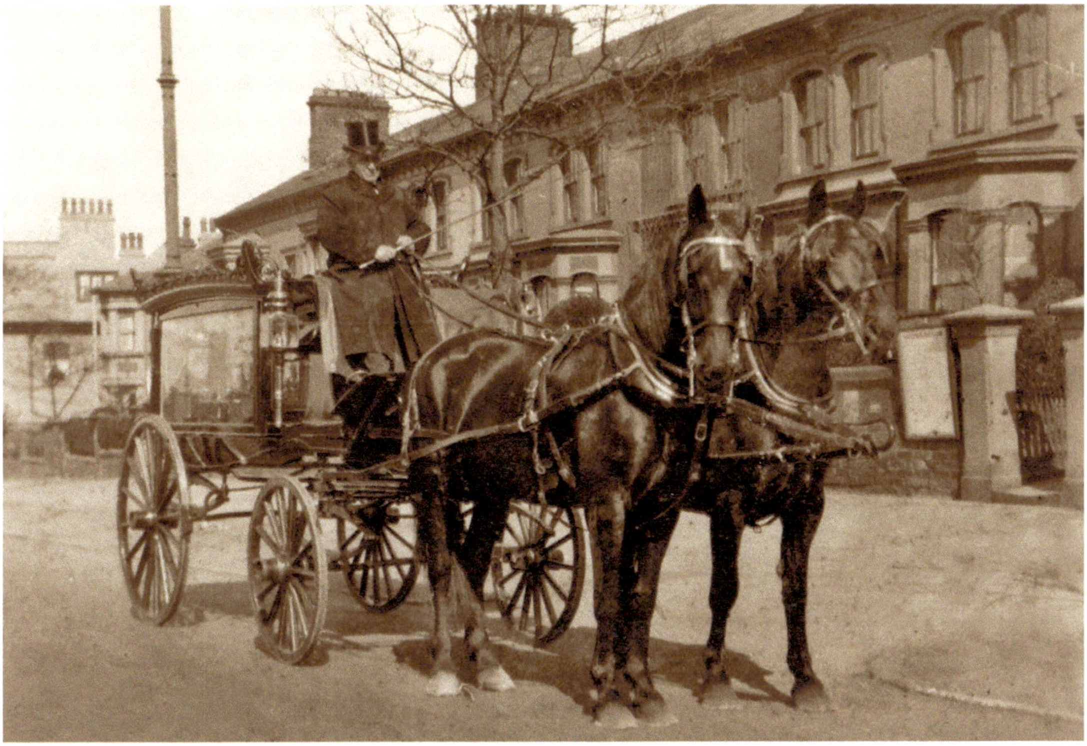

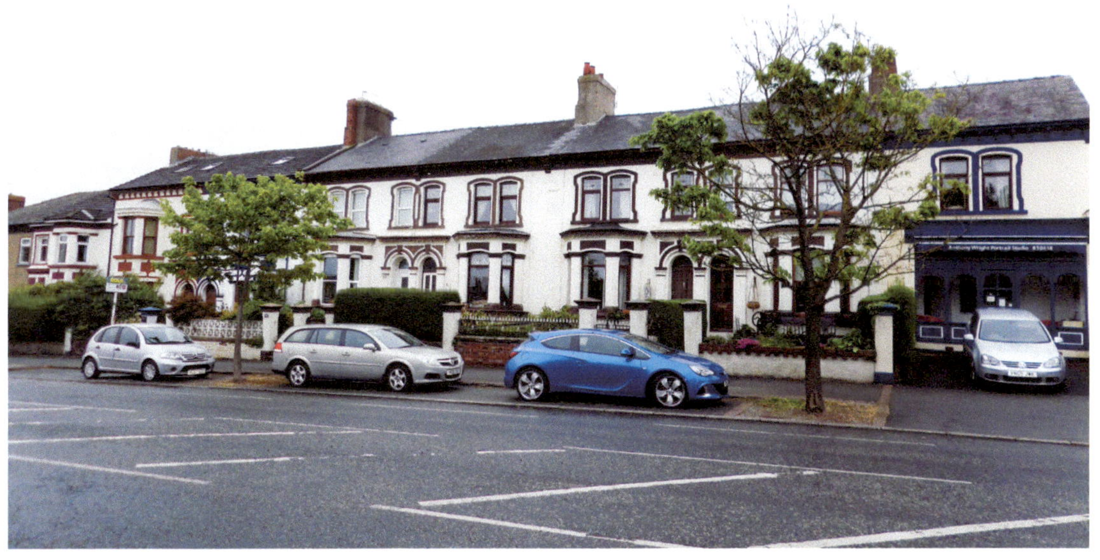

Alexandra Villas, Abbey Road

This terrace behind the hearse is typical of the houses for the aspiring middle class. The houses along Abbey Road became grander and more decorative the further out of town they were. These have a small walled garden at the front and probably a yard at the back. They are larger than the usual worker's terraced houses and are built in the style of the particular builder. William Gradwell was one such builder; based at Roose, he was responsible for many of the houses we see in Barrow.

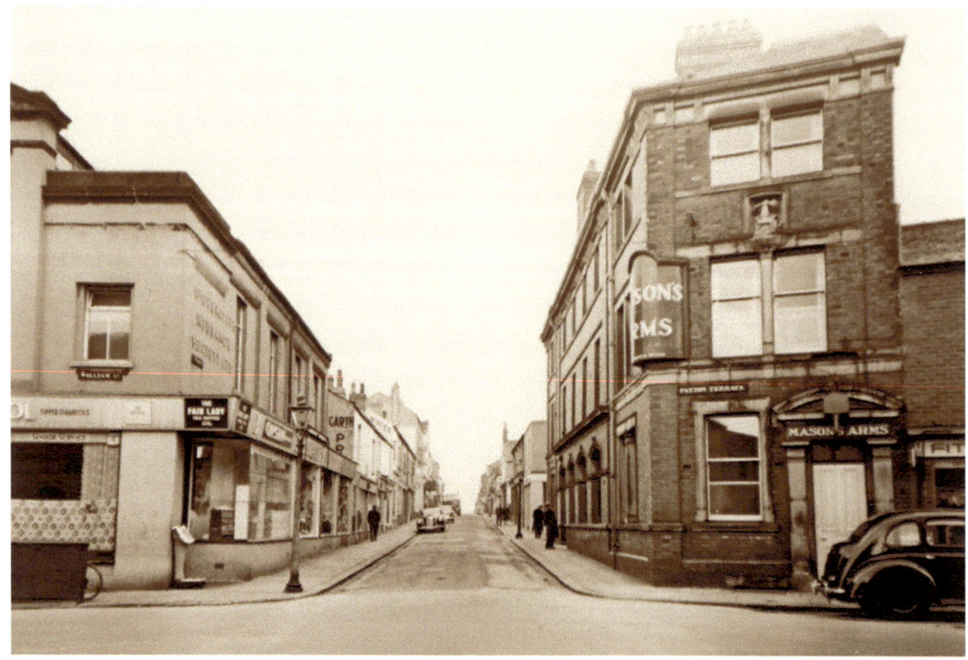

Forshaw Street

This street is allegedly named after Captain William Forshaw of the Manchester Regiment, born 1890 in Barrow. He successfully held his position and defended his comrades at the Battle of Gallipolli in the First World War and won the Victoria Cross for his efforts. He was awarded the freedom of the town for his bravery and so one would assume the street was named after him. However, there has been a Forshaw Street in Barrow from 1870, so it is hard to confirm the assertion. The street is now buried beneath Portland Walk and a multistorey car park.

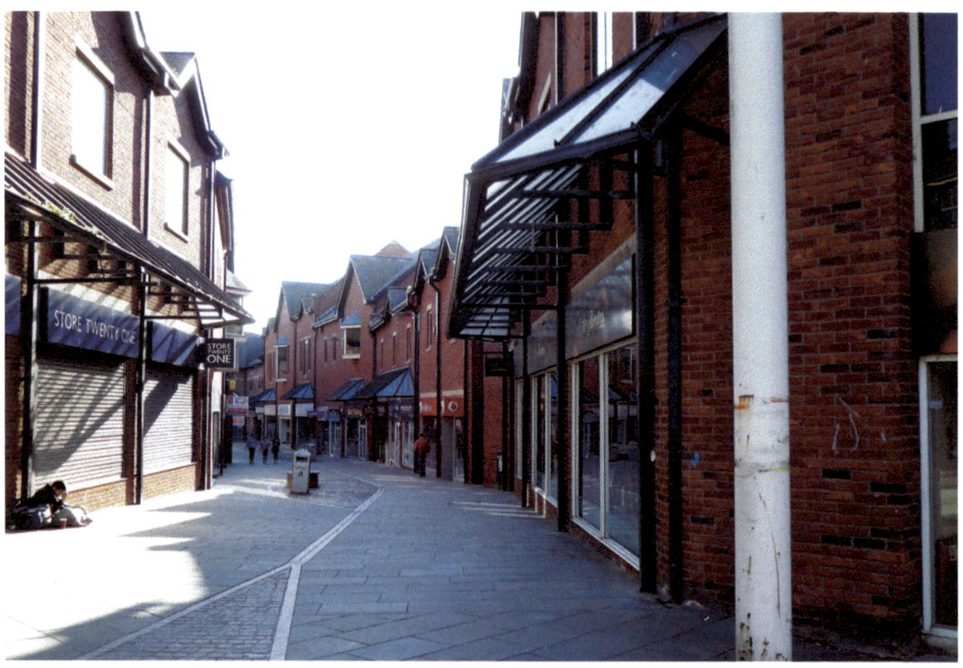

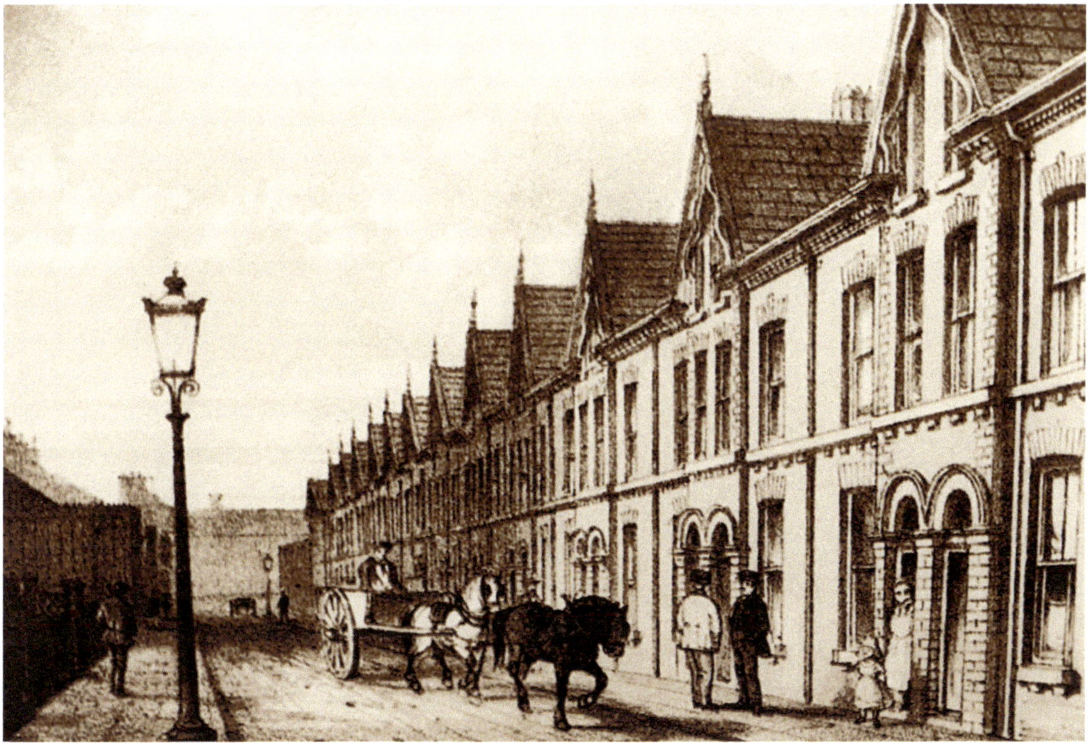

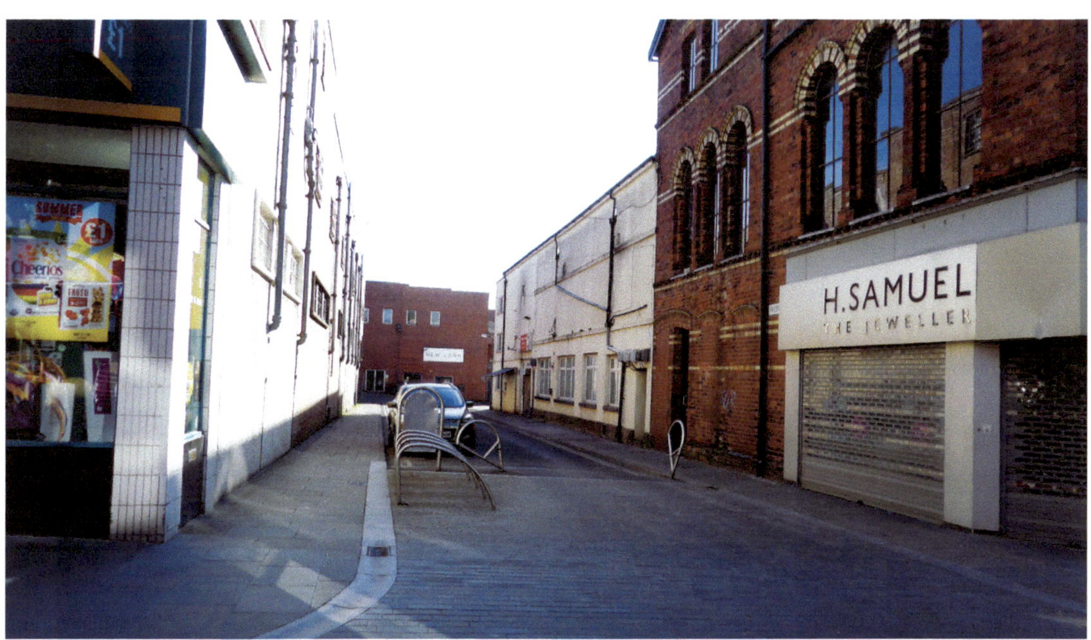

Preston Street

Preston Street is totally unrecognisable when comparing today's view with that of 1880. It originally housed a range of artisans, workmen, small businesses and even a school. Nowadays it has virtually disappeared under Portland Walk and loading bays. A small section remains at the Dalton Road end and is occupied by Preston Street Working Men's Club.

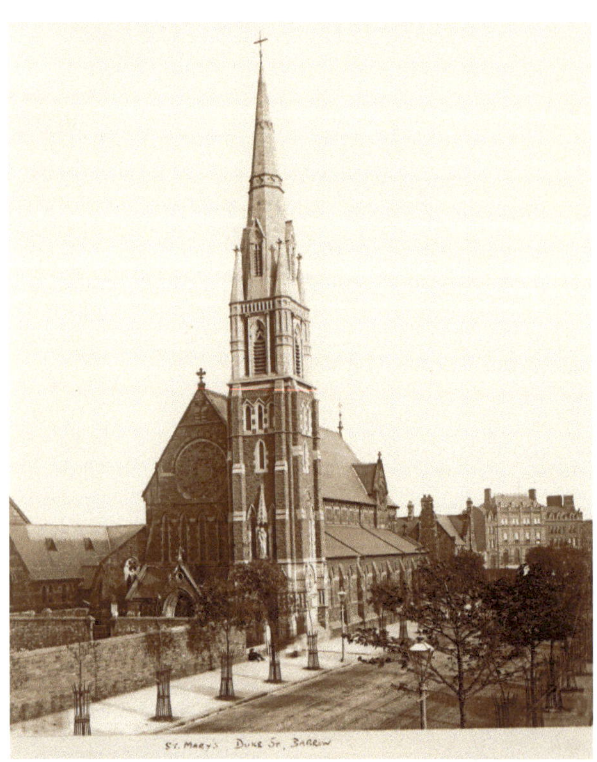

St Mary of Furness, Roman Catholic Church, Duke Street

Roman Catholicism returned to Furness in 1858 with the celebration of Mass in Greengate Street. The huge influx of Irish workers to the town made the building of a church a priority and the Duke of Devonshire donated land and money to enable its construction. E. W. Pugin designed the church and, when it was completed in 1867, it could accommodate some 800 people. A school was added later and opened in 1872. It has since been Grade II listed and has had extensive repairs to the steeple in 2015, funded by the Heritage Lottery Fund.

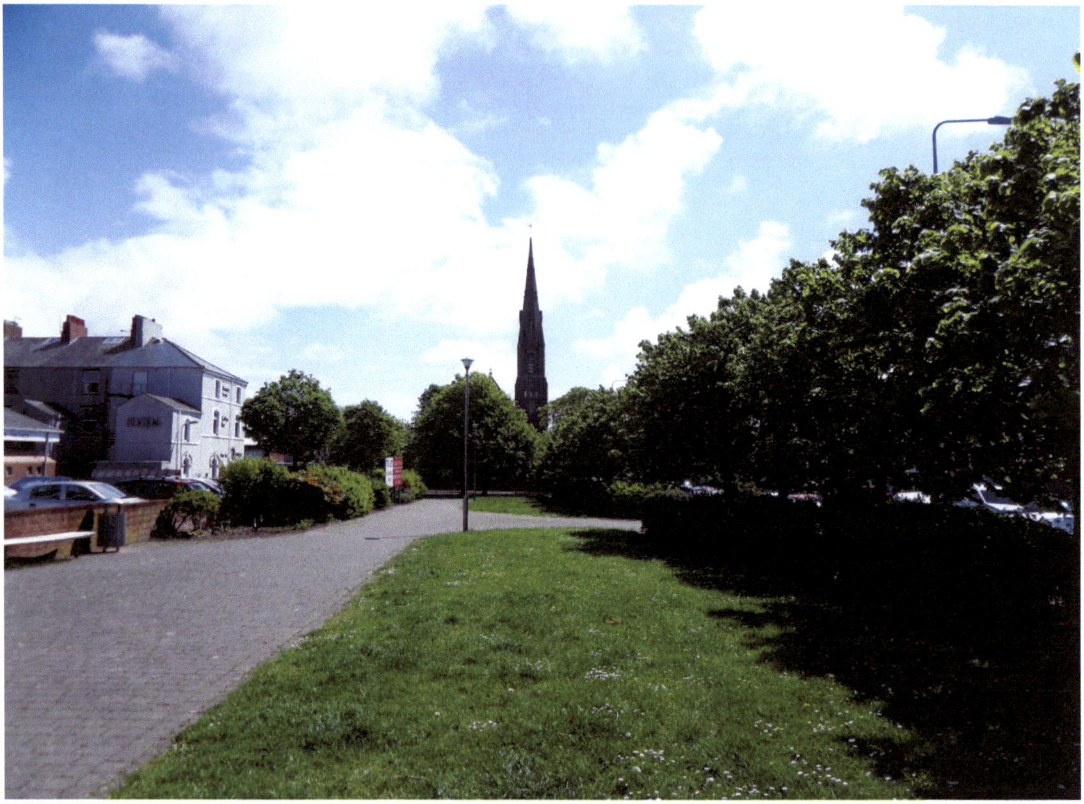

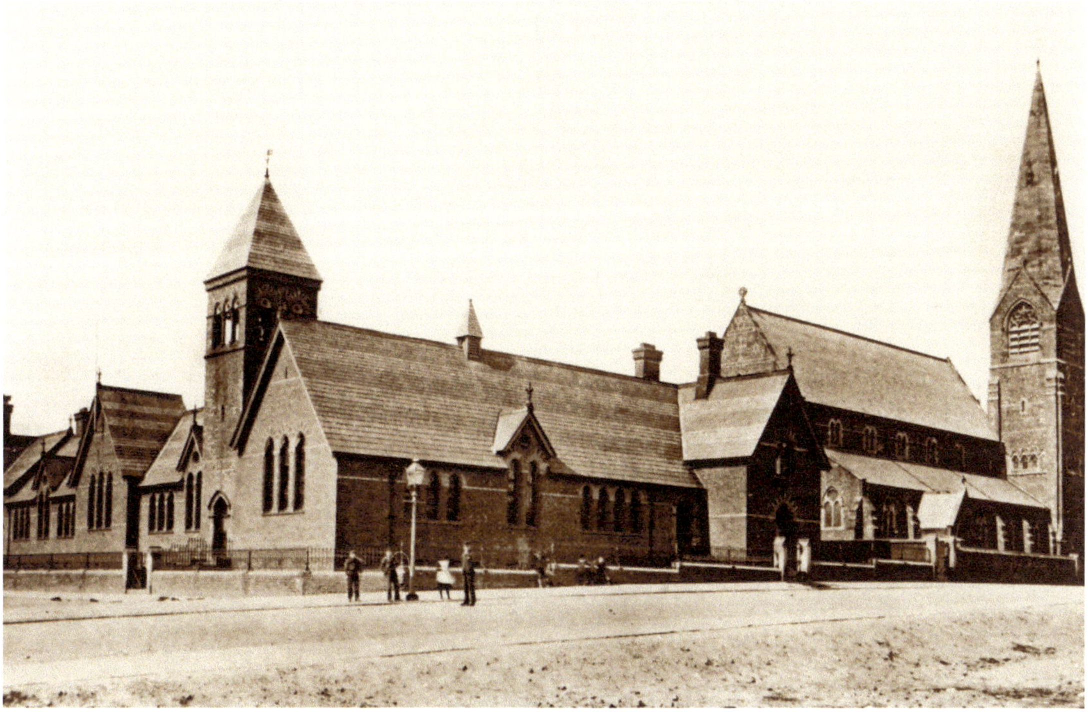

St James' CE Church, Blake Street

Established in 1867, St James' church was completed by 1869, only the second Anglican church to be built in Barrow. It is a large and imposing church, able to hold 1,000 worshippers, though these days it has a waning congregation. It is still a dominant feature on the Barrow skyline and has a spire of over 45 metres high. Restoration work was undertaken in the 1990s and more recently the bells were restored and rehung.

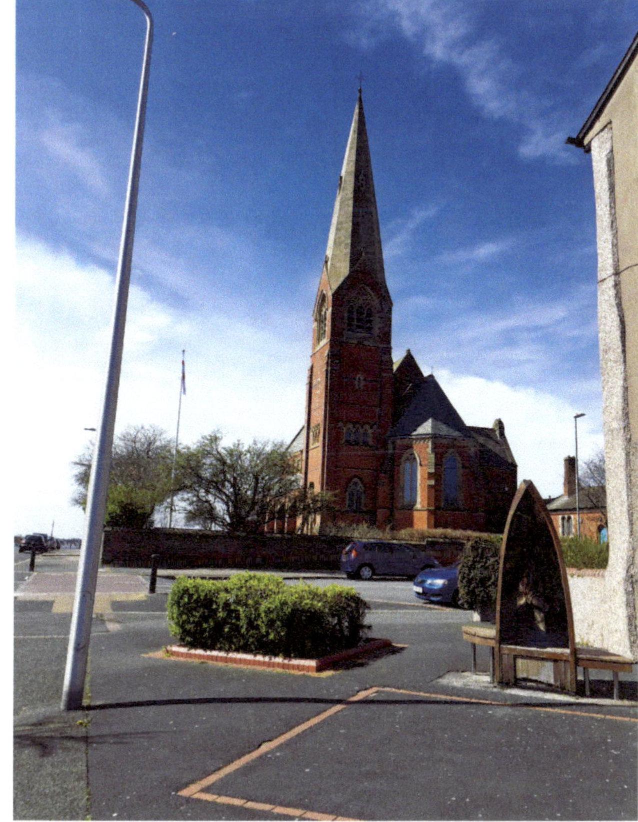

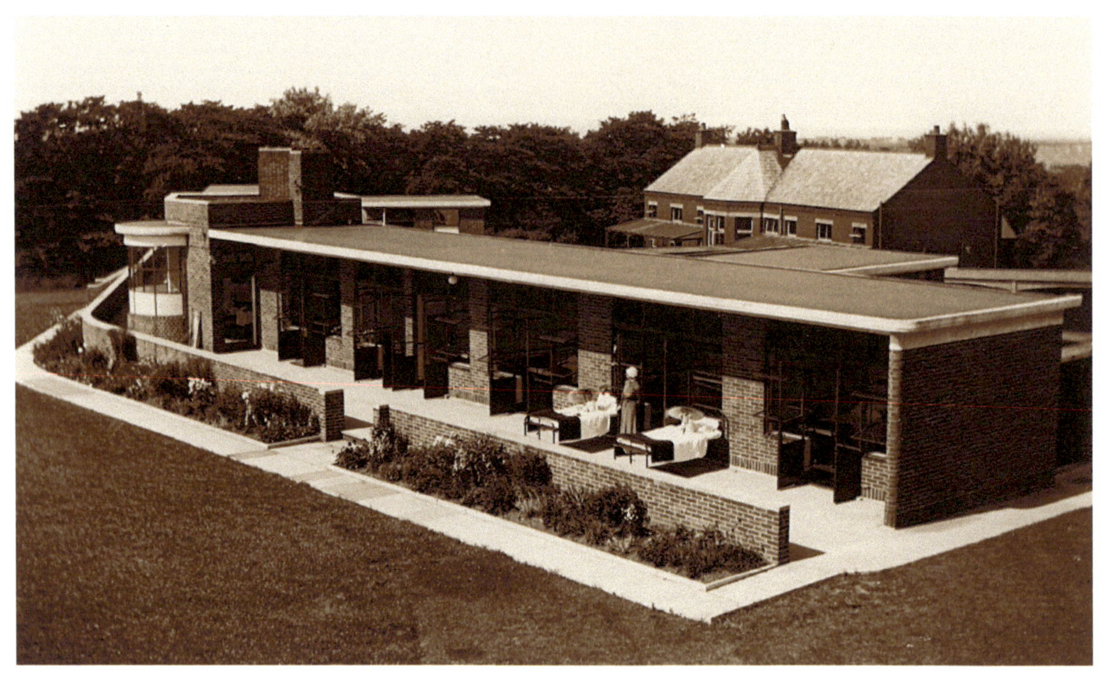

Devonshire Road Isolation Hospital

The hospital's official opening in 1882 was cancelled due to an emergency case being admitted immediately prior to the dignitaries arriving. The hospital dealt with acute cases, such as diphtheria, scarlet fever and tuberculosis. The capacity became insufficient as the town grew and plans were made to extend it by 1930; however, these were rejected by the Board of Health. The hospital had open wards where patients could take the fresh air. The site is now a housing estate which incorporates some of the original building.

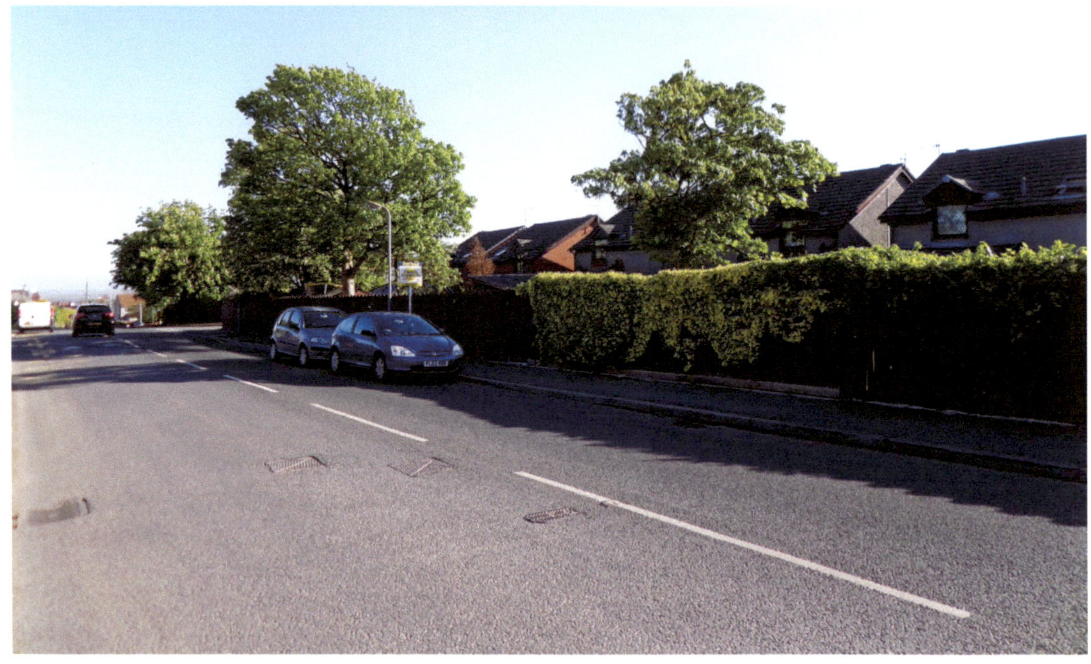

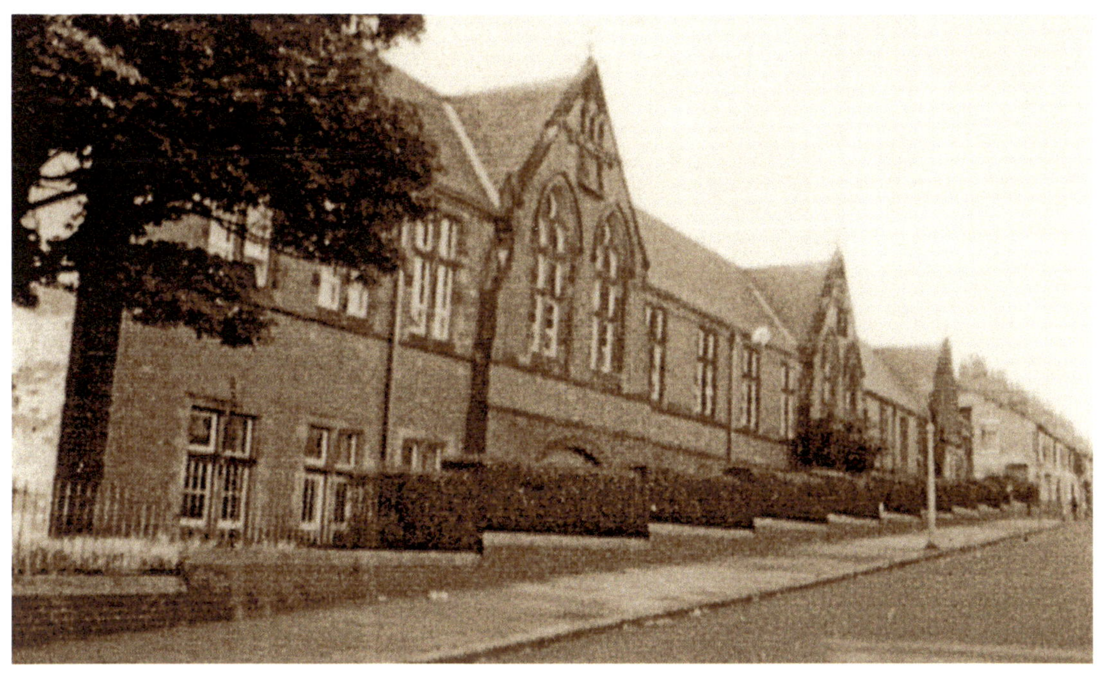

Victoria Junior School, Oxford Street

Constructed in 1884 in response to the rapidly growing population of Barrow, Victoria Junior School was built on Oxford Street, a new residential area. Numbers grew and later an infant school was built higher up the hill in front of the senior school. The Oxford Street site was demolished and a new school was built in 1976 on Devonshire Road, with more space and playing fields. Housing has replaced the school and there is no remaining evidence of what once stood there.

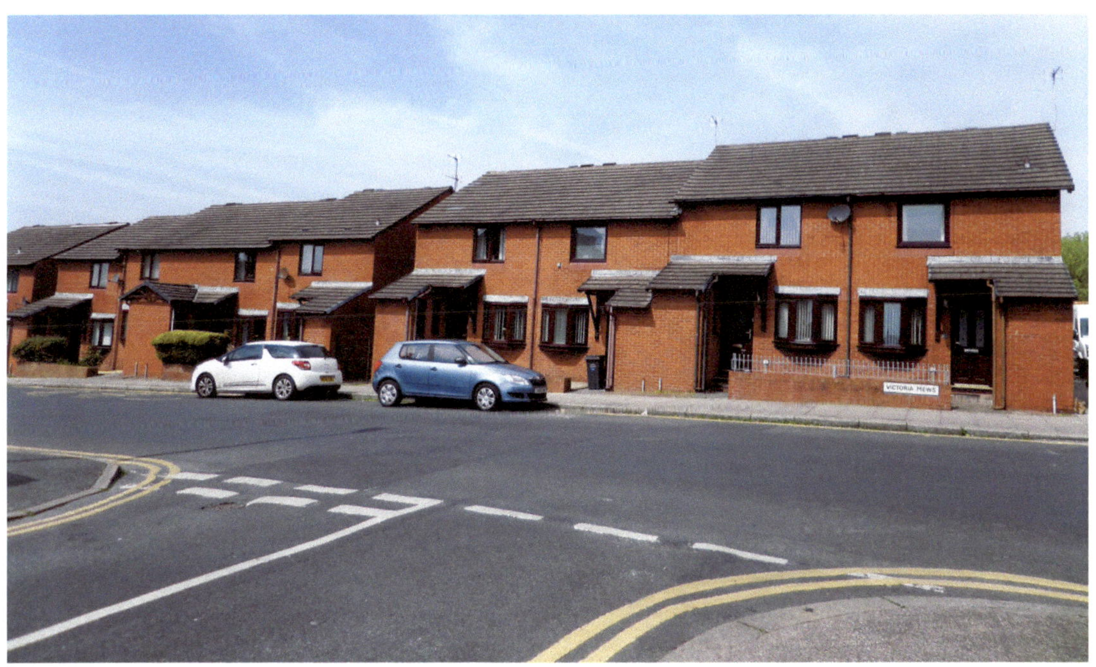

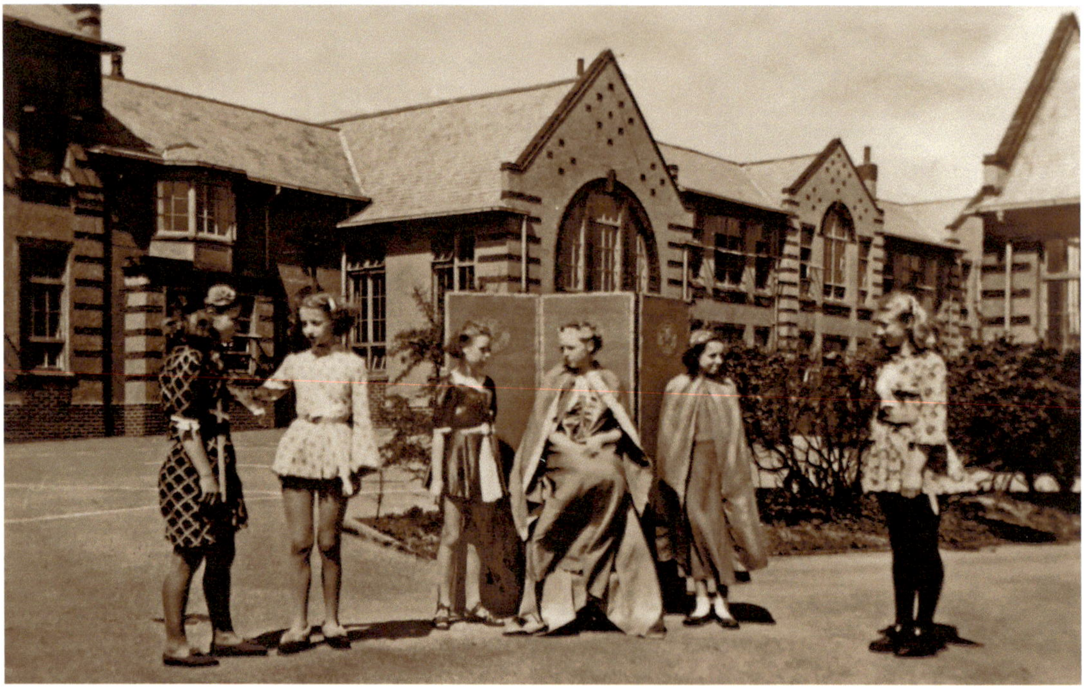

Victoria Infants School, Oxford Street

Barrow Education Committee built Victoria Infants and Ocean Road schools, which were identical in design and completed in 1917. During the Second World War, Victoria Infants School became an Air Raid Centre for fitting gas masks. Forty-one children and two teachers were evacuated in 1940, not returning until the bombing had lessened. The picture shows the old girls' school as well as the infants and was taken in May 1956 during a performance of *The Merchant of Venice*. The school has survived and has adapted over the intervening years. (Picture courtesy of Joyce Fitzsimmons)

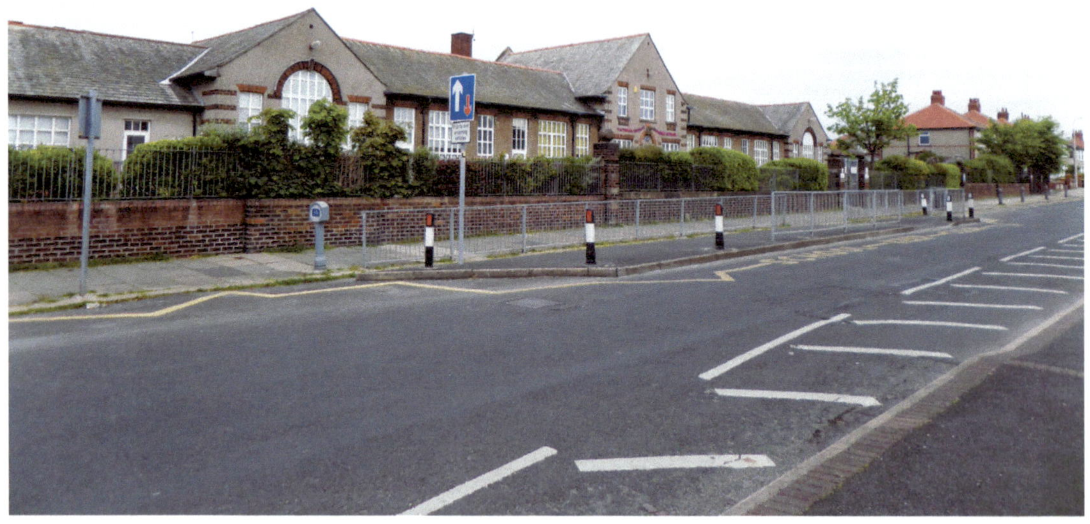

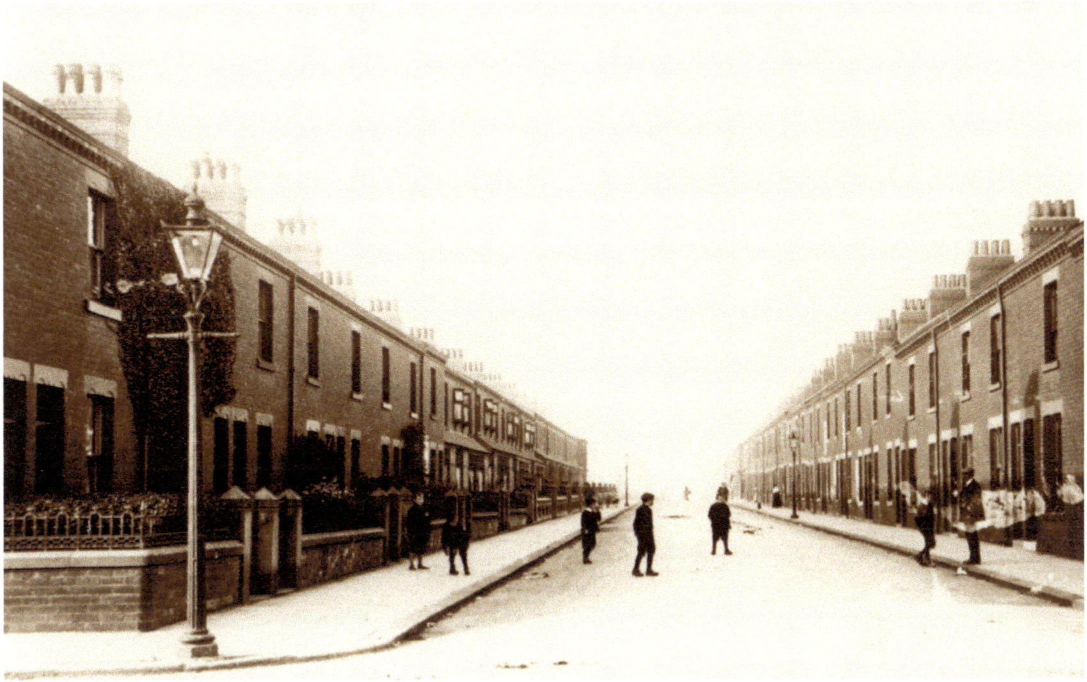

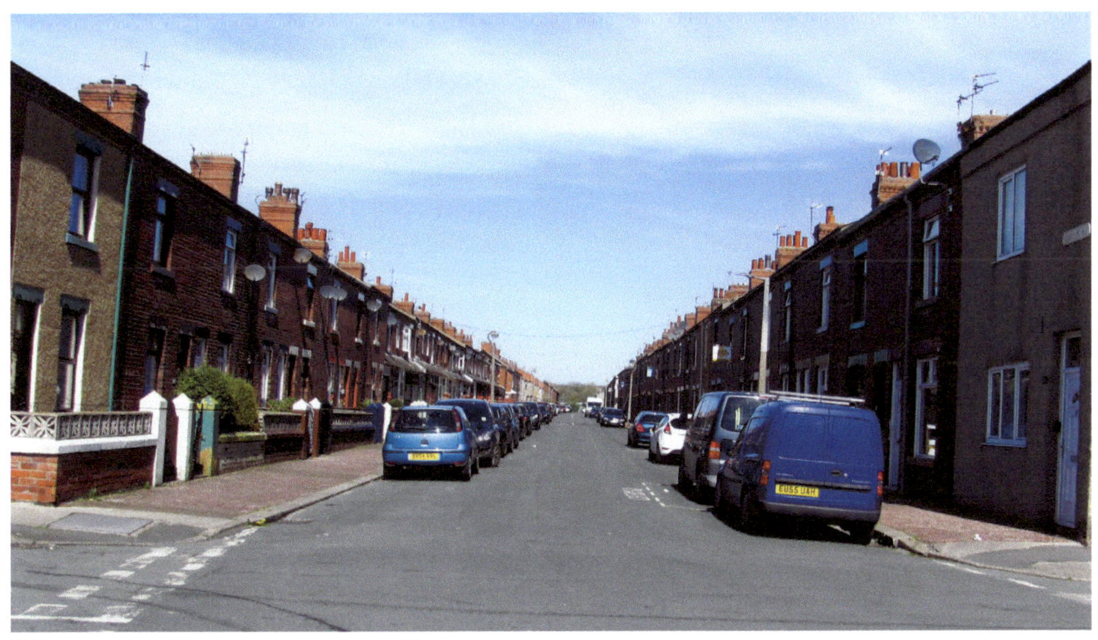

Devon Street

This street view demonstrates the rectilinear street plan. The view is straight and unimpeded. On the left, the houses are higher status with small front gardens for the professional class such as foremen, overseers and tradesmen. The opposite side have doors opening straight onto the street and a simpler design for the labouring class. The style of the housing on the left alters further along, suggesting a different builder. The street is similar today but with modern additions to doors, windows and street furniture.

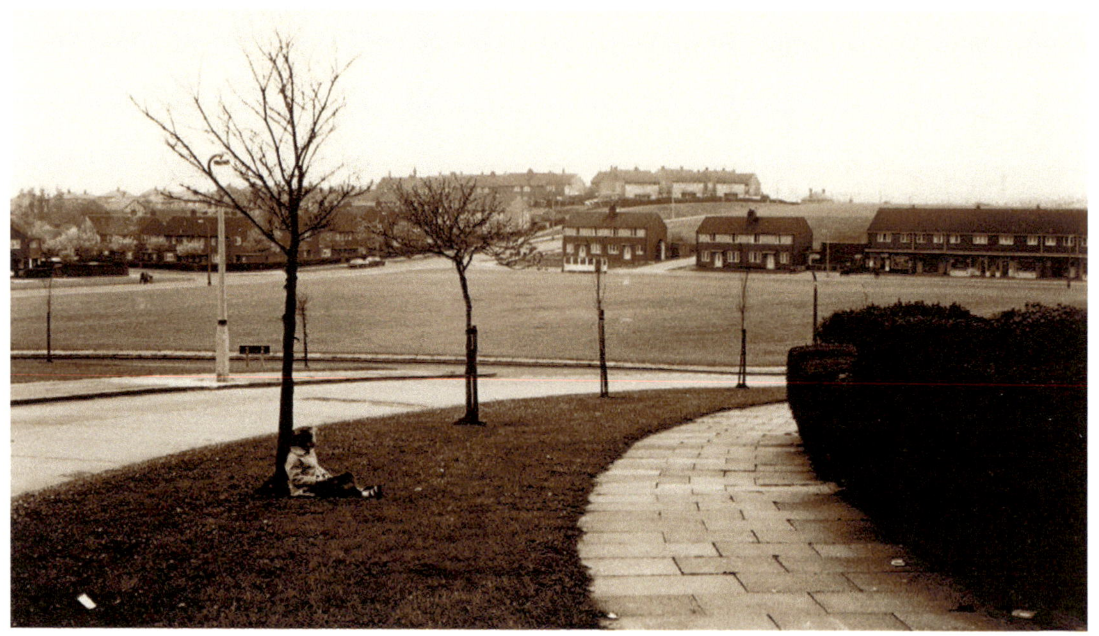

Middle Hill and Lesh Lane

In the post-war era new estates sprang up and Newbarns estate is a good example. Muddiman's Lane, named after the man who ran Risedale Valley Nursery, was renamed Lesh Lane. This planned estate was council social housing, providing modern homes with all conveniences. Provision was made for families with shops, schools and green areas, a far cry from the rigid lines of terraced houses that the Victorians built. The estate remains with a few modern touches, and still offers a pleasant environment in which to bring up a family.

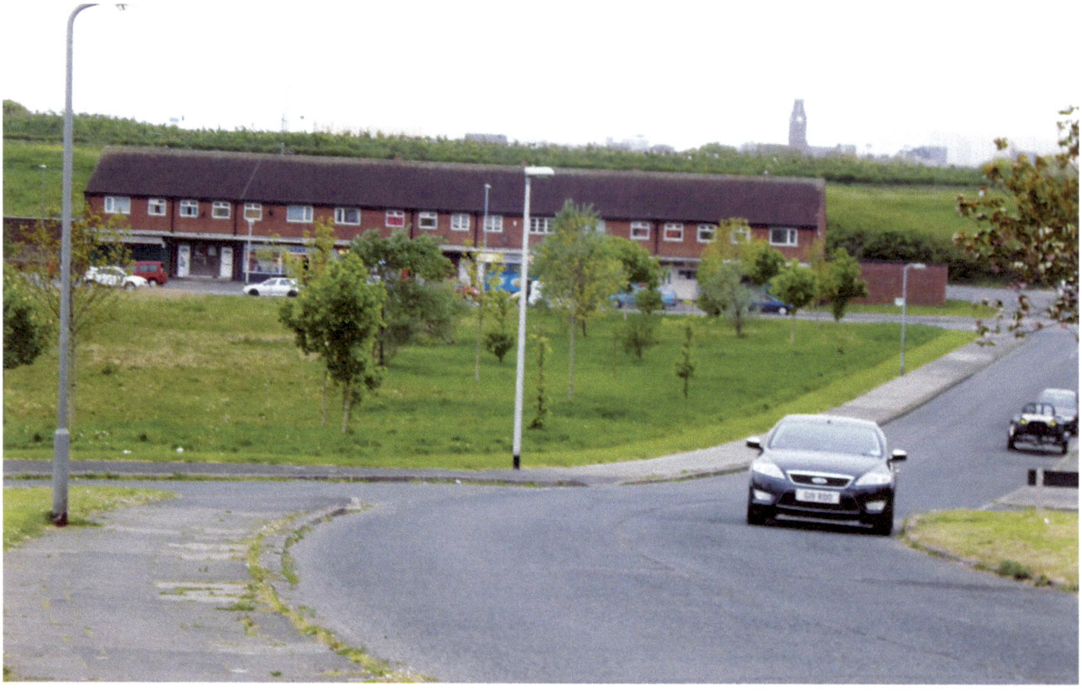

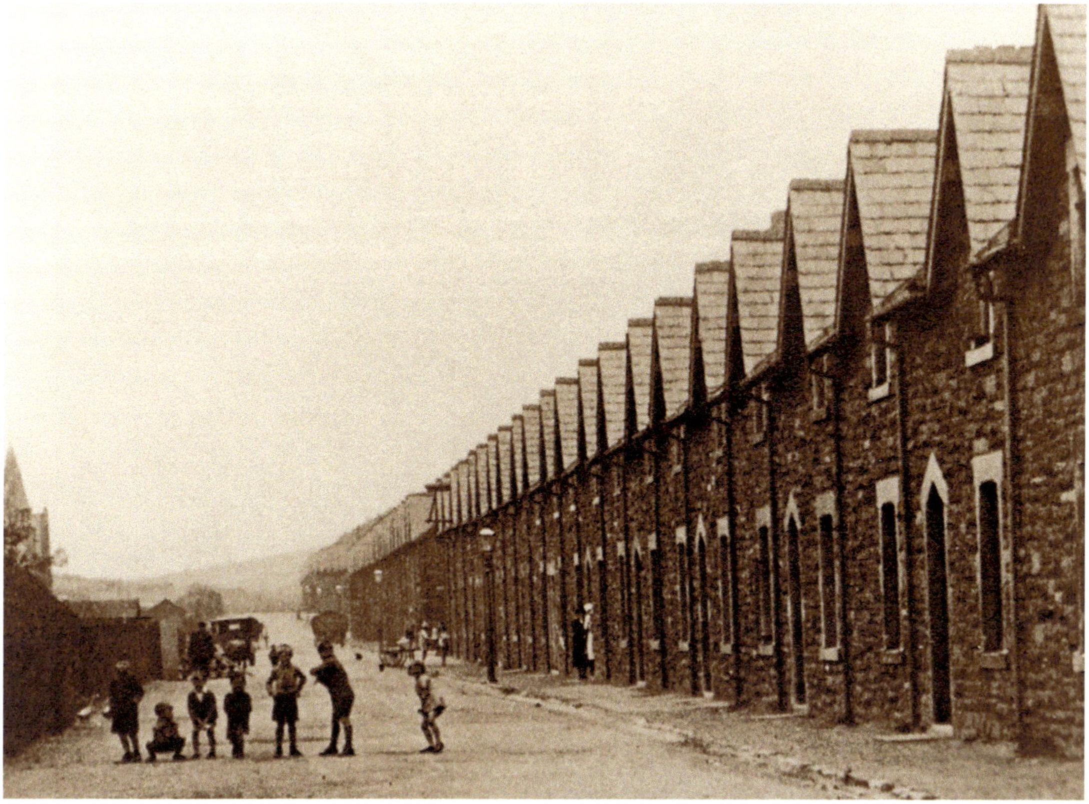

North Row, Roose

Roose was mentioned in the Domesday Book and was part of the Furness Abbey lands. In the nineteenth century the village became the hub of the mining community for Yarlside and Stank mines. The railway ran through the village of sandstone cottages to the mines. Cornish tin miners were brought to work the iron ore seams and their presence is remembered by the family names, the Methodist chapel and St Perran's church, named after the patron saint of Cornwall. The church has just recently been demolished for private housing while the chapel lies unused and derelict.

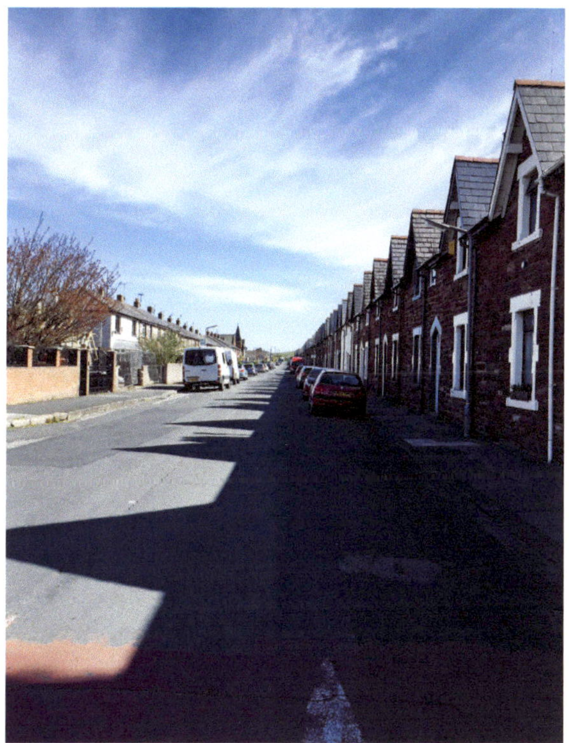

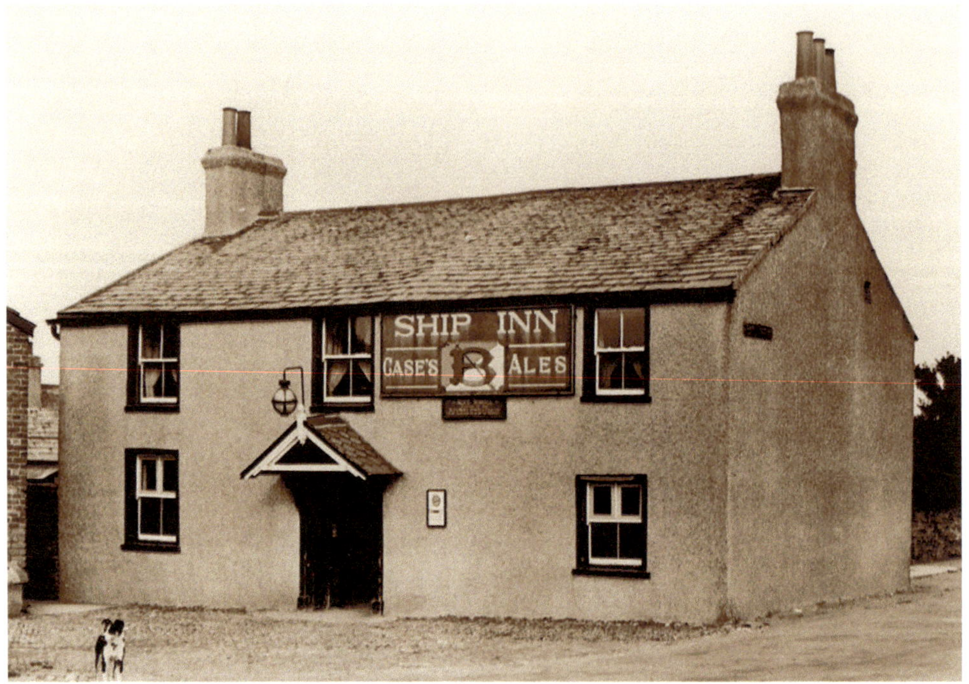

The Ship Inn, Roose

The Ship Inn began life as a simple farm house in the rural backwater of Roose. Situated on a route from Furness Abbey to the coast, the farm was probably linked to an older abbey grange. Most farmhouses brewed their own beer and often made money on the side by selling refreshment. It became established as an alehouse and belonged to Case's brewery until the 1960s. It was subsequently extended and remodelled. It was again refurbished in 2005 and is now a restaurant popular with families.

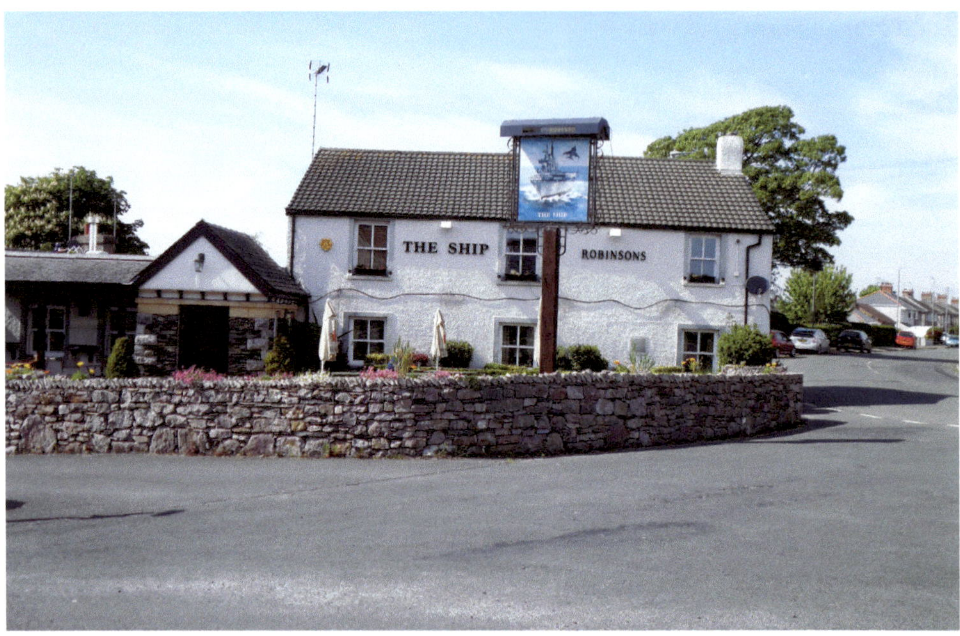

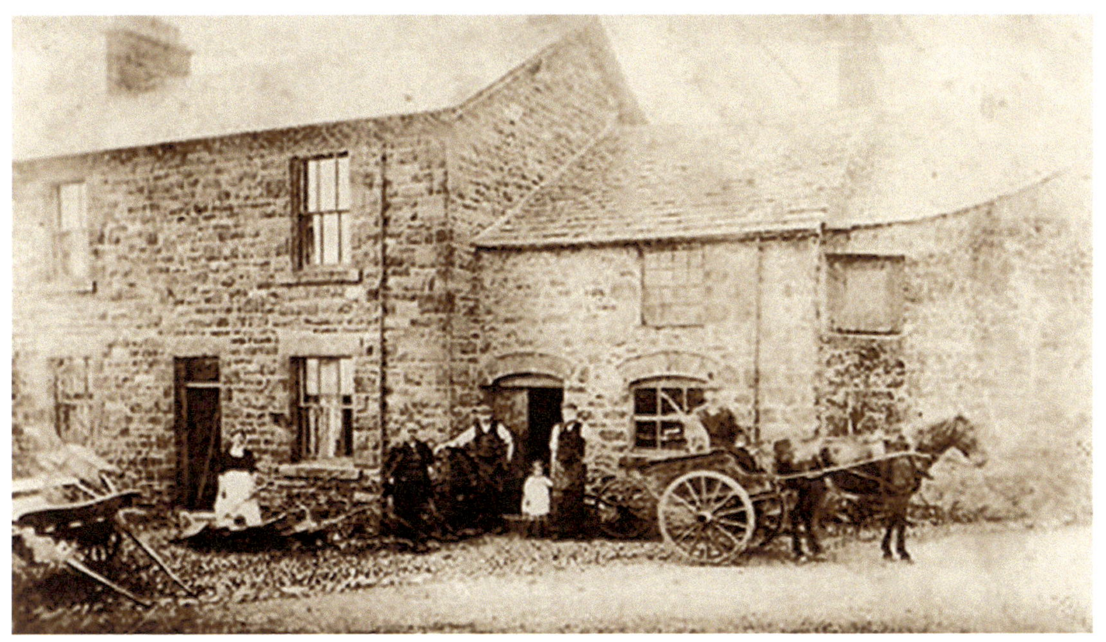

The Smithy, Holbeck

Now a popular fish and chip shop, the 'Smithy', as it is still known, was a thriving blacksmiths. The buildings are constructed from local sandstone and the structure is still generally intact. The frontage has no garden in the early picture and the workshop extends further than today. Today, the shop is whitewashed and pebble-dashed but is still recognisable as the blacksmiths. The position would have been central for a number of farms and no doubt would have been very busy, being on the main route to the coast.

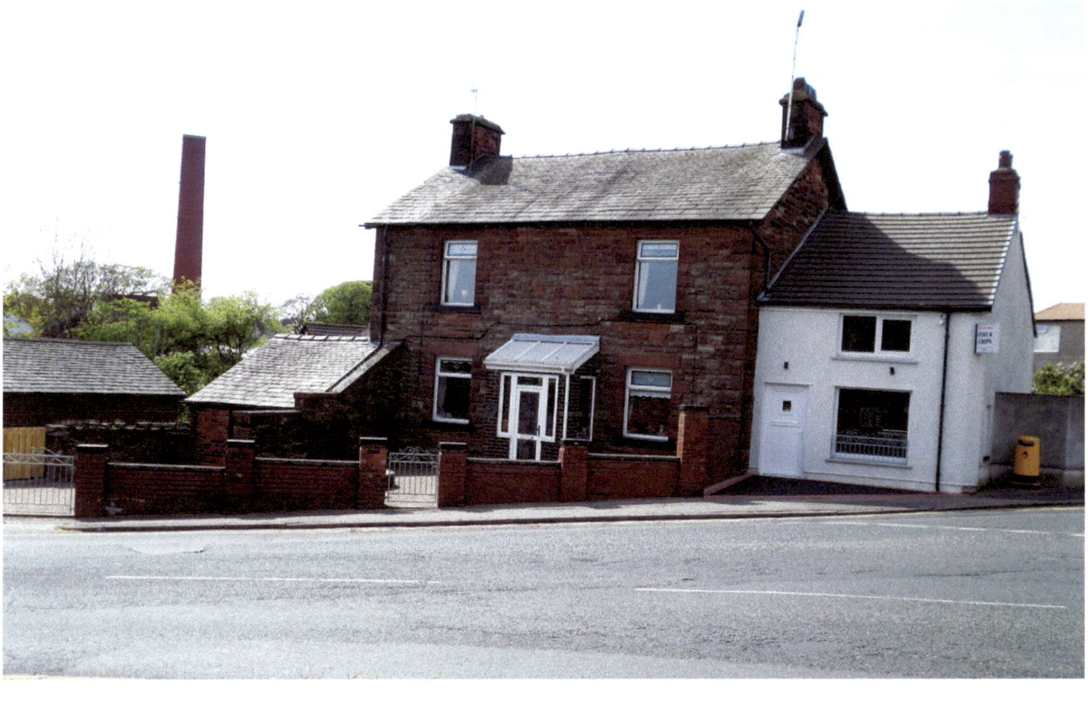

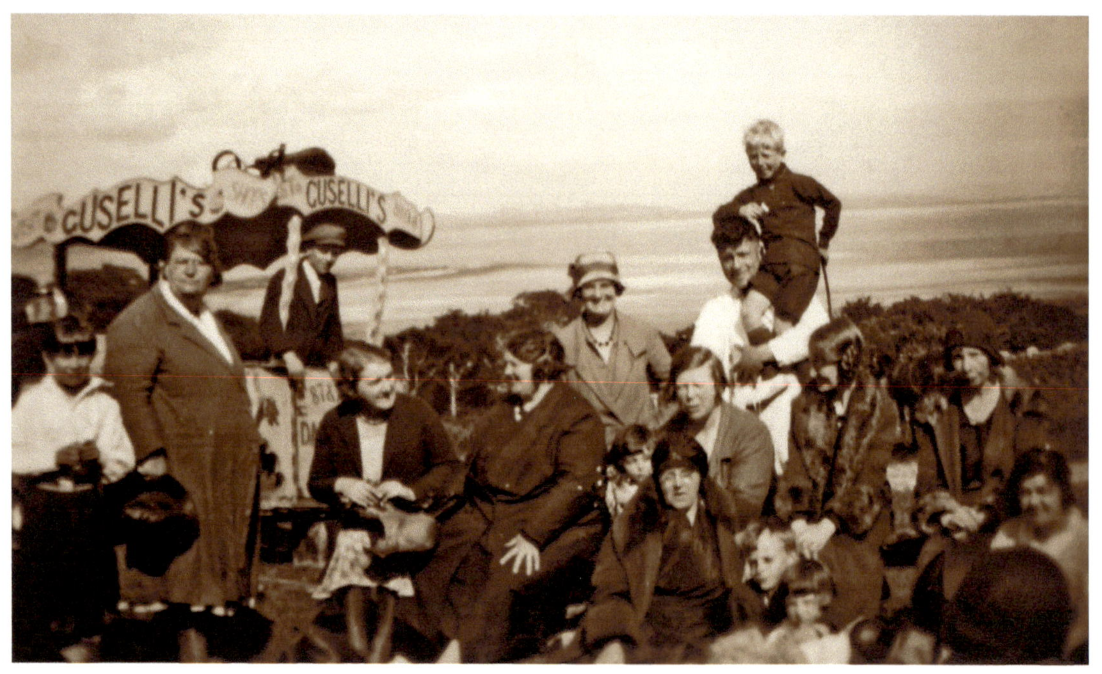

Guselli's Ice Cream Stand, Coast Road

The Coast Road is still a popular location for ice cream sellers and in the summer numerous ice cream vans park along the banking of the beach. Nowadays the vans are motorised and refrigerated, selling ices and drinks. The Gusellis saw an obvious opportunity and early in the twentieth century could be seen with their cart selling cooling ices to the visitors to the beach. The coast road was built by the unemployed in the 1920s. (Picture courtesy of Ray Guselli)

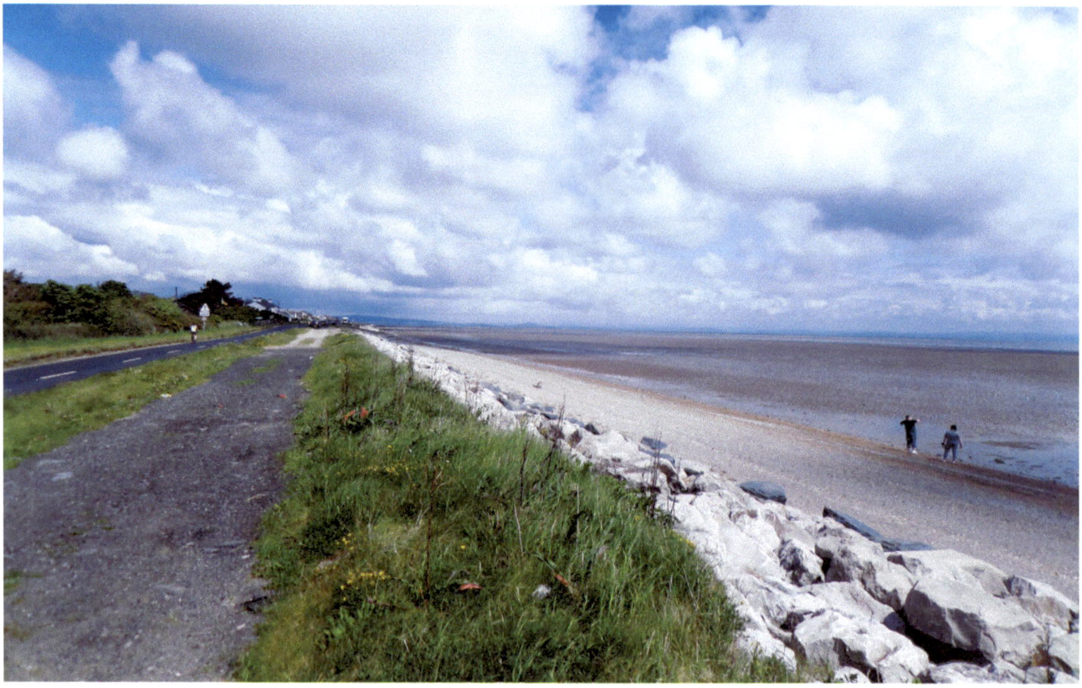

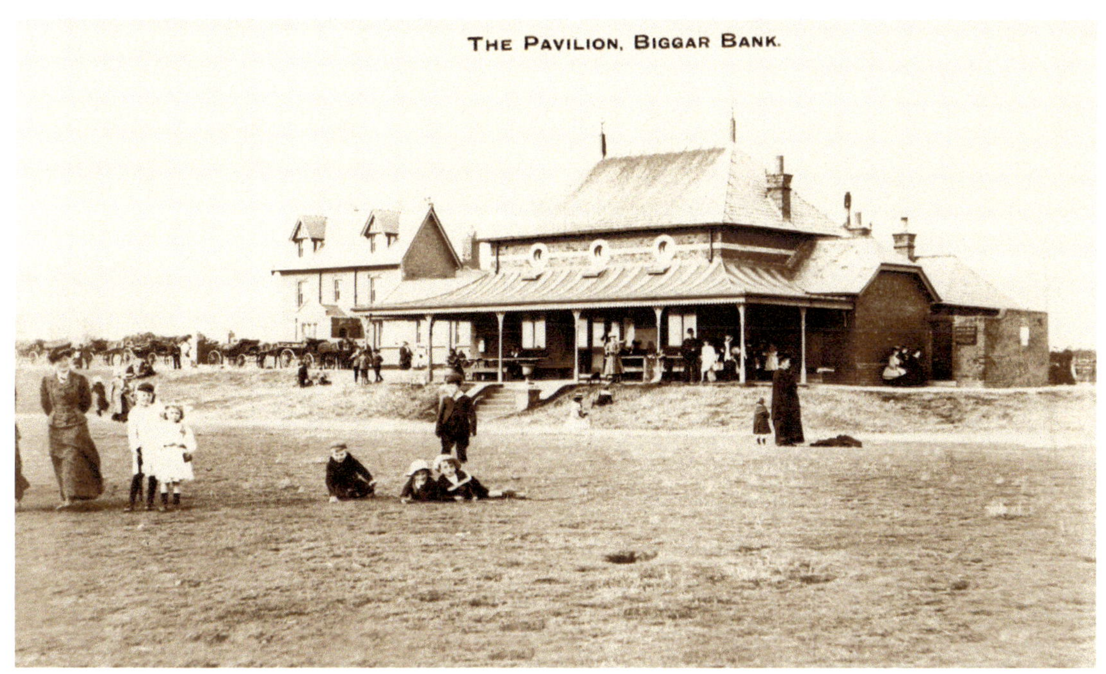

The Pavilion, Biggar Bank

A grand pavilion was constructed to provide refreshment and shelter for visitors to the sea front. There are a number of carriages and horses along the roadside, but most Barrow beachgoers would have walked there, catching the ferry to cross from Barrow. In the background is the Castle House Hotel, which was not granted a liquor license until 1950, after earlier unsuccessful applications in 1899 and 1949. It continues to be a public house and restaurant but Biggar Bank does not attract the same numbers of visitors as before.

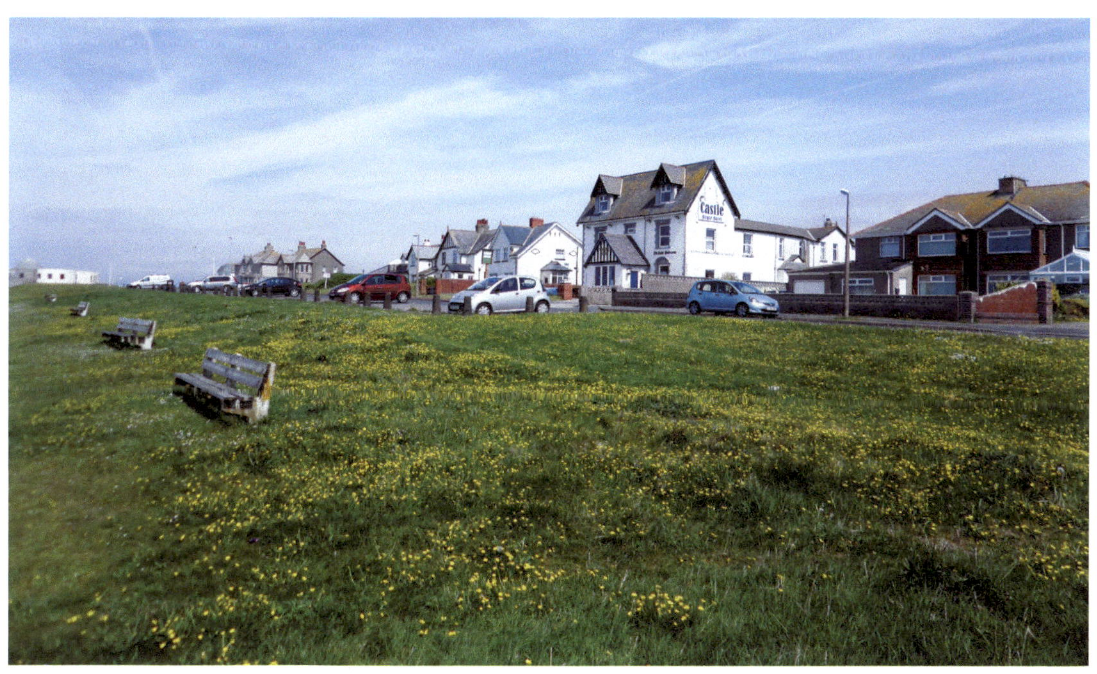

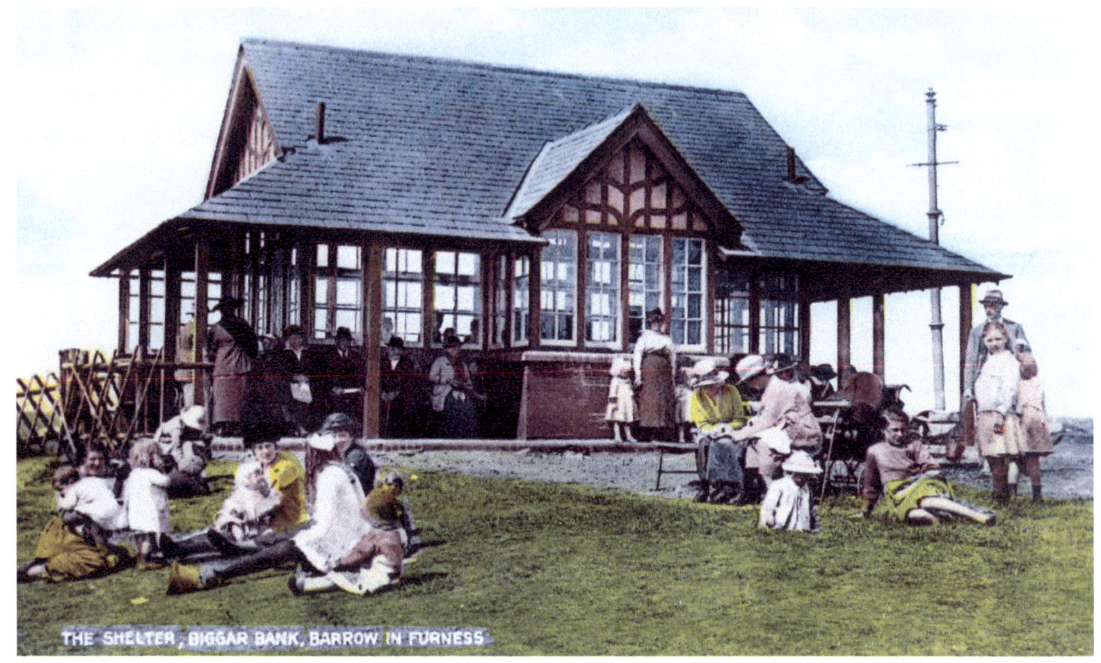

The Shelter, Biggar Bank

A smaller building known as the Shelter was built on the banking above the beach for the use of the public. This continued to be in use for many years but has now sadly gone. In the same vicinity now stands a concrete construction that houses a Chinese restaurant. However, from inside, the views across the Irish Sea are amazing, which makes up for the lack of elegance and beauty on the outside.

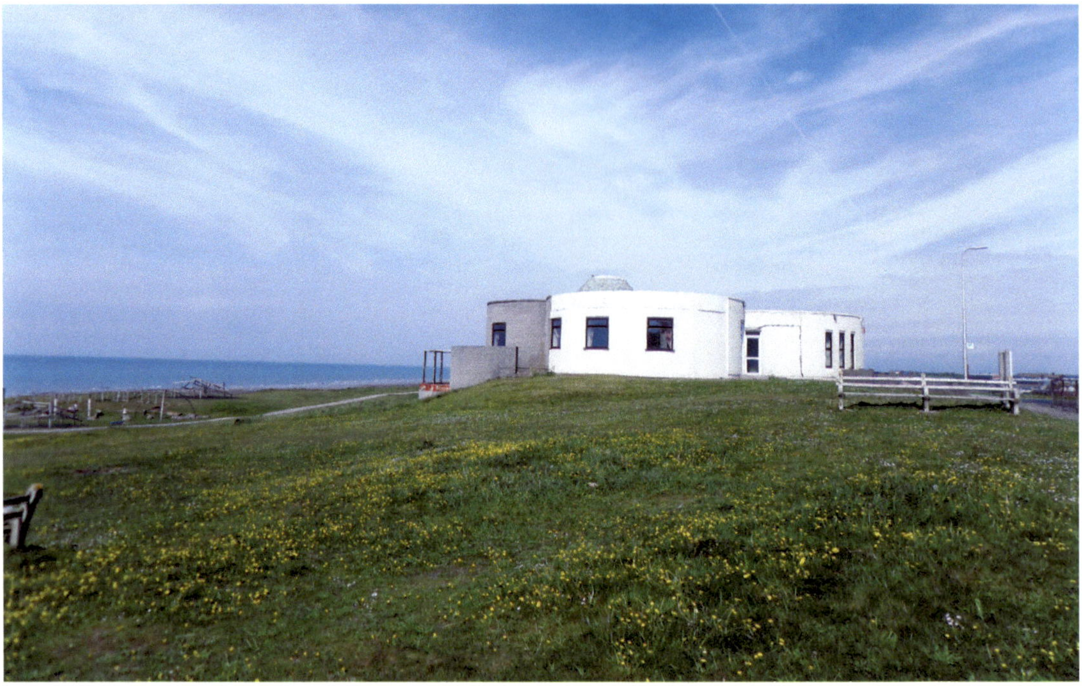

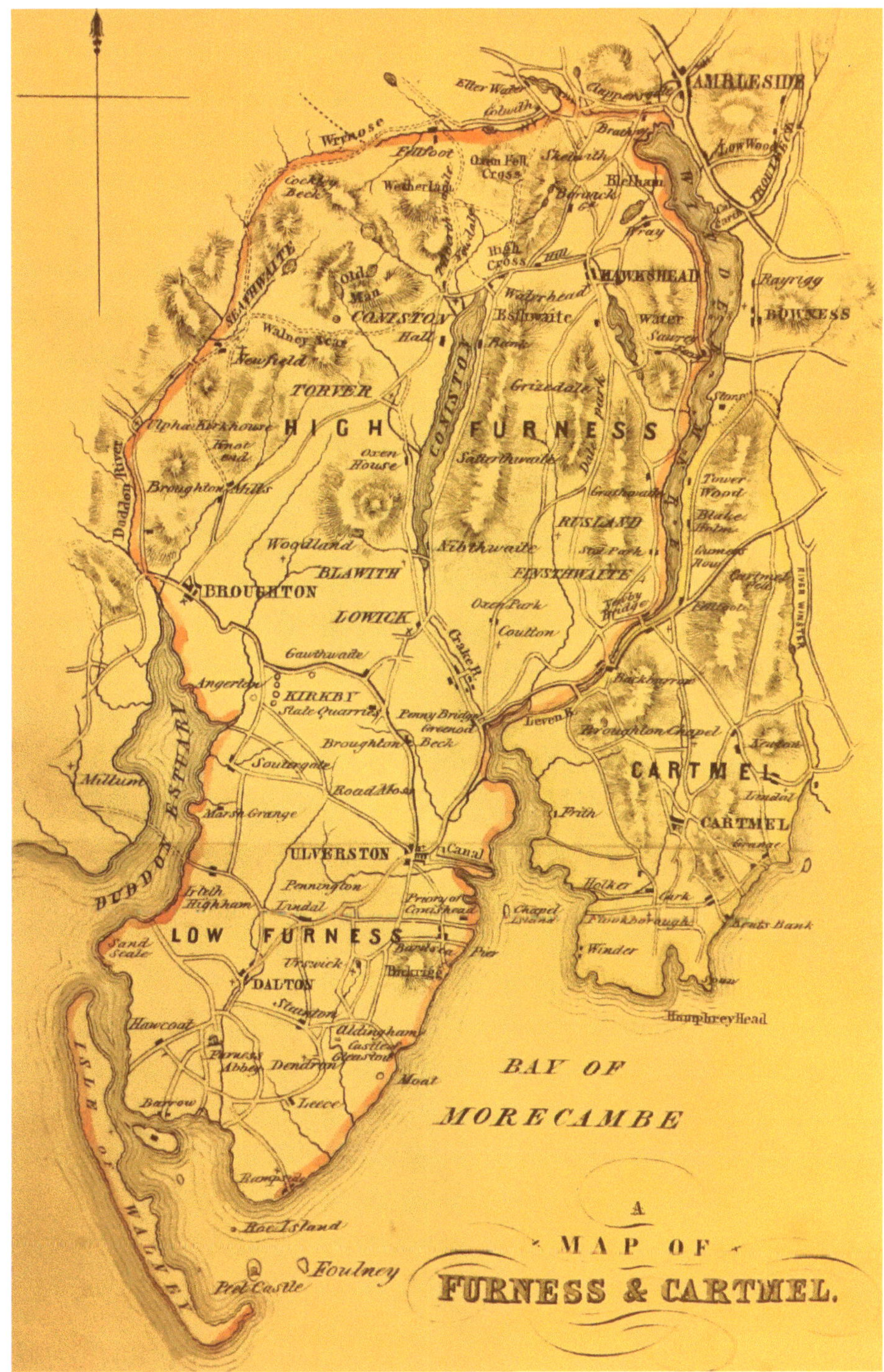

The Furness Pensinsula

This map shows the Furness Peninsula when Barrow was a hamlet and the islands of Old Barrow and Walney were truly islands, before the transformation by Furness Railway and the industries that followed. (Taken from C. Jopling 'Sketch of Furness and Cartmel')

Acknowledgements

The author and publisher would like to thank the following people and organisations for permission to use copyright material in this book: Cumbria Archives and the Barrow Public Library, *North West Evening Mail* and Sabine Skae from the Dock Museum for use of photographs and postcards in the Cumbria Archives Collections, including the Harper Gaythorpe Collection, photographs of dock workers and the aerial view of Barrow Grammar Schools from the *North West Evening Mail* and the image of the Graving Dock from the Dock Museum. Other pictures were sourced and used with permission from the following individuals: Ray Guselli from his family collection and Parkview, Jennifer Foote for Risedale School and Cavendish Dock, Janet Pickering for the dock workers photograph, Sarah Taylor for pictures of Alan Dawes and Barrow Island School, Keith Wallwork for the Bandstand picture, Peter Laird for the Duke of Edinburgh photograph, Joyce Fitsimmons for Victoria Infants School, Martin Millar for DDH, Dock Museum and Devonshire Dock photographs and Katy Millard for postcards of Barrow Park and Walney. Other photographs are from my collection of postcards and photographs including the Wrench series, Raphael Tuck and various unidentified postcards. Prints were taken from West's 'Antiquities of Furness' and Beck's 'Annales Furnessienes'. Every attempt has been made to seek permission for copyright material used in this book. However, if we have inadvertently used copyright material without permission or acknowledgement we apologise and we will make the necessary correction at the first opportunity.